INSIDE AFRICA

INSIDE AFRICA
Contemporary Perspectives

Edited by
A. S. Yaruingam
Rashmi Kapoor

Centre for African Studies
University of Delhi, Delhi

SHIPRA

The views expressed in this volume are of individual contributor and do not represent the viewpoint of the editors or the Centre.

UGC has extended the financial support for this publication.

ISBN: 978-81-7541-712-0

First Published in India in 2013

Inside Africa: Contemporary Perspectives

Published by:
SHIPRA PUBLICATIONS
H.O.: LG 18-19, Pankaj Central Market, Patparganj,
Delhi-110092, Tel: 91-11-2223 5152, 2223 6152
Br.Off.: 4617/18, Ansari Road, Darya Ganj,
New Delhi-110002, Tel: 9650028065, 9810522367
E-mail: info@shiprapublications.com
www.shiprapublications.com

Acknowedgements

Inside Africa: Contemporary Perspectives has been written for the Center of African Studies, Department of African Studies, University of Delhi from the financial assistance granted by the University Grants Commission (UGC). We would like to express our appreciation for this to the UGC. This book would not have been possible without the contribution of several people. First we would like to thank all the contributors for their insightful research papers. They extended full co-operation in the process of bringing out the book. We also owe our thanks to our colleagues who have helped us in the composition of the book. A special gratitude is owed to Mr. S.K. Chauhan, Office-in-Charge, Mr. Gaurav Gupta and Mr. Kuldeep Kumar Sharma, Junior Assistant and Mr. Naresh Kumar, Office Assistant at the Centre for African Studies for their steadfast support.

A. S. Yaruingam
Rashmi Kapoor

Contents

PART III
SOCIETY AND CULTURE

Introduction

All the different phases and epochs in the African history have left indelible marks on the rich African cultures and societies. Contemporary African culture is an interesting mosaic of old and new, ancient and modern, indigenous and alien elements. They are so inextricably entangled that to sift one from the other is not only insurmountable but a perilous engagement. External influences due to exchanges, migration, trade and wars and several different phases of globalization have made contemporary Africa diverse, varied and highly complex and composite society. But rich African history and culture have not been able to counter the strong negative perceptions of widespread conflict, despair, economically disarticulated and impoverished society. The Afro-pessimist discourses have time and again highlighted the ills with which the continent is inflicted. It must be admitted that this cannot be denied. But what is ignored is the fact that despite these ills, there are many scholars who have written about 'Africa rising' or African growth stories. Most African countries could make macro-economic reforms, promote privatization, enable liberalization of markets and trade. These countries were the ones which could promote peace and security. The contemporary realities that are repositioning Africa in the global order should be acknowledged and understood. *Inside Africa: Contemporary Perspectives* has been written keeping in mind the transformative changes that are taking place in Africa; changes that are remarkably altering the African society and integrating it well within the global order. An attempt has been made to explore social, economic, political and cultural trends in Africa today. It is hoped that the efforts of many African scholars and experts will give a new insight to the understanding of Africa and would stimulate African scholars to go for deeper research. It will also enable to put in better perspective the contemporary issues of Africa. The book seeks to provide an alternative view point on contemporary African issues other than the Euro-Centric view point.

The book contains thirteen chapters. The section on Politics and Society has four chapters. Chapter 1 is written by Ian Taylor and is titled Of Big Men and Big Ideas: Can NEPAD'S APRM Make a Difference? NEPAD was an African initiative launched with the hope and expectation that it will enable to eradicate poverty and put Africa on the path to sustainable growth and development and a promise that it will develop a credible peer review process to advance democracy and good government in Africa. Ian Taylor argues that NEPAD can never achieve good governance and democracy in Africa without undermining the position of ruling elites as they are the ones who are delaying the broad based development. In such a situation NEPAD'S APRM cannot be an effective mechanism for Africa's regeneration. Chapter 2 on Revisiting African Development Strategies in the New Millennium: From the LPA to NEPAD by Kyu Deug Hwang gives a detailed discussion on the NEPAD and Africa's development in 21st Century. He critically analyses the role of NEPAD as a development strategy while exploring the three key frameworks of NEPAD including peace and security governance; economic and regional governance; and political and democratic governance. The author insists that Africa has to rethink its development strategy and that NEPAD should be given a chance to be an inclusive and balanced African development strategy. Chapter 3 is on Understanding China-Africa Relations by K. Mathews who discusses the compatibility of the two economies and the political understanding that Chinese and Africans have. Both China and Africa have understood that their co-operation has potential for economic gains. China has acknowledged African sovereignty on equal political terms. No stringent political and democratic strings attached to Chinese loans, aid or grant has strengthened Africa-China relations. What Africa needs to learn from China is their uncompromising stand over China's unity, their nationalism and their entrepreneurial spirit and hence should give prime importance to pan-African identity. Chapter 4 is written by Shubhra Parmar on the Political Participation of Women in South Sudan. This chapter focuses on the gender equality and empowerment of women which is yet to be realized in fullest form in South Sudanese society. This chapter elaborates on the role of women in terms of sustainability of lives, their emerging roles as peace keepers, and their constant struggle for achieving representation in politics, executive and judiciary. It tries to propose new alternatives ways for women to achieve respectable position at social, economic and political level. It explores new opportunities provided to communities, institutions and society to reflect the status of women worldwide and highlights everyone's responsibilities in the vital battle for the advancement of women.

The section on Economy and Society has four chapters. Chapter 5 is on Regional Economic Governance in Africa by Ian Taylor. He discusses three modes of regional economic governance in Africa which evolved as a result of specific political culture therein. These three modes of regional economic governance are neoliberal regional governance, sovereignty-boosting governance and regional shadow governance. The author suggests that sometimes the shadow state becomes 'regional' due to neoliberalism and also due to empty state coffers. The author emphasises that there is a pluralism of modes of regional economic governance in Africa which can occur in different combination that makes Africa a complex and heterogeneous continent. Chapter 6 on Growth and Poverty Reduction in Africa: Political Economy Challenges is authored by Alemayehu Geda and Addis Yimer. The chapter discusses the political economy of policy making. The authors stress that the macro policy making in Africa has been and still is dominated by the policies of International Financial Institutions. The authors argue that the Poverty Reduction Strategy Papers and MDGS macro policy frameworks are the continuation of the SAPs, hence there is a need to have appropriate macro policy that will enable poverty reduction and macroeconomic stability. Chapter 7 on Occupational Health and Safety Framework in the Global Era: A Study of Labour Brokers in the City of Durban by Ivan Niranjan and Sultan Khan is a study that examines the role of labour brokers in creating the conditions for employers to compromise on the health and safety needs of workers in rubber industry in the city of Durban. The study finds that the workers are more than predisposed to serious health risks if they work continuously for longer durations when exposed to noise and volatile chemical substances. The chapter provides an overview of globalization and its effect on the compromise of worker health and safety. Chapter 8 on Financial Constraints to Small and Medium Enterprises (SME) in Africa by Sudhir Kapoor discusses the role and importance of SMEs in Africa. It elaborates on several constraints SMEs face with focus on limited availability of finance as a major constraint. It also discusses the alternative sources of generating finance in Africa and the strategies that SMEs can adopt to become a robust sector of African economy.

The section on Society and Culture has five chapters discussing wide range of African issues. Chapter 9 on Modernizing Process of Religious Identities in African Societies by A.S. Yaruingam discusses the role and importance of religion in everyday life of Africans. He attempts to analyze the process of changing religious identities of contemporary Africa. He critically analyzes the nature and ways in which Africans project their religious identities under different Christian denominations at the same time retaining the core philosophical belief of African Traditional Religion. The author mainly focuses on Christianity to understand African struggle to indigenize it (Christianity). Chapter 10 by Suresh Kumar on Rising Africa and India's Role in Strengthening Education Sector focuses on the importance of higher education for modernization and development of Africa. Africa can gain from Indian experience in finding solutions for Africa's development by assisting in academic and institutional expansion. Several Indian educational institutions are already providing their services in many African countries and this needs to be extended to other people and countries of Africa. Chapter 11 on Climate Change and Agriculture in Ethiopia by Tribhuwan Prasad focuses on various dimensions of climate change affects on Ethiopian agriculture and economy. The chapter estimates the possible impact of rainfall variability on Ethiopian agriculture. The author also discusses the impact on the cost of economy due to climate change and that the country will lose a large per cent of agricultural production over the coming years due to rainfall variability. The author discusses severe poverty implications of the climate change that will make poor more vulnerable. Chapter 12 on Gender and Agriculture in Africa by Rashmi Kapoor focuses on role of gender in agriculture in Africa. It elaborates on how gender inequalities can effect food production and food security. The chapter also discusses the constraints that women face in agricultural production. To address the issue of gender inequality requires interventions at all levels. She argues that women's capabilities be strengthened and the barriers to equal access to opportunities be removed. She stresses that there has to be a paradigm shift in policies and financing programmes for achieving gender equality. Chapter 13 on Islam and Africa: From Stereotypes to Knowledge by Pushpraj Singh demonstrates how history, culture and religion intersect in Muslim Africa communities in Africa. This chapter provides an overview of the development of Muslim societies in Africa with a regional focus on North Africa, Sahara, Sub-Saharan West Africa, the Horn of Africa and East Africa. The chapter examines the process of Islamization and the emergence of regional Muslim culture.

Part I

Politics and Society

1

Of Big Men and Big Ideas

Can Nepad's APRM Make a Difference?

Ian Taylor

The New Partnership for Africa's Development or Nepad was enthusiastically pushed by a select number of countries in Africa, as well as by the G-8, as a means to stimulate what has been termed the "African Renaissance" (*see* www.uneca.org/nepad/nepad.pdf). Nepad was launched in Abuja, Nigeria, in October 2001; it arose from the mandate granted to five African Heads of State (Algeria, Egypt, Nigeria, Senegal, South Africa) by the then Organization of African Unity (OAU) to work out a development program to spearhead Africa's renewal.

Nepad temporarily succeeded in placing the question of Africa's development onto the international table and managed to obtain a fairly high profile and awareness (*see* Taylor, 2005). In doing this, Nepad claimed to be a political and economic program aimed at promoting democracy, stability, good governance, human rights, and economic development on the continent. Nepad was essentially sold as a bargain: African countries would set up and police standards of good government across the continent—whilst respecting human rights and advancing democracy—in return for increased aid flows, private investment and a lowering of obstacles to trade by the West. An extra inflow of US$ 64 billion from the developed world was touted as the "reward" for following approved policies on governance and economics.

In essence, Nepad placed Africa's presidents at the centre of the continent's renewal and as the key agents for driving Africa's renaissance. Indeed, Paragraph 1 of Nepad opened with the statement that 'This New Partnership for Africa's Development is a pledge by African leaders, based on a common vision and a firm and shared conviction, that they have a pressing duty to eradicate poverty and to place their countries, both individually and collectively, on a path of sustainable growth and development'. Paragraph 6 followed with the assertion that 'What is required…is bold and imaginative leadership that is genuinely committed to a sustained human development effort and poverty eradication'. In other words, the continent's progress was seen as being dependent on its leadership.

A great deal of expectations were raised about the possibilities opened up by Nepad, particularly with regard to the promise to develop a credible peer review process to advance democracy and good government in Africa. Much of this, I would argue, was unrealistic as the logic and modus operandi of neo-patrimonial rule meant that Nepad's strictures on good governance and democracy could never be implemented without eroding the very nature of the post-colonial African State and undermining the positions of incumbent elites—an unlikely possibility. Such realities, I argue, derailed Nepad's African Peer Review Mechanism (APRM), the cornerstone of the whole project in many observers' eyes.

What is argued is that Nepad and its promoters fundamentally ignored the reality that power in African politics must be understood as the utilization of patronage and clientelism and operates within neo-patrimonial modes of governance—the antithesis of Nepad's own vision for Africa. The concept of neo-patrimonialism captures the hybridity of African States, in which patrimonial practices coexist and subvert modern State bureaucracies (Van de Walle, 2001: 51). Ruling elites effectively base their authority on their distribution of resources to clients, instead of the legal-rational mechanisms of a Weberian modern state, such as meritocracy, impartial legal structures and political accountability. Clientelism, rent-seeking and corruption are intrinsic to such systems and have become internalised to such an extent that they give 'essential operating codes for politics' (Bratton and Van de Walle, 1997: 63). This is 'accepted as normal behaviour, condemned only in so far as it benefits someone else rather than oneself' (Clapham, 1985: 49).

The irony is that the type of solutions advanced by Nepad would have, if successfully implemented, deprived rulers of the means to maintain their patronage networks. In short, to have an Africa based on the enunciated principles of Nepad would actually have eroded the material base upon which the neo-patrimonial state was predicated. For instance, Section 80 of the Nepad document stated that 'The purpose of the Democracy and Political Governance Initiative is to contribute to strengthening the political and administrative framework of participating countries, in line with the principles of democracy, transparency, accountability, integrity, respect for human rights and promotion of the rule of law' (Nepad Secretariat, 2001: 26). However, transparency and accountability in decision-making would have destabilized the very nature of neo-patrimonial modes of governance, as would the rule of law. And yet Nepad seemed to advance the idea that the very same African elites, who benefitted from the neo-patrimonial State, would now commit a form of class suicide. The possibility always seemed improbable. As Chabal and Daloz (1999: 15) point out:

> If political domination becomes embodied in the recognised juridical universe of the bureaucratic state (as Nepad's strictures on good governance demands), political elites would no longer have to justify their prominence through the fulfillment of their patrimonial duties. What this would mean, however, is that they would have to accept both the supremacy of institutions over individuals and the temporary nature of their political eminence.

With very few exceptions (Botswana, Mauritius, Senegal, South Africa), the majority of the Heads of State involved in Nepad were quintessentially leaders of neo-patrimonial regimes and certainly did not regard their rule as 'temporary' nor that institutional law should constrain their pre-eminence or that their rule be transparent and accountable. In other words, most African presidents behaved in ways that were the exact opposite of what Nepad said regarding good governance. What this meant is that the commitment shown to the APRM by State elites always needed to be taken with a pinch of salt. After all, the countries that far signed on were Algeria, Angola, Benin, Burkina Faso, Cameroon, Congo (Brazzaville), Egypt, Ethiopia, Gabon, Ghana, Kenya, Lesotho, Mali, Malawi, Mauritius, Mozambique, Nigeria, Rwanda, Senegal, Sierra Leone, South Africa, Tanzania, Uganda, and Zambia. Of these, only two would probably pass Nepad's own strictures on clean government and democracy (Mauritius and South Africa), whilst perhaps four others (Ghana, Kenya, Mali and Rwanda) might have been—at the time—given the benefit of doubt regarding efforts towards moving forward to universal standards of governance and democracy. Others were *highly* dubious. Accepting such scepticism, I move to discuss the fate of the much-vaunted African Peer Review Mechanism.

The African Peer Review Mechanism

The APRM was scheduled to be a succession of country reviews conducted by a *Country Review Team* consisting of at least one member from the *Panel of Eminent Persons* and one specialist for each of the four governance areas under the APRM remit. These four areas were democracy and good political governance; economic governance and management; corporate governance; and socio-economic development. A "base review" was to take place within eighteen months of a State's accession to the APRM. After this had been undertaken, the APRM would then engage in periodic reviews of a country's performance every two to four years. A further review *may* have been be inaugurated if there were early warning signs of a looming political or economic crisis (although note that this could only be initiated by the state's ruling leader). In addition to such exceptional circumstances, a review may have been called for by a member of the APRM for its own motivations.

Most focus on Nepad was aimed in particular at the section on Political Governance. As a Scandinavian ambassador commented, 'It was this that captured our imagination and made Nepad that much easier to sell' [Mail and Guardian (Johannesburg) November 8, 2002]. This was because it appeared to suggest a qualitatively different approach to Africa's problems than previous plans and declarations. The Heads of State Implementation Committee (HSIC) in Abuja in March 2002 approved the Draft Report on Good Governance and Democracy and the African Peer Review Mechanism (see UNECA, 2002) and Nepad's promoters forcefully argued that the APRM was a positive and demonstrable effort to encourage African states' commitment to "good governance" (Akinrinade, 2002: 3). It was in this context that Nepad staked its claim to being a different document from previous African declarations. Here, perhaps for the first time, was a promise to self-police African leaders: 'the most significant initiative ever advocated for moving the African continent from crisis to renewal', as one commentary implausibly claimed (Hope, 2002: 397).

According to Nepad's promoters, there would be five stages through which the APRM would proceed. Stage one would see studies commenced to measure the progress that various African countries had made so far towards democracy and good governance (ill-defined, it should be noted). The country to be reviewed was required to supply information to the APR Secretariat to enable it to produce a study of the political, economic and corporate governance and development environment in the country.

This would be based on 'official government documents' as well as 'recent self-assessments and reviews'. During this first phase, participating states would devise a "Program of Action". This would seek to respond to the levels of political representation, institutional effectiveness and accountability, and economic management and corporate governance in each country.

Stage two of the APRM would see an Eminent Persons Review Team visit the country under review to carry out "consultations" with the state administration and its leaders as well as with political parties and legislators. Representatives of civil society were said to be included, although who was to be included and who excluded was not enunciated. The APRM Panel of Eminent Persons comprised the following: Adebayo Adedeji representing West Africa; Bethuel Kiplagat for East Africa; Graça Machel, Southern Africa; Dorothy Njeuma, Central Africa; Marie-Angelique Savané, West Africa; and Chris Stals, Southern Africa. The credentials of these Eminent Persons will be discussed below. The usefulness of a fleeting visit by select elites from within Africa to a country, in order to conduct a "Country Review Visit" was always highly doubtful, to say the least.

Stage three would see the Review Team finalizing its report on the basis of its discussions in stage two and the findings of the studies undertaken during stage one. The material and findings of the Review Team's report would be evaluated against the pointers contained in the UNECA's Declaration on Democracy, Political, Economic and Corporate Governance. The recommendations of the Review Team's report was to focus on how the Programme of Action of the country could be improved to accelerate the "best practice" standards. These recommendations should state specific measures that the country had to include in its Programme of Action. Be that as it may, the report would be considered with the government under evaluation and revisions made. Indeed, 'The Team's draft country review report was to be first discussed with the Government of the country' in order to 'ensure the accuracy of the information'. This process was also designed to 'provide the Government with an opportunity, both to react to the accuracy of the information and the Team's findings and to put forward their own views on how to address the identified shortcomings, including modifying the draft Programme of Action. The responses of the Government (would) be appended to the APR Team's report' (Nepad Secretariat, 2003: 15).

Yet this was highly problematic as at this point all non-state actors were to be excluded and only the government concerned would be involved. In other words, state elites would be given the opportunity, free of civil society oversight, to comment on the "accuracy" of the report as they saw fit. The only limits placed on their activities would be those placed by the Eminent Persons. This was followed by a now well-worn path pursued by Nepad: limited, if not minimal, engagement with civil society. After all, 'until April 2002, no trade union, civil society, church, women's, youth, political-party, parliamentary, or other potentially democratic or progressive forces in Africa were formally consulted by the politicians or technocrats involved in constructing Nepad' (Bond, 2003: 9).

Stage four would witness the revised and final country review report being presented to the APR Panel. The APR Panel was to meet to review the report in accordance with its mandate and submit its recommendations on the report to the APR Forum, which was to meet to consider the report. Upon its adoption, the Country Report would then be publicised through African Union institutions. As part of stage five, the Final APRM Report was to be tabled formally and publicly in key regional and sub-regional structures, such as the Summit of the African Union, the Pan-African Parliament, the African Commission on Human and Peoples' Rights, the Peace and Security Council and the Economic, Social and Cultural Council (ECOSOC) of the African Union, as well as the Regional Economic Community of the region of which the country reviewed was a member (Nepad Secretariat, 2003). This initial stage of the APRM was thus complete, although as noted above, there were instances whereby the APRM might be called upon in the future. Of note, the country reviewed would be left to implement the advice put forward by the Eminent Persons.

However, due to the voluntary nature of the whole process, states did not actually have to implement the APRM panel's advice or even the Country Report. Thus, if state elites were to go back on the recommendations of the Review Team, there were no mechanisms or teeth to do anything about this and even civil society was excluded from being involved. According to Nepad's position, 'the participating states should first do everything practicable to engage it in constructive dialogue, offering in the process technical and other appropriate assistance. If dialogue proves unavailing, the participating Heads of State and Government may wish to put the government on notice of their collective intention to proceed with appropriate measures by a given date' (Nepad Secretariat, 2002: 11). But these 'appropriate measures' continued to be indeterminate and obscure. Indeed, 'these vague measures neither penalize a country for an unfavourable review nor provide it with incentives to undertake the recommendations of the review or take steps to avoid an unfavourable review' (Bekoe, 2003: 5). Yet, 'this mechanism will fail in its task if reviews happen only periodically and rigorous criteria—and the consequences for deviant governments—are not spelled out. It seems that African Heads of State will be left to judge their own performance. The proposed peer review shows that Nepad leaders do not yet recognize accountable governance as a relationship between governments and citizens' (*Zimbabwe Independent* (Harare). May 24, 2002). This is why the nature of the APRM mechanism 'points to the importance of civil society engagement to prevent the reviews from being no more than a window-dressing exercise between governments' (Verwey, 2005: 11).

If a country *did* comply with the Review Team's recommendations, then it would, according to Nepad process, be eventually given a grade: 'Nepad Compliant', 'Aspiring to Nepad Compliance, but in need of assistance', 'Wilfully non-compliant', and 'Post-conflict countries requiring special reconciliation and reconstruction' (*Business Day* (Johannesburg). November 4, 2002). According to the logic within Nepad, this was then supposed to facilitate increased aid and foreign investment into the country, depending on the grade achieved. However, as the whole process was voluntary from the start, 'The toughest aspect of peer review—awarding "pass" or "fail" marks—(was)...neatly dodged, because only those countries likely to make the grade will volunteer to undergo the APR (M)' (De Waal, 2002: 472).

Before discussing the APRM in more detail, it should be noted that no budget was actually set for the APRM. Indeed, the proposed plan called for the APRM to gather its resources primarily from those states that had volunteered to participate in the review process—countries had to pay at least US$ 100,000 to take part. Whilst the APRM (commendably) emphasized the need to keep foreign financial assistance low, in order to avoid charges that it was not African-owned, the financing scheme raised deep concerns that the APRM would end up underfunded and devoid of any real political independence. Firstly, states with no real commitment to Nepad principles could cite the lack of funds as an excuse to duck out of the review process. In addition, 'resources from African states can also be used to bias the peer review. A participating state may refuse to contribute its levy, as a means of protesting an unfavourable review—holding the APRM hostage' (Bekoe, 2003: 6). Certainly, given the historical failure of African states to meet their financial commitments to previous African initiatives, such as paying their dues for membership of, first, the Organization of African Unity and now, the African Union, serious questions needed to be asked vis-à-vis the financing of the APRM and the implications that this had. After all, when the OAU wound down, to be replaced by the AU, the outgoing OAU Secretary General Salim Ahmed Salim indicated that only four countries had paid their dues on time. This improved somewhat by the time of the transformation into the AU: of the 53 OAU members, 16 had settled their dues. This still meant, however, that the AU inherited a multi-million dollar debt. And as it stands, the African Union regularly reports huge arrears.

Prevarication Over the Political

As it was originally conceived (and certainly how it was sold to partners in the G-8), the peer review mechanism pledged to offer a disciplinary device to secure compliance with agreed values and norms in Africa. This was cast as a way to improve the legitimacy of African states in their dealings with outside actors and bolster the possibility of improving governance in Africa as a means to secure greater political and economic stability to reverse Africa's marginalization. The very concept of peer review was portrayed as the examination and appraisal of the functioning of a state by other states (peers), by mandated institutions, or by a combination of these (Economic Commission for Africa, 2002: 2). The end objective was cast as assisting the reviewed state's progress in its adoption of approved best practices and to *ensure* that it fulfilled agreed-upon principles and values.

Indeed, initially the review mechanism was sold as having muscle to rein in malefactors. Such a review process, which Nepad promoters originally insisted, had to include measures to ensure compliance. This was because, according to Obasanjo 'African leaders could no longer remain silent about the shortcomings or abuses of other African leaders' (quoted in Africa Recovery, Vol. 15, No. 4, December 2001: 10). Indeed, Mbeki 'repeatedly stressed the importance of establishing a credible and effective African Peer Review Mechanism to help decide which countries benefit, and to what extent, from membership of Nepad. Peer review is vital to his vision for Africa' (Mail and Guardian (Johannesburg) May 10, 2002). This meant, Mbeki claimed, that the Nepad peer review process should support 'certain standards of behaviour, which are agreed, which are clear, *which are capable of enforcement* (emphasis added)' (South African Press Agency (Cape Town), February 12, 2002).

However, the whole question over what peer review implied quickly led to a somewhat ignominious retreat to a voluntary process with no measures to ensure compliance. Governance review was eventually retained as a watered-down voluntary process. The retreat to a purely voluntary review might be seen as a belated realization by Nepad's promoters that an intrusive review process would never be bought by the bulk of Africa's leaders. In fact, Mbeki quickly realized that if a credible peer review process had been endorsed, then Pretoria would have rapidly been elevated (by the donor countries) to being the de facto policeman of good governance in Africa, a duty that Mbeki—as the debacle surrounding his policies towards Mugabe has shown—is not willing to perform. In addition, the pan-African elite solidarity and the historic reluctance of criticizing fellow presidents on the continent meant that any review mechanism that might seek to enforce best practices and/or judge others' performances, was bound to falter. Furthermore, the volte-face threw into focus the over-selling of Nepad by its promoters and the too easy acceptance by the G-8 of the initial plan—note the comment by one Western diplomat in Pretoria that 'Perhaps we were naïve, but we were very taken by Mbeki going where very few other leaders—and certainly no Africans had dared. It was this that captured our imagination' (quoted in *Mail and Guardian* (Johannesburg) November 8, 2002). But, the type of intrusive peer review system initially sold by Mbeki in the run up to the launch of Nepad was ahead of even the sophisticated and long-standing OECD process and the European Union had not even tried to introduce such a mechanism. As a result, looking at the current situation in Africa, a political peer review system of the type originally sold by Mbeki would only have called attention to wholesale malgovernance and corruption on the continent, thus, immediately sabotaging Mbeki's rhetoric that the "African Renaissance" was already underway. Yet, at the same time, a process with no sanctions or counter-measures against those countries that fail to pass muster meant that the review mechanism had no teeth.

Certainly, the suspicion rapidly became that the evaluation panel restricted itself to rubber-stamping governance reports of countries that were confident of positive evaluations by the panel in the first place. Countries that rapidly volunteered to undergo peer review included Ghana, Kenya, Rwanda and Uganda. The experience of these reviews indicated how effectiveness and value was to be added to Africa's development by the APRM.

When Graça Machel arrived in Nairobi in October 2005, she immediately proclaimed that Kenya's self-assessment report was "candid"

[*Mail and Guardian* (Johannesburg) October 9, 2005], with the *East African Standard* saying, 'The report recognizes some of the good things achieved by the government. There is openness in it'. Yet, as one report critically noted, 'in fact, the report show(ed) that 80 per cent of interviewees feel powerless to change policies that touch their daily lives. Fully three-quarters believe that MPs and councilors are feathering their own nests rather than tending to the needs of the people, who put them in office'. 'Kenyans are dissatisfied with the performance of their elected representatives, widespread corruption in the police force and the justice system' *(ibid)*. Within Kenya, civil society split from the government with regard to the APRM and wanted to present an alternative report to the APRM adjudicators. Machel, however, refused to accept this and urged civil society to 'work with the government'.

As noted above, the Eminent Persons panel (appointed in May 2003) was made up of six initial members. All of these panelists were intimately linked to the elite classes of Africa and immediately brought into question any notion of real independence and objectivity. Certainly, it put into question Marie-Angelique Savané's assertion that 'We are controversial people back at home and we cannot be manipulated' (quoted by *Reuters (Kigali)* March 11, 2004). The six were: Graça Machel (Mozambique), the wife of Nelson Mandela; Adebayo Adedeji (Nigeria) ex-head of the UN Economic Commission for Africa and ex-minister in one of Nigeria's military-run, coup-generated governments; Marie-Angelique Savané (Senegal), former head of the UN Population Fund's Africa Bureau; Bethuel Kiplagat (Kenya), ex-ambassador under Daniel arap Moi; Dorothy Njeuma, ex-minister of education in Cameroon; and Chris Stals (South Africa), ex-head of the South African Reserve Bank.[1] Cynics noted that this line-up would no doubt satisfy those elites in Africa, who were quick to assert that 'Nepad should not be used as a political tool to demand human rights, democracy and other unnecessary conditions' (Namibian Agriculture Minister Helmut Angula, (quoted in *The Namibian* (Windhoek), April 15, 2003). Indeed, the Eminent Persons panel was devoid of credibility if independence from extant elites was a serious criterion. Take for instance, one member, Dorothy Njeuma. In September 2004, during the Cameroonian election, Njeuma told a campaign rally that, 'with (Paul) Biya, there is progress, stability and development… if we want more development, we have to show him our support'. She also stated that the people should vote for Biya, 'on behalf of their sons', because if they do not support Biya, 'their sons may not have the opportunity to be where they are' (*Post* (Buea) September 29, 2004).

Njeuma, it should be noted, is a member of the political bureau of President Paul Biya's governing party. And yet, the Eminent Persons panel is supposed to be independent, free-thinking and willing to critique recalcitrant governments. How does this square with one of its members actively campaigning for a politician, who is routinely held up by observers as being one of the worst examples of a corrupt, neo-patrimonial Big Man? (Mehler, 1998; Van de Walle, 1994).

Certainly, from the perspective of the international community, for the reviews to be considered credible, they should not have diverged too much from what international opinion knew and thought about a country already. But this was a key point: what added value that the APRM process claim to provide to potential investors, which was not already offered by the Economist Intelligence Unit, Standard and Poors credit ratings, Human Rights Watch Africa's reports, Amnesty International's overviews, indeed general knowledge garnered from the media and first-hand experiences? The key answer seemed to be that the APRM was "Africa-owned". But this may not have been so much of a plus point. After all, any repetition of the Zimbabwe debacle or the situation in Rwanda where African monitors gave the presidential elections of 2003 an unrealistically favorable endorsement of the polls, in contrast with the negative opinions of Western observers, would instantly undermine the APRM's worth:

> If the reviews are not credible, then it will depend on what alternative, consistent and transparent monitoring process is applied by the partner countries. To the extent that the developed countries end up paying lip service to superficial or cosmetic reviews, they will simply be helping to entrench an ineffectual political ritual. Therefore, the G-8 and other developed democracies... have to try to make sure that the "reviews" do not simply create a smokescreen behind which corrupt, but influential African governments continue with their old habits, confirming the worst fears expressed by the international NGO movement (Schlemmer, 2002:13).

After all, 'The G-8 supporters of Nepad insist that the African Peer Review Mechanism (APRM) is the jewel in Nepad's crown and have clearly predicated the amount and quality of their financial support on it. Nepad's political difficulties in Western circles have not been helped by how the prognosis of the APRM has become entangled with the controversies over Zimbabwe' (Graham, 2002: 3).

Whilst defenders of the retreat from the original premise of Nepad argued that volunteering for a review would put pressure on those that did not, this was unconvincing. The argument was advanced that an obligatory peer review process under the rubric of Nepad would have undermined the supposedly binding nature of the provisions of the African Union regarding political governance. Yet, as any historian of the AU's predecessor—the Organization of African Unity—will tell you, adhering to "good" political governance was largely neglected by that organization, sacrificed to the pan-African principle of "non-interference" in domestic affairs and, effectively, elite solidarity (Van Walraven, 1999). Why the promoters of Nepad claimed that the AU would be qualitatively different from the OAU when the very same African elites were in power and when the nature of the African state had remained largely unaltered was unclear. After all, as Adeleke notes, any renewal project for the continent 'cannot be meaningful if it is spearheaded and guided by the current African political leadership, those directly responsible for undermining the very foundation upon which a viable pan-African tradition could have been built' (Adeleke, 1998: 533).

Perhaps the main motive for the volte-face was linked to the fear that Nepad would actually result in a split in Africa. If it was to be implemented as a compulsory and credible review process, then, one would see the emergence of various clusters of "winners and losers" within the continent. The main political (and perhaps, economic) beneficiaries would almost certainly be the economically stronger African territories and/or the few leaders on the continent perceived as being serious (i.e. pro-reform liberalisers with an "approved" record on human rights and democracy) by the West. Deviants from this norm and those states with tainted leaders, i.e., "non-acceptable" to the West, would be set aside—unless, of course, their value as guardians of resources warranted a tactical "blind eye". Yet, such a scenario would strike at the heart of one of the very few things the African Union actually stands for: pan-African unity amongst its elites. Increased polarization between these elites was not what Nepad was supposed to be about, even if the logical outcome of its governance agenda would have certainly led to such a milieu. Indeed, the APRM reflected an undeniable contradiction within the whole recovery plan: on the one hand, it had to be as inclusive as possible, in order to obtain pan-African "buy-in", whilst on the other hand, it had to be as exclusive as possible in order to obtain credibility. Furthermore, the APRM as it was initially sold, created what Van der Westhuizen (2003: 389) called the "dual dilemma" of Nepad:

> First, a mechanism to provide a "seal of approval" is required to assure wary foreign investors, but such a mechanism is vulnerable to being perceived by critics as an extension of "Western imperialism"... The second... is the difficulty of relating to sovereignty and non-interference, which prohibits fellow African states from interfering in one another's domestic affairs.

A retreat from such a problematic scenario was, thus, perhaps inevitable.

Whilst obviously "good governance" is but one part of any coherent program to tackle Africa's situation, the way in which Nepad, seemingly, got bogged down (by controversy over the backtracking regarding peer review) was noteworthy. Equally noteworthy was the retreat by Mbeki over his call, linked to the APRM, that the G-8 should hold African leaders to their expressed promises. After all, Mbeki claimed that 'I've been saying to the leadership of the developed world that they need to respond positively... to challenge us, to say "this is what you say but we want to see practical action from you consistent with what you are saying"' (Mbeki, 2002c: 204). Yet, when Commonwealth leaders discussed Zimbabwe and demanded that Mbeki and other African leaders demonstrate 'practical action... consistent with what (they had been) saying' regarding democracy and human rights, Mbeki labelled them racists, who were merely 'inspired by notions of White supremacy' and, who felt uneasy at their 'repugnant position imposed by inferior Blacks' (Mbeki, 2002d).

Concluding Remarks

A key problem facing the continent has long been the ability or otherwise of governance and development initiatives, such as Nepad to successfully operate in the context of neo-patrimonialism and Big Men politics. As Chabal (*2002*) notes, any cool evaluation of the political situation on the continent undermines the potency of the renewal project as a means towards better governance. (*Mail and Guardian*, Johannesburg, July 12, 2002).

Obviously, Africa's regeneration is not simply a question of advancing "good leadership" or "good government"; the structural impediments to African trade are equally important, and we must avoid a voluntarist approach to Africa's development nor neglect the nature of its relationship with the international system. But, it can be said that without the construction of transparent and accountable government, Nepad's ambitious economic plans, whatever their own manifest weaknesses and the wider structural impediments of the global economy (*see* Bond, 2002; Taylor and Nel, 2002) were profoundly compromised. Indeed, the failure to act in any meaningful way regarding governance and human rights as situations presented themselves indicated early on that Nepad would have a rather muted impact. After all, the leaders of Nepad did not need to wait for the APRM to be fully functional before talking out about misrule in places, such as Zimbabwe or Swaziland (Taylor, 2002), or Malawi or the Sudan or Gabon, etc. Whilst one is fully aware of the historical legacies that mean that pan-African elite solidarity reigns, the question that needs to be asked is, for how long will this solidarity trump all else? And can it ever be used to justify inaction and nod-and-wink postures towards malevolent dictators? As Robert Rotberg notes:

> African leaders are expected to demonstrate that they are "fully aware of the responsibilities and obligations to their people, and are genuinely prepared to engage and relate to the rest of the world on the basis of integrity and world respect". This is a tall order. Neither Presidents Mbeki nor Obasanjo have employed peer pressure to halt the growing trend toward dictatorship in today's Africa. Neither leader has publicly condemned electoral theft in Zimbabwe or attempts to breach the constitutions of Malawi, Namibia, or Zambia. Neither they nor many of their contemporaries have criticized denials of media freedom in neighboring countries, corruption, misappropriation or squandering of foreign assistance funds, or said much about the leadership causes of the famine now engulfing 13 million people in southern Africa (quoted in Christian Science Monitor (Boston), June 19, 2002).

The key problem is that there is a 'growing need in this globalizing world to have a strong and credible Africa-wide voice, a voice that draws its legitimacy and authority from being rooted in democratic principles. There are two directions in which this voice needs to speak—internally, to African nations, and externally, to the court of world opinion. Internally, there is a need to show the way, and to persuade and if necessary to sanction, African nations who stray from democracy and basic human rights, and this can best be done by other African nations, through an organization that is founded on these principles' (Kanbur, 2003). However, Nepad was always unlikely to match the heady expectations that greeted its launch and the APRM certainly did not. This was because to do so involved trying to enlist the support of elites, who were bizarrely expected to undermine their own positions and the positions of their clients. As the Rwandan journalist Shyaka Kanuwa noted, this 'brings us to the question, or rather the dilemma: how can rulers, who are themselves clearly the problem be part of the solution?... These men are not troubled by niceties such as respect for human rights, concern for their populations' material welfare or consensual decision-making. Most preside over decaying military or police states. They benefit from a hybrid of African patronage and farcical parliamentary, judicial and other institutional procedures that contrive invariably to act in the big man's interests' (quoted in *Mail and Guardian* (Johannesburg) July 12, 2002).

In addition, to do so would have called into question the manner by which Africa interacted with the global economy (Bond, 2002). It was naïve to expect elites, whose very modus operandi was based on privatized patronage (in Western eyes, malgovernance) and the prohibition and erosion of democracy, to begin implementing and operating by the rubric of "good governance". To do so would not only have damaged their own holds on power, but reduced their ability to maintain lucrative linkages with the external world. That is why it was always strange to have any confidence that the commitments to democracy and good government by members of the HSIC—which included such models as Omar Bongo of Gabon, Paul Biya of Cameroon or Denis Sassou-Nguesso of Congo-Brazzaville went beyond anything more than rhetoric, nor that the involvement of the likes of Adedeji or Njeuma on the Eminent Persons panel amounted to anything serious. When questioned about this contradiction between rhetoric and reality, the chairman of Nepad's steering committee, Wiseman Nkuhlu, was apparently 'not bothered by the criticism' as he had 'a simple answer for the critics'. This answer was that 'all leaders' involved in Nepad 'were democratically elected. So, they represented ruling parties from their own countries' (quoted in Mkhondo, 2004: 19). This of course was patently false.

This skepticism regarding the democratic credentials of a good number of Nepad's signatories was shared by others, including the policy-making community. Stephen Morrison, a former United States State Department adviser and director of the African program at the Center for Strategic and International Studies commented:

> No one is going to stand up and say Nepad is a bad thing. But people are talking about it less and less because they don't believe it will amount to much. The US administration agrees in principle with Nepad's goals. But the inaction over Zimbabwe's persistent breaches of human rights, the inclusion of some very strange

> people on the Nepad steering committee and Mbeki's statement that political criteria are not part of the peer review system give rise to skepticism. The interest level in Nepad wanes as its credibility drops (*Mail and Guardian* (Johannesburg), November 8, 2002).

Thus, it remains that in Africa, a small elite group places self-preservation over and above policies that would benefit the majority of the population. 'In case after case, ruling elites continue to impede the process of sharing political and economic power more broadly' (Schraeder, 1994: 85). This implies that any monitoring of governance standards and the improvement in democratic standards on the continent cannot remain elite-driven as was inherent in the APRM process nor, from the perspective of the donor community, dependent upon the whims of the elites within government. Nor can they be detached from a critical restructuring of Africa's global economic linkages and world trade policies. One of the main positive things about Nepad was that it was an African initiative and that it generated a certain level of debate within Africa with regard to the continent's development impasse. These facets of the project might have been worth building on. However, whilst Nepad remained so dependent upon the Big Men to advance good governance through the APRM, something which went against the very logic of neo-patrimonial rule, as well as promoted neo-liberal policies inimical to long-term and broad-based development, then its project to promote the continent's regeneration in the new millennium, was always likely to be stillborn.

NOTE

1. What is interesting here of course is the fact that before being recruited onto the well-paid and high-profile Eminent Persons committee, Adedeji was a prominent critic of the NEPAD, denouncing it for ignoring his own Lagos Plan of Action and AAF-SAP. In fact, according to Adedeji, the NEPAD was fundamentally flawed because it sought to make Africa 'march towards its future hand-in-hand with its colonial mono-cultural, low productivity and excessively dependent and open economy' [sic] [Adedeji, 2002: 6].

REFERENCES

Adedeji, A. (2002). 'Keynote Address: From the Lagos Plan of Action to the New Partnership for African Development and From the Final Act of Lagos to the Constitutive Act: Wither Africa?', paper prepared for presentation at the African Forum for Envisioning Africa, Nairobi, Kenya, 26-29 April.

Adeleke, T. (1998). Black Americans and Africa: A Critique of the Pan-African and Identity Paradigms, *International Journal of African Historical Studies*, Vol. 31(3).

Akinrinade, S. (2002). Nepad: The New Partnership for Africa's Development. *Bulletin of the Conflict, Security and Development Group*, no. 15.

Bekoe, D. (2003). Creating a Reliable African Peer Review Mechanism. *Chimera.* Vol. 1, issue 4.

Bond, P. (ed.). (2002). *Fanon's Warning. A Civil Society Reader on the New Partnership for Africa's Development.* Trenton: Africa World Press.

Bond, P. (2003). South Africa and Global Apartheid: Is the Reform Strategy Working? Paper presented to the Transnational Seminar, University of Illinois/Champaign-Urbana, 14 November 2003.

Bratton, M. and Van de Walle, N. (1997). *Democratic Experiments in Africa: Regime Transitions in Comparative Perspective.* Cambridge: Cambridge University Press.

Chabal, P. (2002). The Quest for Good Governance and Development in Africa: Is Nepad the Answer?. *International Affairs*, Vol. 78(3).

Chabal, P. and J.P. Daloz. (1999). *Africa Works: Disorder as Political Instrument.* Oxford: James Currey.

Clapham, C. (1985). *Third World Politics: An Introduction.* London: Croom Helm.

De Waal, A. (2002). What's New in the "New Partnership for Africa's Development" *International Affairs*, Vol. 78(3).

Graham, Y. (2002). Nepad's Slippery Milestones. *African Trade Agenda*, No. 5, December.

Hodges, T. (2001). *Angola: From Afro-Stalinism to Petro-Diamond Capitalism.* Oxford: James Currey.

Hope, K. (2002). From Crisis to Renewal: Towards a Successful Implementation of the New Partnership for Africa's Development. *African Affairs*, Vol. 101.

Kanbur, R. (2001). The New Partnership for Africa's Development: An Initial Commentary. *www.people.cornell.edu/pages/skl45*

Mbeki, T. (2002a). Sceptics will Not Stop the Re-building of Africa. *ANC Today*, Vol. 2(38). 20-26 September.

Mbeki, T. (2002b). Critics Ill-Informed About Nepad Peer Review. *ANC Today*, Vol. 2(45). November 8-14.

Mbeki, T. (2002c). *Africa—Define Yourself* Cape Town: Tafelberg.

Mbeki, T. (2002d). Letter from the President: Zimbabwe: "Two Blacks and One White". *ANC Today.* Vol. 2 (10). 8-14 March.

Mehler, A. (1998). Cameroon and the Politics of Patronage. in David Birmingham and Phyllis Martin, (eds.). *History of Central Africa: The Contemporary Years Since 1960.* London: Longman.

Mkhondo, R. (2004). Nkuhlu Unpacks Nepad. *Leadership*, December/January.

Nepad Secretariat. (2001). *New Partnership for Africa's Development, 2001,* www.dfa.gov.za/events/Nepad.pdf

Nepad Secretariat. (2002). *Nepad Action Plans* Midrand: Nepad Secretariat.

Nepad Secretariat. (2003). *African Peer Review Mechanism Organisation and Processes.* Midrand: Nepad Secretariat.

Schraeder, P. (1994). Elites as Facilitators or Impediments to Political Development? Some Lessons from the "Third Wave" of Democratisation in Africa. *Journal of Developing Areas*, Vol. 29(1).

Schlemmer, L. (2002). Getting Real about Democracy in Africa: Nepad and the Challenge of Good Governance', paper presented at an international colloquium on Cultures, Religions and Conflicts, Mzaar, Lebanon, September 18-21.

Taylor, I. (2002). The New Partnership for Africa's Development and the Zimbabwe Elections: Implications and Prospects for the Future. *African Affairs*, Vol. 101, issue 404.

Taylor, I. (2005). *NEPAD: Towards Africa's Development or Another False Start?* Boulder, Colorado: Lynne Rienner.

Taylor, I. and Nel, P. (2002). "New Africa", Globalization and the Confines of Elite Reformism: "Getting the Rhetoric Right", Getting the Strategy Wrong. *Third World Quarterly*, Vol. 23(1).

Van de Walle, N. (1994). Neopatrimonialism and Democracy in Africa, with an Illustration from Cameroon. In J. Widner. (ed.). *Economic Change and Political Liberalization in Africa.* Baltimore: Johns Hopkins University Press.

Van der Westhuizen, J. (2003). How, Not, to Sell Big Ideas: Argument, Identity and Nepad. *International Journal*, Summer.

Van Walraven, K. (1999). *Dreams of Power: The Role of the Organization of African Unity in the Politics of Africa, 1963-1993.* Aldershot: Ashgate.

Verwey, L. (2005). *Nepad and Civil Society Participation in the APRM.* Cape Town: IDASA Occasional Paper.

2

Revisiting African Development Strategies in the New Millennium: From the LPA to NEPAD

Kyu Deug Hwang

Since the continent's independence in the 1960s, development perspectives on Africa have been trapped by contending agendas characterized as a rift between African governments and the international community over approaches to African development (Ake 1996). By the late 1960s and early 1970s, in particular, when Keynesianism as the dominant developmental discourse at the global scale started facing opposition from what has come to be known as neoliberalism, the Structural Adjustment Programs (SAPs) of the International Monetary Fund (IMF) and World Bank (WB) began to take the helm of policy perspectives on the development of Africa. Despite a number of alternative attempts by both within and outside the continent, yet, neoliberal economic policy regime had not disappeared, but had, instead, expanded and deepened, displaying disturbing phenomena for continental leaders and policy makers in Africa in a Post-Cold War international system.

As Africa has entered the twenty-first century, moreover, the continent is faced with a multitude of development problems, including widespread poverty, malnutrition and disease, violent ethnic conflict, corruption, and a broad range of socio-economic quagmire. Against this background, Africa has been considered as the only continent in which living conditions have been deteriorating in the last thirty years (*see*, e.g., Castells, 1997; World Bank, 2000; Hoogvelt, 2002; Guest, 2004). As Saitoti (2003: 13) notes, contrary to the theory of convergence that postulates that poor countries can be expected to grow faster than developed countries, thereby resulting in global convergence in income levels, poor economic situations in Africa has brought forth to divergence. In this sense, he continues to argue that the quality of life enjoyed by the majority of Africans has deteriorated both in absolute and relative terms.

Following some initial progress during the first development decade in the 1960s, in fact, "the development of underdevelopment" has been actualized in many African countries. In this context, *The Economist* in its May 13-19, 2000 issue from the perspective of the so-called Afro-pessimism, called Africa the "hopeless" continent and further characterized the prospects for development in the new millennium as practically non-existent. In order to reverse this condition, the New Partnership for Africa's Development (NEPAD) was created by African leaders in July 2001. Significantly, NEPAD seeks to address Africa's poverty and related structural constraints to place the continent firmly on the path to sustainable development. The advent of NEPAD could, therefore, not have come at a better time and Afro-optimism could not have been unexpected.

What is important to note is, in particular, that NEPAD seeks to develop its developmental strategy by "building up the achievements of the past, as well as reflecting on the lessons learned through painful experience, so as to establish a partnership that is both credible and capable of implementation" (NEPAD 2001: paragraph 27). Diagnosing the earlier African development frameworks in response to the SAPs of neoliberal economic policy, this article begins by discussing the historical, political and economic backdrops of five landmark African development strategies that emerged in the 1980s and early 1990s, which include as follows: the Lagos Plan of Action for the Economic Development of Africa, 1980-2000 and the Final Act of Lagos (1980); Africa's Priority Program for Economic Recovery 1986-1990 (APPER), which was later converted into the United Nations Program of Action for Africa's Economic Recovery and Development (UN-PAAERD) (1986); the African Alternative Framework to Structural Adjustment Program for Socio-Economic Recovery and Transformation (AAF-SAP) (1989); the African Charter for Popular Participation for Development (1990); the United Nations New Agenda for the Development of Africa in the 1990s (UN-NADAF) (1991).

The chapter then pays attentions to the Abuja Treaty establishing the African Economic Community with a view to examining its compositions, modalities as well as its implications for the NEPAD framework. Lastly, this article delves into three key frameworks of NEPAD, including peace and security governance, economic and regional governance, and political and democratic governance. Exploring these frameworks of NEPAD within the diametrically opposing views held by its architects and those of its critics, this article concludes by rethinking African development paths as well as presenting the way forward.

Antecedents to NEPAD: Towards Collective Self-Reliance and Self-Sustainable Development?

The appreciable progress was made in improving the social welfare of the people in Africa in the first decade of independence. Pursuing industrial projects (namely, import substitution strategies), the newly independent governments made a great deal of efforts for expanding the social and physical infrastructure of their countries in a way that widened access to education, transportation, housing, skills development, health, and employment on a scale that exceeded what colonialism provided. For this purpose, and irrespective of the ideological leanings, which they professed, all of the independent governments reserved an important role for the state in the development process; so they undertook varying degrees of planning designed not only to improve the foundations of the economy, but also to continually increase access to opportunities in a context of huge, pent-up demand (Olukoshi, 2002: 6).

During the second decade of independence, however, the slow-down of the economic growth rate was accompanied by increased levels of political repression and exclusion, which further widened the gulf between state and society, popular social forces and the wielders of state power. In addition, SAPs led by the IMF and WB, which triumphed in the quest for reversing the dwindling economic fortunes of Africa not only exacerbated the crisis of decline, but also struck the final nail in the coffin of the post-colonial model of accumulation and the social contract that was built into it (Olukoshi, 2002: 7).

The Advent of the LPA as a Response to the African Crisis

In April 1980, nevertheless, the UN Economic Commission for Africa (UNECA) and the OAU devised the Lagos Plan of Action (LPA) identifying actions that needed to be taken to implement the objectives of the Monrovia Declaration adopted by the OAU in 1979. With the LPA and the Final Act of Lagos (FAL), African countries attempted to initiate a development model based on the principle of individual autonomy and collective self-sufficiency. In its diagnoses, that is, the LPA focused on the exogenous factors that led to and sustained *dependent capitalism,* which was supported by the theory of dependency in International

Relations. In the beginning of the Preamble, the LPA asserted that "the effect of unfulfilled promises of global development strategies has been more sharply felt in Africa than in other continents of the world" (OAU, 1980: paragraph 1). In lieu of producing substantial development, the global development strategies had made Africa "more susceptible than other regions to the economic and social crises suffered by the industrialized countries" (*Ibid.*).

Within this context, the structural weaknesses of African economies as one of the main causes of the African economic crisis can be firstly pointed out. In agriculture, this is mainly a function of low production and productivity, and rudimentary agricultural techniques. In the area of trade, it manifests itself in over-dependence on the export of primary products (agricultural and minerals), which exacerbates openness to external shocks (OAU, 1980: paragraphs 7, 9). The second important cause of the crisis is lack of adequate capacity (capital, skills and technology) for the development of the rich natural resource endowment. In this situation, there was a considerable dependence on foreign transnational corporations for the development of a narrow range of African natural resources selected by these corporations to meet the new material needs of the developed countries (OAU, 1980: paragraph 76). The third one is the developed countries' negative and hostile attitude towards efforts being made by African countries for accelerated industrialization in the region through import substitutions industrializations (ISIs) (OAU, 1980: Chapter II).

In response to the crisis, which can be identified as fundamentally structural and the hostile external environment at least in relation to the developed countries and the foreign transnational corporations, the LPA's strategy for orienting Africa towards a sustainable development path involved 'collective self-reliance and self-sustainable development' at the stages and modalities of its short, medium and long-term implementation framework.

However, the focus of the LPA was overwhelmingly on economic factors, such as inter-African trade and investment through regional cooperation and integration schemes. Due to the fact that, "by 1980—when the LPA was adopted—almost all the economic cooperation schemes optimistically launched in the 1960s—the halcyon days of African integration had become largely moribund" (Asante, 1985: 82). In this sense, Herbst argues that "the tendency of the LPA was to list the problems that African countries were facing; suggest, without even a vague hint of how these could be financed, and then recommend the creation of numerous international institutions to help African countries" (Herbst, 1993: 139).

Searching for the Alternative Development Strategies in the Era of SAPs

Meanwhile, a year later, in 1981, the World Bank responded to the LPA with a special report entitled *Accelerated Development in Sub-Saharan Africa: An Agenda for Action*, more commonly known as the Berg Report. In particular, the report also stressed the interdependency of countries throughout the world and maintained that African countries should pursue their 'comparative advantage' by striving to improve production of their export products. But, this was criticized and rejected by African governments because they believed that implementation of such a policy would most certainly leave their countries in a permanent structure of dependent capitalism in which African countries should continue to export primary commodities, like coffee and use their foreign exchange earnings to import essential manufactured goods and even their food requirements.

Although various adjustment packages had been implemented in Africa before the 1980s, the Berg Report was to usher in a new era in African political economy, that is the era of SAPs. In brief, the Report pursued a dual strategy of privatization and liberalization for African countries with a view to resolving the debt crisis within the context of SAPs. The debt crisis experienced by many African countries since the late 1970s up to the present forced most of them to turn to the IMF and WB for financial assistance under the conditionality of SAPs. But the evaluation of the SAPs experience across African countries has unfolded that as the dominant economic program foisted on Africa in the 1980s and 1990s, SAPs have been a catastrophic failure. It has contributed to increasing mass poverty and the collapse of the real economy of production in various sectors across the region, and promoted deindustrialization, rising inflation and the growing marginalization of Africa. This manifest failure of a dominant paradigm in Africa made the implementation of alternative development paradigms more imperative (Onimode, 2004: 23). Thus, the supposed 'one-size-fits-all' approach, which characterized much of the SAPs, produced a counter-reaction in the form of the Africa's Priority Program for Economic Recovery 1986-1990 (APPER), which was adopted by the OAU. It was later transformed and repackaged as the United Nations Program of Action for Africa's Economic Recovery and Development (UN-PAAERD), yet, the effect of both programs was no more than a failure.

The impact of SAPs on Africa reappeared in July 1989 with the UNECA's *African Alternative Framework to Structural Adjustment Program* (AAF-SAP), which was adopted by the OAU and endorsed by the General Assembly of the United Nations as the most elaborate and most technically sophisticated alternative recovery-with-development paradigm for Africa (UNECA, 1989). However, like almost all previous plans in Africa, the AAF-SAP never took off, mainly due to the lack of commitment by both those African leaders, who had signed the Framework and the International Financial Institutions (IFIs) and Western governments (Taylor, 2006: 20). Rather, as soon as the AAF-SAP emerged, the World Bank, in its traditional parallelism of imposing alternative blueprints to those prepared by Africa, launched its laborious Long-Term Perspective Study (LTPS) in 1989 (World Bank, 1989). Indeed, this has been a main cause of the avoidance of the AAF-SAP by African countries and their failure to implement it to date.

Just as the LPA had been followed by the Berg Report, the AAF-SAP was followed by a new World Bank report in 1989, *Sub Saharan Africa: From Crisis to Sustainable Growth*. The distinct argument of this new report is that "African governments and foreign financiers (commercial banks and export credit agencies as well as donor agencies) must share responsibility. Foreign financiers and suppliers promoted capital exports with attractive credits, and poor coordination among donors caused duplication and waste" (World Bank, 1989: 27). Within the shifted context from its previous hard-nosed stance towards the role of the state, it can be pointed out that the report took into account human resource development together with a social welfare issues, which used to be belittled and even ignored by the World Bank. This report, however, does not mean that the World Bank was to abandon the normative principles of neoliberalism. Rather, while it is to encourage the policies of a social safety net that have positive effects on have not groups, at the same time to share the blame between endogenous and exogenous factors: to varying degrees, indeed, this emerged as defining principle, which has been maintained to date and which informs NEPAD's own formulas (Taylor, 2006: 20).

Another attempt by African countries to address their own problems developed at the UNECA's Arusha conference on Popular Participation for Democracy in Africa, namely *The African Charter for Popular Participation in Development and Transformation* (1990), which was adopted by the African Heads of States and Government at the Addis Ababa Summit of the OAU in July 1990. Considering the main argument of Charter stating that "there must be an opening up of political processes to accommodate freedom of opinion, and tolerate differences" (Lone, 1990: 1), it is feasible to infer that "the blame for Africa's demise could be sourced to a large degree (but not, obviously, exclusively) from within Africa-or rather, from within the palaces of African presidents" (Taylor, 2006: 21).

Within this context, the international community renewed the commitment to Africa that it made five years earlier in the UN-PAAERD by projecting the UN New Agenda for the Development of Africa (UN-NADAF 1991). Like a number of other previous initiatives, the UN-NADAF had not fully reached its objectives to be implemented. However, one important goal of the UN-NADAF that was evaluated as partly progressive, in particular, is pursuing regional and sub-regional economic cooperation and integration with the ultimate goal of establishing the African Economic Community (AEC). Although serious problems still remain internally within the Regional Economic Communities (RECs), the treaty establishing the AEC should be considered as an important road map on how to achieve the pan-African economic community, in which the treaty needs to be reviewed.

The Abuja Treaty: Establishing the African Economic Community (AEC)

The formation of the AEC in 1991 heralds a new historical mark of African integration efforts. The AEC was established by the Abuja Treaty at an OAU summit in June 1991, but only entered into force on 12 May 1994 after the required numbers signed up for ratification. In 1980, in fact, when the OAU Extraordinary Summit adopted the Lagos Plan of Action, the LPA attempted to develop itself as a major step towards the goal of African integration.

The AEC Treaty (known as the Abuja Treaty) provided for the African Economic Community to be set up through a gradual process, which would be achieved by coordination, harmonization and progressive integration of the activities of existing and future regional economic communities (RECs) in Africa. The RECs are regarded as the building blocks of the AEC. That is, the Abuja Treaty has accorded special recognition to the critical role of the RECs in the stages of establishing the African Economic Community. Accordingly, a Protocol has been concluded on relations between the AEC and RECs, which should serve as an effective instrument and framework for close cooperation, program harmonization and coordination as well as integration among the RECs on the one hand, and between the AEC and RECs on the other.

The major characteristics of the AEC is that it is being established in six stages, according to the provision of the Abuja Treaty (Articles 6 and 88), mainly activities of the RECs. This makes the AEC different from other integration organizations established in Africa. In fact, the Abuja Treaty makes it clear that the establishment of the AEC is the final objectives towards which the activities of all the RECs (existing and future) shall be geared (Article 88). In recognition of this fact, the Abuja Treaty has set up the modalities for establishing the AEC; the implementation of the Abuja Treaty is a process that will be done in six stages over 34 years, i.e., by 2028. Each of the stages consists of specific activities to be implemented concurrently.

Despite the six stages, the Abuja Treaty states that the cumulative transitional period shall not exceed forty years from the date of its entry into force. It also provides for measures to be taken concurrently, with regard to the formulation of multinational projects and programs for the promotion of a harmonious and balanced development among Member States. However, the stages are not inflexible; the process can be expedited with regular verification of completion of the stages. The main objectives of the AEC are to promote economic, social and cultural development as well as African economic integration in order to increase self-reliance and endogenous development and to create a framework for development, mobilization of human resources and material. The AEC further aims to promote co-operation and development in all aspects of human activity with a view to raising the standard of life of Africa's people, maintaining economic stability and establishing a close and peaceful relationship between member states (Treaty Establishing the African Economic Community (Article 4) 1991: 8-9).

Many of these ideals are further advanced by and evolved into NEPAD in the new millennium. Indeed, the AEC Treaty argues that "Any Member State, which persistently fails to honor its general undertakings under this Treaty or fails to abide by the decisions or regulations of the Community, may be subjected to sanctions by the Assembly" (Treaty Establishing the African Economic Community (Article 5) 1991: 9). Within the progressive and evolutionary context, such general undertakings that pay attention to the recognition, promotion and protection of human and peoples' rights and good governance open up a good chance to understand and explain the genesis and *modus operandi* of NEPAD, constructed by Africans for Africans in order to provide Africa with the opportunity to extricate itself once and for all, from the malaise of underdevelopment and exclusion in a globalizing world.

Table 2.1: Main Initiators, Characteristics and Outcomes of Pre-NEPAD Initiatives in Africa

Initiatives	*Main Initiator(s)*	*Key Characteristics*	*Outcomes*
LPA (1980)	UNECA/OAU	Economic Self-Reliance	Failed
APPER (1986-1990)	OAU	Economic Recovery	Failed
UN-PAAERD (1986-1990)	UN	Economic Recovery and Development	Failed
AAF-SAP (1989)	UNECA/OAU	Sustainable Development	Failed
UN-NADAF (1991)	UN	Regional Cooperation/Integration	Partly Progressive
AEC (1994)	OAU	Establishing African Economic Community	Partly Progressive

Source: Author

NEPAD and Africa's Development in the New Millennium

NEPAD was created out of a number of the past initiatives and extensive consultations among a group of African Heads of State. It was previously called the New Africa Initiative (NAI), which was renamed NEPAD in October 2001 in Abuja, Nigeria following a merger of two processes, the Millennium Africa Recovery Plan (MAP) and the Omega Plan (that was produced by President Abdoulaye Wade of Senegal). The MAP originated from the attendance at the G8 meeting in Okinawa, Japan in July 2000 when three key African leaders took the helm of international forums: the former Presidents Thabo Mbeki (South Africa), Olusegun Obasanjo (Nigeria) and Abdelaziz Bouteflika (Algeria) served as chairperson of the Non-Aligned Movement (NAM), the G77, and the OAU, respectively (Gelb, 2002: 1).

According to its own documents, NEPAD is a 'comprehensive and holistic integrated strategic framework for the socio-economic development of Africa'. In fact, the architects of NEPAD recognized and accepted globalization as the new economic reality, which requires Africa to utilize different strategies from the introverted ones of the past. From the NEPAD's outset, African leaders admitted that the roots of Africa's crisis are internal and deeply connected to such African home-grown problems as insecurity, conflicts and bad governance. This idea stands in sharp contrast to earlier positions asserting Africa's problems as externally originated.

Although NEPAD was initially criticized BY others, who viewed it as an overwhelming neoliberal orientation (Bond, 2004: 5-43), it has been acclaimed to be an opener of new chapter of history in Africa to achieve a common vision and a firm and shared conviction to eradicate poverty and to place Africa on a path of sustainable growth and development (NEPAD, 2001). That is, NEPAD was constructed as Africa's organic political product designed to pull the continent out of its past developmental limbo by setting it on the path to peace, security, democracy, good political and economic regional governance, and respect for the rule of law in the new millennium (NEPAD, 2001; Posthumus, 2003; Nwonwu, 2006).

Key Frameworks of NEPAD Revisited

Peace and Security Governance

NEPAD places emphasis on peace and security as prerequisites for development. The NEPAD Initial Action Plan presented to and endorsed by the inaugural summit of the African Union (AU) in Durban, South Africa, in July 2002, clearly underlined this. The Action Plan indicated that NEPAD was based on a three-pronged strategy, the first element of which was establishing conditions for sustainable development, including peace and security and improved governance. To reinforce this, it proposed a Peace and Security Initiative, designed to support the efforts and conflict management mechanisms of the AU and regional organizations. The AU Summit in 2002 underscored particular elements of the NEPAD Initial Action Plan by adopting a Protocol establishing a Peace and Security Council (PSC). The Council is envisaged as the collective security mechanism for the continent, and it is intended to ensure timely and effective response to conflict and crises.

The PSC in conjunction with the chairperson of the commission, can institute sanctions whenever an unconstitutional change of government takes place in a member state. That is, it has the power and authority not only to undertake peace-making and peace-building functions, but also to recommend to the assembly intervention in situations where the national independence and sovereignty of a member state is threatened by acts of aggression. Although security was traditionally regarded in predominantly military terms as maintenance of territorial integrity or national sovereignty, it is now considered as a much broader, and as inextricably linked to development. Indeed, it is increasingly apparent that while insecurity threatens development, so too lack of development undermines security. In this sense, Cilliers argued that "where resources are scarce, as is the case across much of the continent, the object of political contestation is to secure economic consumption, which in turn is best guaranteed by capturing state power or replacing the state in a particular region, such as in the Kivu's in eastern DRC" (Cilliers, 2004: 25).

Although NEPAD ties its ability to maintain peace to the availability of 'peace funds', lack of funds has been pointed out as the main reason for the difficulties facing the AU peace-keeping force in Darfur. The mission is reported to face severe shortages of resources, making it difficult to reach out to the hungry and starving people in the region. In order to make it successful, the mission requires funds from the international community for motor vehicles, helicopters, and ambulances, and this is where NEPAD looks upon the foreign partners for assistance (Nwonwu, 2006: 10).

As an evolving new security architecture in Africa, nevertheless, the AU/NEPAD security regime pursues strengthening the capacities of regional organizations in conflict management and resolution through maximizing the use of domestic, but also external resources. In this context, NEPAD has already served to attract external resources from Africa's development partners towards peace and security. Although these various assistances have been limited to logistics, NEPAD has played its important role in providing opportunities for cooperation between Africa and western powers in strengthening the fragile security structures on the continent.

Economic and Regional Governance

NEPAD is geared towards establishing an enabling environment for FDI in the continent. That is, the FDIs occupy the center stage in NEPAD's development strategy and resource mobilization. In this sense, NEPAD postulates that increased private capital flow to Africa is an essential component of a sustainable long-term approach to filling the resource gaps (NEPAD, 2002: paragraph 153). Given that Africa's inability to deal with the process of globalization is an outcome of structural impediments in the form of resource outflows and unfavorable terms of trade (*Ibid.*: paragraph 34), nevertheless, it seems uncertain that FDIs help address these problems as long as globalization has "increased the ability of the strong to advance their interests to the detriment of the weak, especially in the areas of trade, finance and technology" (*Ibid.*: paragraph 33).

Admittedly, NEPAD faced resistance from others, who regarded it as an attempt by more powerful countries to entrench their domination. Within the context of the neoliberal programs embodied in NEPAD centered on the free market, informed by the logic of trickle-down economics and with a number of conditionalities, some critics pinpoint that NEPAD can at best worsen rather than reduce poverty (*see* Bond, 2003; Onimode, *et al.*, 2004; Taylor, 2006). The skeptics see that the local benefits from globalization are far outrun by the globalizers' activities that deplete local resources without generating development.

Another important NEPAD's mission is to pursue debt reduction and cancellation. Over US$200 billion debt burden for Africa is the single biggest obstacle to the continent's development. Most of this debt is illegitimate in nature, having been incurred by despotic and unrepresentative regimes. African countries spend almost US$14 billion annually on debt service. In order to address the debt burden, thus, the Heavily Indebted Poor Countries (HIPC) program was initiated by the World Bank and IMF in 1996. Yet, Africa's recent disappointment came from the G8 meet in Gleneagles, Scotland in July 2005. In fact, the G8 deal fell short of the promises of 100 per cent debt cancellation made by G8 officials in 2004, and it did not take full effect up to now. The deal still leaves majority of African countries on "debt row", required to meet harmful economic conditions as a condition for future debt relief or cancellation.

Since the IMF has restructured HIPC in 1996, nonetheless, the initiative has had notable success, both in terms of the levels of relief it has delivered, and in ensuring that this relief is channeled towards poverty reduction. To date, relief totaling more than US$60 billion has been agreed for 32 countries [23 (18 African countries) countries have received full cancellation], reducing their debts by around two-thirds, and freeing up resources for spending on poverty reduction. Poverty-reducing expenditures in countries that receive HIPC assistance are projected to have increased from 6.4 per cent of GDP in 1999 to 8.4 per cent of GDP in 2007. Yet, the debt relief under HIPC, though necessary for some short-term economic growth, is certainly not sufficient for long-term sustainable development. And it has come to most of African countries under HIPC with serious socio-economic problems, such as unemployment through donor dictated structural policies of privatization. Moreover, these countries are threatened to be stripped of many strategically important national assets through a reckless privatization program that was not adequately monitored for its economic and social effects on the people (Zulu, 2004: 5). Thus, although HIPC attempted to tackle its shortcomings by expanding its definition of unsustainable debts, making greater relief available to more countries, and by making relief available sooner, it still remains to be seen whether the money spent in debt repayment will be re-channeled towards just reducing poverty or ultimately eradicating it in Africa and seize the momentum of development.

For a long-term development strategy, indeed, NEPAD recognizes sub-regional and regional approaches as necessary for achieving economic growth and sustainable development through improving Africa's competitiveness, considering that as markets, most African countries are small (NEPAD, 2001). The NEPAD document notes that "the five sub-regional economic groupings on the continent must be strengthened" (*Ibid.*: paragraph 94), and that sub-regional and regional approaches to development "will also go a long way in kick-starting the regeneration of the continent" (*Ibid.*: paragraph 191).

As noted earlier, regional governance approaches within the LPA and the Abuja treaty establish that the AEC employ the term 'region' or 'regional integration' to refer to geographically-based regional groupings within Africa. Since the NEPAD's inception, in fact, the NEPAD initiators intended to use the RECs as the building blocks of NEPAD and have the role of guiding and facilitating the implementation of projects and programs under the NEPAD framework. Common markets that connect member states and encourage interregional economic cooperation contribute to the realization of this goal.

In this context, it can be noted that the Common Market for Eastern and Southern Africa (COMESA) is one of such formation that generates regional and interregional trade and economic cooperation; however, basing economic integration on geographic location often leads to the questioning of the rationale regarding the inclusion of members from outside the geographic vicinity. Considering that NEPAD failed to go beyond referring to 'the goals of achieving a Common Market and an African Union', moreover, it needs to further strengthen regional integration mechanisms through developing and evolving the AEC plan.

Currently, more important and urgent task to address is that rationalization and capacity building must be undertaken before the RECs can fully discharge their responsibility for implementation. According to NEPAD (2008), in fact, no rigorous assessment of the capacity of national governments and the secretariats of the RECs was conducted before assigning them responsibility for leading the implementation of NEPAD programs. Thus, it essentially required strong political will to lead rapid rationalization of the RECs through strengthening capacity building, which has been initiated with the support of the African Capacity Building Foundation, though the progress of capacity building remains slow.

Political and Democratic Governance

The African Peer Review Mechanism (APRM) is designed to monitor and assess the progress made by African countries in meeting their commitment toward achieving good governance and sustainable development. A positive aspect of the APRM is that it notes that governance problems are central determinants of Africa's development challenges (Hope, 2005:289; Mathoho, 2003:1). Indeed, one of the most innovative features of NEPAD has been referred to the APRM. Given that the principle of non-intervention into the internal affairs was of paramount importance for African leaders to maintain their regime security, moreover, an introduction of the APRM can be highly acclaimed for opening a new history of establishing a governance instrument targeted at domestic issues. In this regard, it is argued that "the APRM presents opportunities for strengthening democracy to ensure that the basis of governance transcends the narrow confines of personal rule, patron-client relations or ethno-religious politics" (Akokpari, 2004: 253). The peer review is done by a seven-member Independent Panel of Eminent Persons (IPEP), which conducts countries through various stages of the review process.

Instead of policing the actions of the acceding governments, the ultimate goal of the APRM is to assist governments in their commitment to good governance through helping countries adopt optimal policies, standards, and practices that lead to political stability, economic growth, and sustainable development (NEPAD, 2003). Thus, submission to the review process is 'voluntary' and there does not exist any sanction placed upon wrongful governments. In this context, countries, which signed up, have possibilities to opt out if the process proves intrusive. Moreover, the AU lacks the power to compel countries to either sign up to the review process or comply with standards of good governance. This is a major limitation that has left the APRM under the aegis of the AU as a "lame leviathan" (Akokpari, 2005: 6).

Within this context, another critical point for the APRM to overcome is the issue regarding its ranking system. The ranking system was recommended by the Canadian Prime Minister Jean Chretien, in his speech delivered at the UN Summit in Monterrey, Mexico on 21 March 2002. Under the system, African countries would be ranked from 1 to 53, in three areas: good governance, human rights and corporate governance. The idea of ranking countries is that the top performers will be eligible for an enhanced package of aid and investment from the developed countries (Thompson, 2002). However, African leaders tend to be reluctant to criticize each other on human rights and on sensitive political issues. For this reason, even though the APRM requires African governments to agree on certain performance standards, and the criteria of evaluating their performances in terms of economic, corporate, and political governance, it is intrinsically limited to achieve good results.

Moreover, some critics have expressed fears that the Western powers could attempt to utilize the APRM to sanction African countries selectively, as has occurred over Zimbabwe. That is, the review mechanism could become an instrument through which "donors impose collective penalties on African countries in cases where African leaders, who are declared pariahs by external actors, are not sanctioned by their African peers" (Bekoe and Landsberg, 2002: 2).

The aforementioned critical perspectives on the APRM has opened up considerable room for African civil society organizations to seek out parallel processes to hold African governments and leaders accountable to their stated commitments and decisions (Nwonwu, 2006: 15). Indeed, civil society participation in the APRM process is crucial to the credibility of the review process as it will help ensure that the review report represents a consensus of views on a country's quality of governance, rather than being limited to what the government in question would like to make public (Verwey, 2005: 20). In this sense, civil society is seen to act as a watchdog over the credibility of the country reviews. However, civil society can and should be more than just a watchdog. It often has more information on local circumstances and specific issues than the government—information which can add range and depth to the peer review. Most importantly perhaps, peer review represents a window of opportunity for civil society to influence policy and translate policy into credible commitment. Although it would be naive to think that the peer review process will induce massive governance improvements in no time at all, this does not mean that the process cannot lead to real changes within a meaningful time span (*cf* Verwey, 2005).

Table 2.2: Key Frameworks, Drivers, Characteristics and Challenges of NEPAD

Key Frameworks	*Drivers*	*Characteristics*	*Challenges*
Peace and Security Governance	AU-PSC	Conflict Management/ Resolution	Shortages of Resources/Funds
Economic and Regional Governance	IFIs/ RECs	Sustainable Development	Slow Progress of Capacity Building
Political and Democratic Governance	AU-APRM	Voluntary Mechanisms	Lack of Compelling Power and Limited Role of Civil Society

Source: Author

Conclusion

Ever since the initiative was created, a number of scholars and civil society organizations have acutely criticized NEPAD as a top-down, elitist and state-centric approach bound to fail. In this context, Nwonwu (2006:22) states that "NEPAD is widely considered to be a closed system that has shut its doors against *bona fide* stakeholders including civil society organizations. The organization is still undergoing an acceptability test from the African citizenry, who were not consulted at the formative stage of the initiative". Hence the debate on how to engage the activities and further expand the reciprocal relationships between NEPAD and civil society organization should be upheld. It is encouraging, however, that the debate on the APRM has opened up space for African civil society organizations to establish "parallel processes" to hold African leaders accountable to their stated commitments. Indeed, the continent has witnessed a multitude of conferences involving civil society actors, NEPAD officials and African leaders, although this has not been diffused throughout the whole continent (*see*, e.g., Cilliers, 2003; Mashele, 2006).

From the perspective of Afro-pessimism, NEPAD has been severely attacked by the critics, who argue that the initiative has undertaken *a priori* a commitment to uphold and strengthen the Development Merchant System (DMS) and its neoliberal economic policy, perpetuating economic dependence, instead of promoting economic self-reliance and self-sustainment (Onimode, *et al.* 2004: 233-255). Nonetheless, it is important to note that the problem with Africa is not a matter of greater openness and/or integration. This implies that the real problem with Africa is not openness or a need for greater integration *per se*, but rather it is the nature of its openness/integration: that is, dependence on primary commodities, lack of diversification in export, and the unfavorable terms of trade is a source of the vulnerability of African economies. Hence, these structural impediments to tackle will be key to the future direction and success of NEPAD in particular dimension of economic and regional governance.

Despite the aforementioned skeptical concerns, an important aspect of the NEPAD initiative is that, instead of donors and development institutions prescribing policies that they would assist, the NEPAD initiative calls for development partners to support policies and programs that are initiated and created by Africans themselves, though they are not yet fully inclusive of whole African people including the grassroots, civil society and a host of other stakeholders. That is, the initiative attempted to take Africa away from the era of conditionality to where Africans themselves can set priorities and impose conditions of good governance on themselves with a view to addressing the fellow states' problems of 'ownership' and 'partnership' (Saitoti, 2003: 26-27).

Thus, how NEPAD can be distinct from previous African development strategies, such as the LPA, is that the former is defined as an Africa-owned program at least in theory with its own self-prescribed conditionalities in practice. Indeed, unlike the externally-imposed conditionality of the IMF and the World Bank, which overshadowed the African continent for the last two decades, the NEPAD architects developed self-identified and self-imposed conditions for improving the prospects for reform sustainability in Africa.

Yet, the question of NEPAD's "ownership" remains to be controversial in that the African continent has depended (and is depending) so much on external actors for its financing. In fact, the unequal relationship between the west and Africa is intrinsically linked to the lack of "reciprocity, complementarity or symbiosis that characterize genuine partnerships" (Akokpari, 2005: 5).

To some extent, nonetheless, the sense of optimism created with the advent of NEPAD in Africa can be compared to the euphoric mood of past development experiences. Just when the continent got deeply trapped into the state of darkness and despair, African leaders have succeeded in putting a new face on the international image of Africa by introducing an initiative that has managed to attract the attention of even the cynics inside and outside the continent. Given that NEPAD seeks to build on the achievements of the past, as well as reflect on the lessons learned through painful experience, so as to establish a global, regional and local partnership that is both credible and capable of implementation, thus,

NEPAD should be given a chance to evolve into its inclusive and balanced African development strategy in the 21st century.

REFERENCES

Adesina, Jimi O., Y. Graham, and A. Olukoshi. (2005). *Africa and Development Challenges in the New Millennium: The Nepad Debate*. London and New York: Zed Books.

African Union. (2002). Protocol relating to the establishment of the peace and security council of the African Union. 9 July

Ake, Claude. (1996). *Democray and Development in Africa*. Brookings Inst. Press.

Akokpari, John. (2004). The AU, NEPAD and the Promotion of Good Governance in Africa. *Nordic Journal of African Studies*, Vol. 13(3): 243-263.

Akokpari, John. (2005). Africa's Quest for Long-Term Development: Does NEPAD Provide the Necessary Policy Framework? *Presented at the 11th CODESRIA General Assembly*, Maputo, Mozambique 6-10 December 2005, at http:*www.codesria.org/Links/conferences/general_assembly11/papers/akokpari.pdf.*

Asante, S.K.B. (1985). Development and Regional Integration since 1980", In Adedeji A. and T. Shaw (eds.). *Economic Crisis in Africa: African Perspectives on Development Problems and Potentials.* Boulder: Lynne Rienner.

Bekoe, Dorina A. and Chris Landsberg. (2002). NEPAD: African Initiative, New Partnership? *International Peace Academy (IPA) Workshop Report.* 16 July 2002.

Bond, Patrick. (2003). Can NEPAD survive its Proponents, Sponsors, Clients and Peers? *Organization for Social Research in Eastern and Southern Africa (OSSREA) Newsletter* Vol. 21(3): 12-19.

Bond, Patrick. (2004). South Africa and Global Apartheid: Continental and International Policies and Politics. *Disscussion Paper* 25, Uppsala: Nordiska Afrikainstitutet.

Castells, Manuel. (1997). *End of Millennium*. London: Blackwell.

Cilliers, Jakkie. (2003). Peace and Security through Good Governance — A guide to the NEPAD African Peer Review Mechanism". *ISS Occassional Paper*, No. 70. Pretoria: Institute for Security Studies (ISS).

Cilliers, Jakkie. (2004). *Human Security in Africa: A conceptual framework for review*. Monograph for the African Human Security Institute. Pretoria: Institute for Security Studies.

Dare, Sunday. (2001). A Continent in Crisis: Africa and Globalization. *Dollars and Sense*, July/August, pp. 1[illegible]-14.

DeLancey, Virginia. (2001). The Economies of Africa. In April A. Gordon & Donald L. Gordon (eds.). *Understanding Contemporary Africa*, Boulder: Lynne Rienner Publishers.

De Villiers, Les. (2008). *AFRICA 2008*. Connecticut: The Corporate Council on Africa and Business Books International.

Gelb, Stephen. (2002). The New Partnership for Africa's Development (NEPAD): A Brief Overview. *Global Insight*, Issue No. 19, June 2002.

Guest, Robert. (2004). *The Shackled Continent: Africa's past, present and the future*. London: Macmillan.

Herbst, Jeffrey. (1993). *The Politics of Reform in Ghana, 1982-1991*. Berkeley: University of California Press.

Hope, Kempe Ronald. (2005). Toward Good Governance and Sustainable Development: The African Peer Review Mechanism. *Governance: An International Journal of Policy, Administration, and Institutions*, Vol. 18(2): 283-311.

Hoogvelt, Ankie. (2002). Globalization, Imperialism and Exclusion: The Case of Sub-Saharan Africa. In Tunde Zack-williams, Diane Frost, and Alex Thomson (eds.). *Africa in Crisis: New Challenges and Possibilities*. London: Pluto Press.

Kouassi, Rene N'Guettia. (2007). The Itinerary of the African Integration Process: An Overview of the Historical Landmarks. *African Integration Review,* Vol.1(2): 1-23.

Lone, Salim. (1990). Africas Adopt Bold Charter for Democratization. *Africa Recovery* 4 (April-June), pp. 14-17.

Mashele, Prince. (2006). The New Partnership for Africa's Development - Four years of a promising attempt or hollow optimism? *ISS Occasional Paper 125*, February 2006.

Mathoho, Malachia. (2003). An African Peer Review Mechanism: a panacea for Africa's governance challenges?. *Policy Brief 29*, Center for Policy Studies, Johannesburg: South Africa.

Mucavele, Firmino G. (2006). The New Partnership for Africa's Development. *Progress Report—Towards Development*, 8th February 2006.

NEPAD. (2001). *The New Partnership for Africa's Development*. Midrand, South Africa: NEPAD Secretariat.

NEPAD. (2002). *Declaration on Democracy, Political, Economic and Corporate Governance*. Midrand, South Africa: NEPAD Secretariat.

NEPAD. (2003). *African Peer Review Mechanism: Organization and Processes*. Midrand, South Africa: NEPAD Secretariat.

NEPAD. (2008). NEPAD: a look at seven years of achievement and the challenges on the way forward. *NEPAD Dialogue*, Online Weekly Issue 209, 25 January 2008.

Nwonwu, Francis. (2006). NEPAD: A New Agenda or Another Rhetoric in Africa's Political Adventurism? *Africa Policy Journal*, 2: 1-30.

Organization of African Unity (OAU). (1980). *Lagos Plan of Action for the Economic Development of Africa (1980-2000)*. Addis Ababa: OAU.

Organization of African Unity (OAU). (1986). *Africa's Economic Recovery and Development (UN-PAAERD)*, Addis Ababa: OAU.

Organization of African Unity (OAU). (1991). *Treaty Establishing The African Economic Community*. Addis Ababa: OAU.

Ochieng, Zachary. (2006). APRM: Time to Address Government and Civil Society Concerns. *News from Africa*, 6 November 2006.

Olukoshi, Adebayo. (2002). Governing the African Political Space for Sustainable Development: A Reflection on Nepad. Presented at the African Forum for Envisioning Africa to be held in Nairobi, Kenya, 26-29 April 2002.

Onimode, Bade. (2004). Mobilization for the Implementation of Alternative Development Paradigms in 21st-Century Africa. In Lawrence O. C. Agubuzu *et al.* (eds.) *African Development and Governance Strategies in the 21st Century: Looking Back to Move Forward.* London & New York: Zed Books.

Onimode, Bade *et al.* (2004). *African Development and Governance Strategies in the 21st Century: Looking Back to Move Forward.* London: Zed Books.

Owusu, Francis. (2003). Pragmatism and the Gradual Shift from Dependency to Neoliberalism: The World Bank, African Leaders and Development policy in Africa. *World Development*, Vol. 31(10): 1655-1672.

Posthumus, Bram. (2003). A Conference Report. In Bram Posthumus (ed.). *NEPAD: A New Partnership?* Amsterdam: Netherlands Institute for Southern Africa.

Saitoti, George. (2003). Reflections on African Development. *Journal of Third World Studies*, Vol. 20(2): 13-29.

Taylor, Ian. (2006). Partnership through Accommodation? African Development Initiatives and Universal Policy Descriptions. In Henning Melber (compiled). *Africa, Regional Cooperation and the World Market: Socio-Economic Strategies in Times of Global Trade Regimes.* Uppsala: Nordiska Afrikainstitutet.

Thompson, Allan. (2002). Rethinking Foreign Aid: Chrétien Urges a Ranking System. *World Press Review*, Vol. 49(6), at http://www.worldpress.org/Americas/536.cfm.

UN Economic Commission for Africa (UNECA). (1989). *African Alternative Framework to Structural Adjustment Programs for Socio-Economic Recovery and Transformation (AAF-SAP).* Addis Ababa: UNECA.

UN Economic Commission for Africa (UNECA). (1990). *African Charter for Popular Participation in Development.* Addis Ababa: UNECA.

UN Economic Commission for Africa (UNECA). (2002). The African Peer Review Mechanism: Process and Procedure. *African Security Review*, Vol. 11(4): 7-13.

Verwey, Len. (2005). Nepad and Civil Society Participation in the APRM. *Occasional Papers*, IDASA-Budget Information Service-Africa Budget Project, at *http://www.idasa.org.za*.

World Bank. (1981). *Accelerated Development in Sub-Saharan Africa: An Agenda for Action.* Washington DC: World Bank.

World Bank. (1989). *Sub-Saharan Africa: From Crisis to Sustainable Growth*, Washington DC: World Bank.

World Bank. (2000). *Can Africa Claim the Twenty-first Century?* Washington DC: World Bank.

Zulu, Jack Jones. (2004). Zambia's experience with HIPC. *Policy Brief: Promotion of Social Justice and Concern for the Poor.* Jesuit Center for Theological Reflection, at *http://www.jctr.org.zm/downloads/HIPCbrief_280604.pdf*

3
Understanding China-Africa Relations

K. Mathews

China's Rise

The peaceful rise (development) of China in recent years may well prove to be the most momentous happening in the early 21st century. The first and early second decade of this century witnessed unprecedented growth in China's vastly increased engagement with Africa and other parts of the world. Recently China has become the world's second largest economy after the USA. Its GDP is about US$ 8 trillion (2012). China's rapidly growing economic, political and cultural engagement and influence around the world is undeniable as it is remarkable. China has emerged as an engine of global economic growth with over US$ 3 trillion in foreign currency reserves (May 2013) and plans to apply hundreds of billions of dollars of this to international investment through its sovereign wealth fund. Its driving need for all kinds of commodities, from oil and uranium to cement and copper, has driven up world prices. China is now the largest foreign holder of US debt, the second biggest consumer of luxury products and the planet's top buyer of gold and mobile phones China is also the first major economy to recover from the recent global financial and economic crisis and is indeed leading the world out of it. Rapid industrialization has boosted China's import demand for oil and minerals (e.g., iron ore, bauxite, and nickel, copper) which Africa can supply. China is now Africa's second largest trading partner. The dramatic rise of China and other emerging powers like India, Brazil, etc. has profound consequences for the emerging new world order.

China's rapid growth has also transformed its relationship with Africa. The rapid economic modernization of the Chinese economy since the 1979 post-reform period and its subsequent global expansion, particularly its growing presence on the African continent, has provoked conflicting commentary and sparked controversy among scholars and policy makers. In some quarters China's increasing demand for resources is regarded as creating a new scramble for Africa. In others, it is seen as providing a much desired alternative to Western imperialism and neo-colonialism. Western political forces and media have criticized every aspect of China's activities in Africa, while the Chinese, with significant support from Africans, have mounted a spirited defense. Media reports about China in Africa have often highlighted huge aid packages, support for pariah regimes and the ruthless exploitation of workers and natural resources in some of the poorest countries in the world and these have sparked fierce debates.

The common concern has been whether China's new Africa policy marks a sea change in Africa's international economic and political relations, and if so the impact of that on the interests of Africa's Western development partners. According to some analysts China's involvement in Africa will not be different from the West who plundered and continue to plunder Africa's resources through various guises. Yet others see the rising Chinese presence in Africa as part of China's grand design to take full 'control' of the whole world. For others still, China's 'Africa project' is a natural progression of a people who have successfully outgrown their own market and therefore are on the 'prowl' for more markets as well as resources. It is to these people 'simple profit motives' rather, 'than complex political and strategic considerations' that underpin the rise of China and its expanded engagement in Africa.

Some important questions to be examined in discussing the contributions of China-Africa economic relations include:

(1) Is China really offering Africa a better development aid option than the West?
(2) Is China just the latest in a line of exploiters of Africa's rich natural resources who put their economic interests above humanitarian, environmental or human rights concerns?
(3) How far China's engagement is an extension of South-South Cooperation?
(4) Does China's engagement enable African countries to free themselves from the tyranny of debt and conditionality that, through two decades of Structural Adjustment Programmes (SAPs) have reversed most of the gains of independence?
(5) Will Chinese aid move Africa towards achieving the Millennium Development Goals?

(6) How can Africa and African countries and Institutions position themselves for a genuine China-Africa-win-win relationship?

For examining these questions it may be helpful to provide a brief historical background to the development of China-Africa relations in an attempt to contextualize their specific contributions.

Historical Background

Broadly, Sino-African relations can be divided into three distinct historical stages. The first of these three stages was the 15th century mercantile expansion of China associated with the Ming Dynasty, which saw China 'discover' much of the eastern coast of Africa as far south as Mozambique nearly 100 years before the first arrival of the Europeans. It was the famed explorations by the Chinese Moslem Admiral Zheng He during the Ming Dynasty (1368-1644). The admiral made seven voyages between 1416 and 1423, two of which reached the east African coast. Or in all it is estimated that he had between 48 and 317 ships with a crew of over 28,000 men. During each of Zheng's voyages, he brought back diplomats from other countries or encouraged ambassadors to go to the then Capital Nanjing on their own, according to historical records. Zheng He brought with him products to conduct commerce with local people. However, China's self-imposed withdrawal from the world under the Qing Dynasty (1644–1911) coincidentally followed Portuguese navigational exploits along the eastern African coast, which effectively shut out further Chinese efforts at maintaining contacts with Africa. Under the Guomindang, following the 1911 revolution, Africa again retreated to a position of irrelevance for the republican government.

It was only during the second stage, after the Communists took power in 1949 that China pursued an active foreign policy in Africa. In the immediate post-colonial period, China forged a series of political relationships with the newly independent states, and supported liberation movements in Angola, Mozambique, Zimbabwe and South Africa. This stage remained distinctly political, underpinned by the Cold War rivalry of the period. During the immediate post-revolutionary period, Chinese Communist foreign policy was greatly influenced by the Soviet Union's support, signified by the Sino-Soviet Alliance of 1950. Because of American support for the Guomindang during the Civil War, China viewed the United States as being firmly opposed to the Communist regime in Beijing.

The landmark Bandung Asia-Africa Conference in April 1955 is seen as the foundation stone of modern Sino-African relations. It was at this Conference that Communist China first made its tentative links with the African continent. The relations between 1955 and the mid 1990s, despite important economic projects like the TANZAM railway, was mainly political in orientation, China seeking support and influence in Africa and championing the cause of the 'Third World' in international discourse. African countries in turn saw opportunities to escape the clutches of the super power Cold War with its expectation of satellite states.

In the period between 1960–1965, Beijing achieved great diplomatic successes, with PRC entering into relations with 14 newly independent African countries (Ghana, Mali, Somalia, Zaire, Uganda, Burundi, Kenya, Benin, Central African Republic, Congo (Brazzaville), Tanzania, Tunisia, Zambia and Mauritania.) At the end of 1963, Chinese Prime Minister, Zhou Enlai, embarked on his much publicized ten-nation tour of Africa. The main purpose of which was to rationalize Chinese policies in Africa, then as part of PRC's anti-Soviet offensive. It is well known, China took a keen interest in freeing Southern Africa from the control of colonial and minority governments. In the early 1970s, at the height of the chaos of the Cultural Revolution, China built the most prestigious, Tan-Zam Railway—Africa's longest railway, nearly 2000 kilometers— stretching from the copper mines of land-locked Zambia through Tanzania to the sea.

During the 1980s, the relationship shifted towards economic cooperation based on common aims. After the end of the Cold War IN 1989-90, China attached importance to both political and economic benefits and portrayed itself as an attractive economic partner and political friend. For African governments, this presented an alternative to the "Washington Consensus" and was termed "Beijing Consensus", i.e., support without interference in internal affairs.

Expanded Engagements

The third (current) stage in China-Africa relations could be traced from about the mid-1990s. The forces unleashed by China's Open Door Policy of 1979 created a significant momentum in China's interest in Africa. This time the focus is primarily economic. Bilateral trade with Africa reached US$ 200 billion by the end of 2012, which was US$ 114 billion in 2008 up from a mere US$ 10 billion in 2000. The Chinese government's "Going Global Policy", which encouraged Chinese companies to become multi-nationals, has supported a rise in China's FDI in Africa to US$ 5.4 billion in 2009, up from a negligible amount just a decade ago. According to the Chinese Ministry of commerce, between 1979 and 1990, China invested US$ 51.19 million in 102 projects in Africa. By the end of 2008, Chinese investors had set up around 1,600 companies in Africa, while the cumulative Chinese direct investment net stock reached US$ 7.8 billion, which was 4.2 per cent of China's total outward direct investment stock.

In the current stage of China-Africa relations has witnessed China's strong engagement with Africa, driven by its post-reform economic imperatives and the demands for growth and modernization. The renewed importance of Africa in China's foreign policy came to light in 1996 during President Jiang Zemin's tour of Africa, when the idea of creating the Forum for China-Africa Cooperation (FOCAC) was raised. A brief survey of the FOCAC process may provide interesting insights in understanding the expanding nature of growing China-Africa relations.

Forum on China Africa Cooperation (FOCAC) Process

Launched in 2000, the Forum on China Africa Cooperation (FOCAC) has become an effective mechanism for collective dialogue and multilateral cooperation between China and Africa. It has put in place an important framework and platform for a new type of China-Africa partnership. Relations between China and African countries have historically been focused on bilateral relations. However, FOCAC provides an all encompassing dialogue on areas related to economic, diplomatic and social engagement. It serves as a multilateral forum within which the relationship between China and Africa has evolved since 2000. FOCAC provides a platform for Chinese and African government representatives to engage with each other on areas of mutual interest and towards a common vision. FOCAC thus serves to set the direction of rapidly expanding Sino-African relationship. Besides, FOCAC has served as a mechanism to implement China's Africa policy.

The First FOCAC Ministerial Summit was held in Beijing on 10-12 October 2000, set the basic procedures, structure and contents of this new phase in China-Africa Cooperation, which were gradually developed in subsequent ministerial meetings. It focused on two major areas: how to promote and establish a just and equitable new international order and to further strengthen cooperation between China and Africa on economic and social development. The Forum reached consensus on a wide range of issues and adopted two important policy documents—the Beijing Declaration and the Programme of Action on Economic and social Development. The Beijing Declaration (2000), works as a founding document of the Forum.

The 'Programme for China-Africa Cooperation in Economic and Social Development 2001-2003' provided an extensive list of areas for cooperation. The main areas of cooperation lined up in this first Action Plan included: promotion of high level exchanges, provide development assistance to support policies of receiving countries, provide preferential access to China, play a leading role in bi-lateral cooperation, infrastructure, financial cooperation, debt relief, tourism, migration, agriculture, natural resources and energy, science and technology, medical care and public health, education and human resources development, environment and biodiversity and cooperation in multilateral forums.

The Second FOCAC Ministerial Meeting was held in Addis Ababa, Ethiopia, on 15-16 December 2003. Forty four African countries participated. China was represented by its the then new Premier, Wen Jiabao. The Meeting reviewed the implementation of the two Documents adopted at the First Summit and explored new ideas and measures to deepen China-Africa cooperation. The Meeting concluded with the adoption of the Addis Ababa Action Plan 2004-2006 which reflected consensus by both sides on political issues and other important international issues of common concern. The major concrete measures that China promised to undertake included the following: granting some African countries tariff-free treatment for their exports to China, expediting increased revenue and alleviating poverty by exempting import tariffs for certain commodities of least developed countries, increased assistance and channel more resources to African Human Resource Development Fund.

On political affairs, emphasis was put on peace and security issues through the intensification of China's participation in peace-keeping operations in Africa as well as the de-mining activities, fighting terrorism and tackling non-traditional security issues. In terms of multi-lateral cooperation the Action Plan proposed to intensify consultation between China and Africa within the international multilateral institutions so as to safeguard common interests and strengthen cooperation in areas identified by NEPAD (such as infrastructure, health, agriculture and human resources.) The question of economic development contained the largest number of cooperation fields, namely, agriculture (technological and human resources development), infrastructure, trade and investment (mutual greater market access), tourism, debt relief, development assistance, natural resources, energy development and social development.

The White Paper on China's Africa Policy released by the Chinese government in January 2006 set forth China's long term strategic plan for deepening and strengthening cooperation and consultation with African countries. Part of this long term plan included the aspiration to "establish and develop a new type of *Strategic Partnership*" with Africa featuring political equality and mutual trust, economic win-win cooperation and cultural exchange. FOCAC III reflected this new dynamism.

The Third FOCAC Ministerial Summit was held in Beijing on 4-5 November 2006, named "the Year of Africa" in Chinese diplomacy. Chinese President Hu Jintao and the Heads of state and government of 48 African countries attended the Summit. The Beijing Declaration (2006) adopted at the end of the Summit made a call for enhanced South-South Cooperation and North-South dialogue in order to promote African development. At the opening ceremony of the Summit, President Hu Jintao unveiled an Eight Point Plan supporting African development in the next three years (2006-2009) in a bid to promote the bilateral cooperation in a wider scope and on a higher level: The Eight new initiatives were:

(1) Double the 2006 level of assistance by 2009;
(2) Provide US$ 5 billion in preferential loans and credits within the next three years;
(3) Provide US$ 5 billion to support Chinese companies to invest in Africa;
(4) Construct a new Conference Centre for the African Union (AU);
(5) Cancel debt owed by the Heavily Indebted Poor Countries;
(6) Increase zero tariff items to China from 190 to 440 from the least Developed African countries;
(7) Set up 3-5 trade and economic cooperation zones in Africa;
(8) Send Chinese experts to Africa and train African professionals in the areas of agriculture, health, education, science and technology.

The Beijing Declaration 2006 also reiterated the appeal made in the previous declarations for the reform of the United Nations and other multilateral institutions (IMF and WTO) and the pledge of supporting Africa's NEPAD goals through FOCAC's Action Plan. It signaled the upgraded bilateral cooperation by setting up a strategic partnership between China and Africa and advanced a large number of concrete tasks to be achieved during 2007-2009 Action Plans, most of which were in fact, achieved ahead of time. The Action Plan at the FOCAC III is by far the most focused and ambitious of all three so far, advancing a range of concrete measures to be taken by China.

The Fourth FOCAC Ministerial Meeting was held in Sharm el-Sheikh, Egypt on 8-9 November 2009. It took place during a rather tumultuous time in global history, as compared to the prosperous period experienced by both sides in the previous Summit in Beijing in 2006. From 2006 to 2008 China-Africa trade almost doubled from US$ 55 billion to over US$ 100 billion, while China experienced double digit economic growth figures. It is also estimated that China provided its highest levels of funding towards infrastructure construction in Africa peaking at US$ 4.5 billion in 2006. However, the run up to the FOCAC-IV saw China facing a number of domestic challenges resulting from a global economic downturn that threatened world markets, trade flows and financial volatility. Domestic growth decreased over the past two years from double digit figures of 10-11 per cent in 2006-2007 to 9.6 and 8.7 per cent 2008-2009.

FOCAC-IV also adopted two documents: the Sharm el-Sheikh Declaration and the Action Plan for 2010-2012 to chart the path for further China-Africa cooperation. The Declaration served to contextualize the role of Sino-African relations, specially within the global context. In particular the document high-lighted the effects of the global financial crisis on African development, while emphasizing that the current global economic climate should not detract from African development issues. An anticipated decrease in aid flowing from the developed West was noted and the important role of development assistance from the developed world was acknowledged in the effort towards poverty eradication and economic growth in Africa. The FOCAC-IV aimed to provide significant impetus to existing trade and investment flows as Premier Wen Jiabao reported that approaximately 1,600 Chinese companies active in Africa had already concluded investments of around US$ 7.8 billion on the continent.

The Sharm el-Sheikh Declaration and Action Plan emphasized the need for "practical cooperation" and the creation of "sustainable development" towards a "new type of strategic partnership" and a number of initiatives were created that could serve as a catalyst towards this. China committed to the following measures in the Sharm el-Sheikh Action Plan to be implemented over the next three years, 2010-2012, among others:

(1) Sending 50 agricultural technology teams to Africa, training 2,000 agricultural technicians for African countries and

increasing to 20 the total number of agricultural technology demonstration centers in Africa;

(2) Providing US$ 10 billion of preferential loans to African countries towards Infrastructure and social development projects;

(3) Granting tariff exemption treatment to 95 per cent of exports from the least developed countries (LDCs) in Africa having diplomatic relations with China;

(4) The establishment by Chinese financial institutions of a special loan of US$ 1 billion for African SMEs;

(5) Training a total of 20,000 people in various human resource sectors in Africa and contributing US$ 1.5 million to support NEPAD's projects to train nurses and maternity assistants in Africa;

(6) Building of 50 China-Africa Friendship Schools, training 1,500 African School Headmasters and teachers and increasing the number of Chinese Government scholarships to Africa to 5,500;

(7) Implementing a China-Africa joint research and exchange plan to strengthen Cooperation and exchanges between scholars and think tanks in China and Africa.

However, questions are asked as to whether the FOCAC-IV 2009 commitments illustrate a new development agenda in China's engagement with Africa. The 2009 FOCAC document certainly alludes to the idea that greater levels of participation at the continental and regional levels are possible. The experience and practice of FOCAC over the past 12 years (2000–2012) indicate that it is an important platform and effective mechanism for conducting collective dialogue between China and African countries and exchanges on governance, promoting mutual trust and carrying out practical cooperation.

The Fifth Ministerial conference of the FOCAC was held in Beijing on 19-20 July 2012. Foreign Affairs Ministers from China and 50 African countries and the Chairperson of the African Union commission participated in the conference. The two sides applauded the progress of FOCAC in the past twelve years since its inception in 2000. The Beijing Declaration 2013 and the Beijing Action Plan (2013-2015) adopted at the Meeting laid down a very elaborate and ambitious plan for the future growth of China-Africa cooperation, covering particularly areas such as political affairs and regional peace and security, cooperation in international affairs, economic cooperation, cooperation in the field of development, cultural and people to people exchanges and cooperation, among others.

It is true that over the years China has spent billions of dollars in assisting African countries with over 900 projects including textile factories, hydro-power stations, stadiums, hospitals, schools, etc. all over Africa. Some 1600 Chinese companies are currently operating in Africa, engaged in trade, manufacturing, natural resource exploitation, transportation, agriculture and agricultural processing, thus helping, among others, to create employment opportunities for African countries. The question now needs to focus on how Africa can achieve maximum benefit and development from the implementation of these commitments. Premier Wen Jiabao's assertion that "China will encourage more enterprises to invest in Africa and ask them to shoulder more corporate social responsibilities (CSR) and live in amity with the local people" (2009) is an encouraging sign that corporate social responsibilities can be strengthened in the future.

An Assessment

China's ever growing economic, political, cultural and other engagement in Africa continue to draw variable responses from all manner of people and places. Not least is the notion that China's is just another re-colonization of Africa or at best the capture of the resources of Africa. In this they will not be different from the West who plundered and continue to plunder Africa's resources through various guises, some say. Yet others see the rising Chinese presence in Africa as part of China's grand design to take full 'control' of the whole world. For others still, China's 'Africa project' is a natural progression of a people who have successfully outgrown their own market and therefore are on the 'prowl' for more markets as well as resources. It is to these people 'simple profit motives' rather, 'than complex political and strategic considerations' that underpin the rise of Chinese investments in Africa.

These concerns, coming particularly from the West, are not surprising as China's trade with Africa has increased from US$ 3 billion in 1995 to 106 billion in 2008 and US$ 200 billion in 2012. The European Union, however, remains Africa's largest trading partner, with trade totaling more than US$ 315.2 billion in 2006. Whatever the real intentions of China in Africa are, it is certainly not a humanitarian mission given that China has its own needs to satisfy in Africa. Thankfully they have not hidden their intentions in Africa. This they did, among others by launching the comprehensive China Africa Policy in 2006. The challenge so far is for Africa to clearly come out with its own side of the bargain, in a meaningful and comprehensive way, so as to make great returns from the Chinese engagement.

It should be stressed that the strategic partnership between China and Africa assume global significance, not just meaningful to their own bilateral relations. Currently there are many concerns expressed both in the West and Africa about China's perceived impact on political systems and economic development in Africa. If there is no doubt that China's breaking into the African scene is good for the continent because it brings a new actor which is willing to invest, and gives to the Africans an opportunity to chart another path to social and economic development other than the unfettered capitalism forced upon them by the Western countries, there are nonetheless some question marks to be raised about some controversial aspects of Chinese engagement in Africa.

Some scholars have argued that China's supporting of dictatorships in Africa is counter-productive both for long-term Chinese policy towards Africa, and to the African people. It is noted that China's involvement currently benefits primarily the elites, an opportunistic practice for which it has been criticized by humanitarians and others. The Chinese Model is proving attractive to corrupt African leaders who are flocking to Beijing to learn how to stay in power in exchange for growth.

Besides, mainly by Western countries who accuse China of "neo-colonialism". It is noted that Africa sells raw materials to China and China sells manufactured products to Africa. This is a dangerous equation that re-produces Africa's old relationship with colonial powers. Like Africa's old colonial masters, China has entered into secret deals with African leaders. In Angola, DRC, etc. China has secured billions of barrels of oil in exchange for electricity and road infrastructure. It is also said that China's export strategy of sending vast amounts of cheap manufactured goods of all kinds is contributing to the de-industrialization of some middle income countries.

Importing labor from mainland China and of flooding African markets with goods of very poor quality, in stark contrast to the selected articles of particularly good quality destined for Western markets. This sounds like discriminatory trade practices against the Africans. African products face competition from low cost imported Chinese goods, particularly in the textile sector. The growth of the informal sector is also stifled, provoking acute tensions and Chinese traders drive their African counterparts out of business. In some cases, factories are closed and jobs are lost. China's 'win-win paradigm', according to which no Chinese partner can turn out to be a loser, sounds more and more hollow to the extent that some are assimilating it to a disguised neo-colonial market penetration strategy. It is this which prompted former Tanzanian President Julius Nyerere to describe Chinese and Africans as "Most *Unequal Equals*".

It is further alleged that thousands of Chinese convicts have been pressed into service on infrastructure projects undertaken by state-owned Chinese companies in Africa, reminiscent of exports of convicts to Australia at the height of British imperialism. The export of unwanted peoples is not only blocking unemployed local youths from new job opportunities but it may lead to deep social problems in the long run.

African countries are regular buyers of Chinese weapons and military equipment. Reports say that between 1955 and 1977, China sold US$ 142 million worth of military equipment to Africa, and the pace of sales has picked up significantly since then. It is noted that China's arms sales to Africa made up 10 per cent of all conventional arms transfers to the continent between 1996 and 2003. China's main clients include: Sudan, Equatorial Guinea, Ethiopia, Eritrea, Burundi, Tanzania and Zimbabwe. In such an unstable region as Africa, already saturated with weaponry which is deadly and used against civilians across the continent, pouring more guns in this volatile situation cannot be welcome. The routine Chinese response "business is business and China separates business from politics" sounds rather cynical, mostly if we consider Chinese troops participation in peacekeeping missions in the continent to avert these very killings.

Oil represents a lifesaver for all industrialized countries which, until the terrorist attacks of 9/11 on America, had taken for granted a free access to steady oil supply with, in addition to the latitude to be able to control its trading price. Africa is the only soft target left for mineral resource predators to battle it out. But the last thing Africa wants and needs is to be the battleground in an economic and political cold war style confrontation. This can even, given that oil represents, virtually, a question of life and death for these economies; escalate into military confrontation between the belligerents, conveniently in a region far from their own shores in which they have all have military presence.

The Americans, who import 1.5 million barrels of oil a day from West Africa, have established strategic bases to safeguard output. Under the guise of the "war on terror", the Americans have set up the African Crisis Response Initiative (ACRI), the Djibouti-based Trans-Saharan-Counter-Terrorism Partnership and above all the AFRICOM (US Africa Command). Aircraft carriers patrol the Indian Ocean to protect their oil supply. For their part, the French maintain five military bases in Ivory

Coast, Djibouti, Gabon, Senegal and Chad, with 10,000 men placed in permanent state of alert to protect French interests on the continent. 4,000 Chinese Peoples Liberation Army (PLA) troops have been deployed to southern Sudan to guard an oil pipeline. With all these occupying armies, another area of concern is the risk of some kind of oil-induced cold war in the region whose main protagonists would be France, the United States, the UK and China.

The Darfur conflict is a perfect illustration of that fear. In spite of its declared faith in non-interference, China, because of its extending interests in the Sudanese oil, kept impeding any solution of the UN Security Council with regard to sanctions against the Khartoum Government, whose troops and government-aligned militias have been perpetrating genocide against Darfurians, using Chinese-made helicopter gunships, based at airstrips maintained by Chinese oil companies.

Another issue is that of alleged corrupt business practices. There is a tradition of bribery included in the way China does business. That, combined with the rampant corruption that plagues Africa can bring an explosive chemistry, highly damaging to the anti-corruption campaign underway in the region. It is pointed out that some of the most invited and feted African Heads of States in Beijing have been leaders whose wide corrupt practices have been documented and reported, making headlines in the world press. (Examples include Omar Bongo of Gabon, Denis Sassou Nguesso of Congo Brazzaville).

Question of Social Conflicts in Africa: Social conflicts connected to controversial Chinese practice in Africa have also beset countries such as Zambia, Senegal, South Africa, Nigeria, and Cameroon, among others. In Zambia, for example, the Chinese public Company NFC Africa, a subsidiary of the Chinese State-owned, Foreign Engineering and Construction Company, in 1998 bought an 85 per cent stake in the Chambisi Copper Mine. Tensions between the new owners and their African employees were rife because of low salaries and poor working conditions, which in 2005, cost the life of 49 miners. The following year in 2006, an anti-police riot squad repressed a rally of workers protesting the lack of security. As a result, one of the protesters was killed and five others were hospitalized. The situation was such that in the presidential election of 2006, one of the candidates, Michael Sata, had run an anti-Chinese campaign. China threatened to sever economic ties with Zambia if Sata were elected. This should be a matter of concern for all African countries since China will not hesitate to make forays into Africa politics if its economic interests are threatened.

Yet another issue relates to China's Africa Trade Imbalances. African countries sell raw materials to China while buying manufactured goods from Beijing. This is the result of a chronic negative trade balance. In South Africa, the main Chinese partner in the continent, this situation has led COSATU, the country's powerful trade union, to level threats of boycotting the traders of Chinese products accused of contributing to the increase in unemployment. The same tune is being played in the streets of some other African capitals such as Dakar and Dar-es-Salaam, filled with cheap Chinese shoes and drugs while textile factories are on the brink of closure due to Chinese competition.

Human rights violations constitute another serious issue of contention. Democratic deficits and poor human rights records beset both China and Africa. Economic growth without social justice is just another form of denying to the majority of the people their rights to decent living conditions for the benefit of a tiny rich minority. Human rights organizations, particularly in the run-up to the 2008 Summer Olympics criticized China for its supportive relationship with the government of Sudan, which is accused of mass killings in Darfur.

Positive Side

No matter how valid the above criticisms levelled against China's activities in Africa, they are only too familiar to all those acquainted with developments in Africa. They are the same criticisms that are leveled against the Western powers, the IMF, the World Bank, colonialism and indeed all the woes that are besetting Africa and its people. Many African leaders and scholars have hailed the friendship between China and African countries pointing out that the relations have brought much benefit to the whole African continent.

The latest symbol of China's dramatic emergence as Africa's closest development partner is the gift of the US$ 200 million gleaming new headquarters of the African Union in Addis Ababa, Ethiopia, inaugurated on 28 January 2012 by Jin Qinglin, Chair of the Chinese People's Consultative Conference. Termed "China's Gift to Africa", the edifice was constructed by the China State Construction Engineering Corporation with over 90 per cent Chinese labour. Among the other main contributions of China-Africa engagement the following may be highlighted:

The first relates to recent revival of Africa's Economic fortunes. It is widely believed that China's growing economic engagement in Africa has greatly contributed to the revival of Africa's economic fortunes within a globalizing world economy. China's activities in the continent have improved the economic outlook of Africa after a decade of average growth of 5.4 per cent, rate that is similar to those in the rest of the developing world and actually today exceeds the rate of growth in most advanced economies.

China also creates a win-win equation. Undoubtedly, close economic ties with Africa have secured China the raw materials essential for its industrial development. For the continent it has yielded previously unimaginable growth rates and helped end its much decried economic marginalization. The Chinese have poured tens of billions of dollars into vast infrastructure projects—highways, railways, bridges and power generation plants—which are transforming the inter-African trade. At the same time it is also a huge new market and boosting prices for agricultural commodities that are African peasants' economic lifeline. China also sells Africa inexpensive technologies which have lifted millions of small entrepreneurs out of poverty through access to farm machinery and transport.

China's seemingly unlimited ability to cultivate intimate economic ties with Africa must rankle Western managers seeking to do the same. But they are constrained by good-governance legislation which does not permit the deals that China's state-controlled enterprises thrive on. But the fact is that the dramatic rise of China is based not on this advantage but on its clear, long-sighted identification of its own—and Africa's—economic self interests and goals, something the West never really bothered to comprehend. The West instead focused on achieving political and military influence, through which much-needed African resources were also to be obtained. An excellent example of the two blocs' divergent approach to securing Africa ties is exemplified by the establishment of the US Africa Command (AFRICOM) in February 2007, which claimed would "promote our common goals of development", whereas China has been negotiating energy deals and multibillion-dollar aid agreements. It is obvious that AFRICOM would militarize African-US relations, as witnessed in the past six-seven years. It has also led to armed interventions to protect, topple or install governments as in Libya, Ivory Coast and Somalia (2011). In the same period China has been busy dotting the African landscape with massive road and rail projects, power stations and football stadiums and the like. And yet, the question being regularly asked is not whether the West is re-colonizing Africa, but the supposed colonizer is China, which does not have any military base on the continent, and has not been in any way politically involved in any political power struggle.

Besids, as pointed out by some scholars, the strategic partnership between China and Africa, the largest developing country and home to the largest concentration of developing countries, takes on wider significance, not just meaningful to bilateral relations. In this context, implications of China-Africa Cooperation for South-South Cooperation, African Renaissance and Harmonious world can be relevant. As an important element of international cooperation for development, South-South Cooperation (SSC) offers viable opportunities for developing countries and countries with economies in transition in their individual and collective pursuit of sustained economic growth and sustainable development. Economic cooperation among countries of the South having common colonial experiences, resources and production complementarities was seen as a panacea for reducing dependence on Western powers,

From a geopolitical point of view, cooperation between China and Africa and other developing countries such as India will help boost the influence of the developing world as a whole and also help bringing about a more just political and economic order in the world. With their ties strengthened the developing countries will have more say in world affairs. In the World Trade Organization negotiations on agriculture, for example, the developed countries had to make concessions on the issue of farm produce subsidies, thanks to the orchestrated actions on the part of the developing world, including China, India and leading African countries. Besides, China and African nations adopt the same or similar stances on important international issues such as opposing unilateralism, upholding the authority of the United Nations and increasing the representation of the developing world in the UN Security Council. Working together in international affairs is of great significance to boosting the developing countries' influence on world affairs. From the perspective of South-South Cooperation, this kind of partnership can facilitate in bring about widely shared prosperity among developing countries, while taking care of China and African countries.

Another relevant dimension is African renaissance. In recent years, particularly after the liberation of South Africa from apartheid in 1994 the creation of the African Union (2002) and the adoption of the New Partnership for Africa's Development (NEPAD, 2001), the realization of African renaissance has become the main preoccupation of African leaders and people. For centuries African countries have been bound up with the traditional rich Western countries but still held the poorest place in the world. Now with the involvement of the emerging powers; particularly China, India, Brazil, etc. in Africa in recent years, a lot of positive changes are taking place on the continent. Africa is no longer "a Hopeless Continent". (*Economist*, 13 May 2000). Ten years later Africa has become 'an unexpected bright spot on the global economy'. Today, the notion of an 'emerging Africa', a giant continent awakening from poverty, dictatorship and disaster, bustling with hope and opportunity, has become fashionable. The new narrative of a 'Rising Africa' can well be regarded as the manifestation of the process of African renaissance. Undoubtedly the involvement of China and other emerging powers in Africa has a key role in this African transformation in the positive direction

Conclusions

The one thing that stands out in China-Africa relationship is the relative absence of historical and political complications. This is as opposed to the historical baggage that shadows the relation the continent has with the West, its traditional patron. In addition to the compatibility of the two economies the 'poliitical understanding' that Chinese leaders and their African counterparts seem to have reached have helped further strengthen the unprecedented economic and business ties they are forging. The Chinese partnership model that is based on mutual benefit and respect seems to resonate in most African capitals. This has helped China to gain access to African resources and do business with almost every country in the continent, even in places that alleged human rights violations have been carried out. Ofcourse this has led many in the West to doubt China's seriousness in carrying out its responsibilities as a world power. In almost every corner of Africa, there is something that interest China. The continent is rich in natural resources that promise to keep china's booming, fuel-hungry economy on the road.

The Beijing Action Plan (2013-2015) approved at the fifth Ministerial conference of FOCAC in Beijing in July 2012 has explained the future course of China-Africa cooperation. As Africa's economy heads for a take-off, the need for massive investment is becoming evident by the day. With the biggest foreign reserve in the world, US$ 3.2 trillion at the end of 2012, according to the world Bank, China has a real potential to solve the capital shortage in the continent.

Africa needs a transparent and effective government to get the best out of this partnership. Fair competition will also prove to be essential to

Sino-African relations. And China could also play a dominant role in the industrialization of the continent, but this calls for a strong and regulatory framework from African governments. Environmental protection will be a critical factor. Besides, a reduction in tariffs related to African goods should be made in order to allow for their market entry at competitive prices. Additionally, African countries should impose limits on Chinese involvement, such as higher tariffs and regulations to avoid lopsided agreements resulting in unequal relationship and public resentment.

The basic principles that guide China's engagement with Africa—respect for sovereignty and mutual economic benefit—indicate that China is committed to engaging political and economic equals. Both China and Africa have recognized the potential economic gains in fostering cooperation. Deeper engagement with China and other emerging powers is both desirable and inevitable for Africa. The politics and economics of globalization have stripped African countries of their assets and natural resources and left them with an unbearable debt burden. The emerging "Beijing Consensus" underlines a clear divergence between China's current activities in Africa and the political agenda of the colonial era in which European states overtly pursued policies of territorial, and economic dominance. Nowhere in colonial agendas was there room to acknowledge African sovereignty on equal political terms. Furthermore, not until the final decades of the colonial era did the notion of "economic benefit" to African people enter the picture.

China's seeming non-interference in the internal politics of African countries has been seen by some as an issue that endears it to African countries. Again no stringent political or democratic strings are attached to Chinese loan, aid or grant as opposed to the conditionalities that normally accompany Western ones.

African states can and should do more to ensure that relations with China work to their advantage. The onus is on African leaders to evaluate critically their countries' engagement with China and to use this unprecedented opportunity of influence to secure real advantages for their citizens. In partnership with China, African leaders should insist on developing the growth of an economic middle class, stifled during the colonial era and first half-century of independent rule, by providing robust and widespread training opportunities for African entrepreneurs and managers. At the same time, African leaders could insist on preferential trading conditions to be extended to the tens of thousands of African entrepreneurs who currently live and do business in China. African leaders would be also wise to examine China's treatment of the environment in its own context and insist on environmental measures and controls to safeguard the resources that its citizens—and its economy—will require for future economic stability and growth. The burden of envisioning, planning and implementing partnerships with China and ensuring advantages for Africa lies squarely with African leaders.

If African countries want to challenge the negative effects of globalization and end the deplorable plight of Africans, they also will have to achieve their unity. What Africans ought to emulate from the Chinese is their uncompromising stand over China's unity, their fierce nationalism and their entrepreneurial spirit. It is therefore, of paramount importance that Africans put the building of a pan-African identity and their unity at the top of their agenda in discussing cooperation with China.

Whatever China's good-will towards Africa, it remains a great power looking after its own interests and it is up to the Africans to do the same. China is neither on a 'civilizing' nor humanitarian mission in Africa. It is for Africa to satisfy its needs.

Undoubtedly, Africa needs to be cautious in its dealings with China. Obviously, the West's and Africa's interests do not coincide.

Africa needs to have a clear vision, a development strategy and be able to imbibe and apply global best practices in the management of its development process. Above all, it must avoid appearing as a helpless development partner and also shed the inordinate tendency to beseech partners for aid that was a constant in Africa's engagement with the rest of the world in the past. Africa needs to be aware of the context in which the strategic partnership with China is being developed. This strategic partnership should address what Africa can do with China as a partner, rather than what China can do for the continent. Even though trade is the main feature of the contemporary China-Africa relationship, China's increasingly multifaceted engagement in Africa will shape the continent for good.

NOTE

Revised version of a paper presented at the International Conference on "Contributions of Sino-African Relationship", Shanghai Institutes for Innternational Studies (SIIS), Shanghai, China, May 18, 2012.

REFERENCES

African Agricultural Technology Foundation. (2009). *Study on the Relelvancce of Chinese Agriculturlal Technologies to African Small Holder Farmers*.

African Union Commission, Doc. "Meeting the Task Force on Africa's Strategic Partnership with the Emerging Powers: China, India and Brazil, September 2006.

Alden, C. and Alves, A. (2008). History and Identity in the Construction of China's Africa Policy. *Review of African Political Economy*, Special Issue: 'The New Face of China-Africa Co-operation', Vol. 35(115).

Alden Chris. (2007). *China in Africa: Partner, Competitor, or Hegemon*? London: Zed Books.

Ampiah, Kweku and Naidu, Sanusha (eds.). (2008). *Crouching Tiger, Hidden Dragon? Africa and China.* Pietermaritsberg: University of KwaZulu Natal Press.

Angang, Hu. (2011). *China in 2020: A New Type of Superpower.* New Delhi: Harper Collins Publishers.

Bergsten, Fred, *et al.* (2009). *China's Rise: Challenges and Opportunities.* Peterson Institute of International Economics, Centre for Strategic and International Studies, Washington D.C.

Brautigam, Deborah. (2009). *The Dragon's Gift: The Real Story of China in Africa.* Oxford University Press.

China in Africa Project, South African Institute of International Affairs. *The China-Africa Toolkit: A Resource for African Policymakers*, SAIIA, September 2009.

China's Environmental Protection Policy. (2007). Available online: http//pacific environment.org

Chinese Government, '*China's Africa Policy', January 2006.*

Farndon, John. (2008). *China Rises: How China's Astonishing Growth Will Change the World.* Virgin Books, Random House.

Forster, V. *et al.* (2008). *Building Bridges: China's Growing Role as Infrastructure Financier for Sub-Saharan Africa.* Washington D.C.: World Bank and PPIAF.

Grimm, S. *et al.* (2009). European *Development Cooperation to 2020: Challenges by New Actors in International Development,* Working Paper N. 4.

Guo S, and J. Blanchard. (eds.). (2008). *Harmonius World and China's Foreign Policy.* Plymouth: Lexington Books.

Harneit, Axel-Sievers; Marks, Stephen and Naidu Sanusha. (eds.). (2010). *Chinese and African Perspectives on China in Africa.* Pambazuka Press, HBF, Nairobi and Foundation Publishers, Kampala.

He Wen Ping. (2009). China's Africa Policy: Driving Forces, Features and Global Impact. *Africa Review* (New Delhi), Vol. 1(2).

Herman, Hayley. (2010). FOCAC 2009: A New Courtship or More of the Same? Paper presented at the Special Symposium on *China in Africa,* Syracuse University, New York, USA, 8-10 April, 2010.

Hongwu, Liu and Jiemian, Yang. (2009). Fifty Years if Sino-African Cooperation: Background, Progress and Significance. Yunnan University Press.

Jacques, Martin. (2009). When *China rules the World: The Rise of the Middle Kingdom and And the End of the Western World.* Allen Lane: Penguin Books.

Kragelund, P. (2010). *The Potential role of Non-Traditional Donors in Africa.* (ICTSD Issue Paper. No. 11.

Mathews, K. (2010). Forum on China-Africa Cooperation (FOCAC): Opportunities and Perspectives for Africa. Paper presented at the Seminar on "China-Ethiopia and China-Africa Relationship in a Mutually Beneficial and Win-Win Manner", organized by the Embassy of China and the Ethiopian International Institute for Peace and Development (IIPD), held at Hilton, Addis Ababa.

Mathews, K. (2010). India's Engagement with Africa in the 21st Century. Paper presented at the Special Symposium on *Africa and China.* Syracuse University, New York.

Mukanga, Chola and Lone, Salim. (2012). Do China's activities in Africa amount to recolonisation of the continent. *BBC Focus on Africa.* April-June 2012:30-31.

Naidu S., Corkin, L., and Herman, H. (2009). China's Re-Emerging Relations with Africa. in *Politikon.* Vol.36 (10).

Naidu, S. (2007). The Forum on China-Africa Cooperation (FOCAC): What Does the Future Hold? In *China Report.* Vol. 43(3).

OECD, The Rise of China and India: What's in it for Africa, May 2006 Report.

Rotberg R. (ed.). (2008). *China into Africa: Trade, Aid and Influence.* Cambridge & Massachussets: World Peace Foundation.

Taylor, I. (2009). *China's New Role in Africa.* London: Lynne Rienner Publishers.

Tull, Denis M. (2006). China's Engagement with Africa: Scope, Significance, and Consequences. *Journal of Modern African Studies,* Vol. 44(3).

Vines, Alex. (2007). China in Africa: A Mixed Blessing. *Current History*, Vol. 106(700).

4
Political Participation of Women in South Sudan

Shubhra Parmar

South Sudan is a land lock country in the east-central Africa with its capital at Juba. It covers an area of 619,745 km. It is bordered with Ethiopia to the east, Kenya, Uganda, and the Democratic Republic of the Congo to the south; and the Central African Republic to the west. South Sudan is ethnically and linguistically highly diverse. South Sudan is the 54th country of Africa and 193rd nation of United Nations. South Sudan has an estimated population of 8 million. South Sudan gained independence from Sudan on 9 July 2011 as the outcome of a 2005 peace deal that ended Africa's longest-running civil war. Formed from the ten southern-most states of Sudan, South Sudan is a land of expansive grassland, swamps and tropical rain forest. South Sudan has federal, presidential, democratic republic character with its first elected president Salva Kiir Mayardit and Vice President Riek Machar Teny. The constitution establishes a mixed Presidential system of government headed by a President who is head of state, the head of government, and commander-in-chief of the armed forces. It also establishes the National Legislature comprising of two houses: a directly elected assembly, the National Legislative Assembly; and a second chamber of representatives of the states, the Council of States. The constitution also provides for an independent judiciary, the highest organ being the Supreme Court.

Women in South Sudan have suffered and are still suffering because of the long 21 years of civil war. During the struggling period of bifurcation of Sudan and South Sudan, violence against women, including rape, remains widespread, particularly in Darfur in and around camps for internally displaced persons (IDPs). Throughout Sudan, the government routinely repressed human rights defenders, political opponents and ordinary civilians, subjecting many to torture and other forms of ill-treatment. There were ethnic clashes, rebel group conflicts, competition of resources and governmental issues in Sudan and South Sudan which directly and indirectly created disturbances of displacement, internally displaced refugees, sexual abuse, insecurity, homelessness, fear, doubt, prejudice, unemployment in the life of men, women and children. Women and children were disproportionately affected due to these massive violence and displacement.

Women and girls are routinely deprived of the rights subjected to degrading practices such as forced and early marriage, wife-inheritance, and the use of girls to pay debts, and various forms of domestic violence. Domestic disputes are resolved by traditional courts that often apply discriminatory customs. Female refugees face daily threats of harassment, exploitation and violence, and the persistent fear, constant struggle for daily basic sustainability. In regions plagued by conflict women have been subject to some of the worst marginalisation, oppression and violence perpetrated by various groups within and outside the region. These various crises have inevitably transformed women into heads of households without granting them the legal status, political power and other social, symbolic and cultural benefits.

Since the signing of the Peace Agreement (CPA) in 2005, South Sudan also has committed itself to ensuring women's participation, including through a quota system to ensure gender parity in government. South Sudanese women played a very central role in their society, in physical and psychological welfare as well as conflict prevention and peace building. The majority of female and male politicians in South Sudan acknowledge the roles that women played during the conflict as well as their roles as peacebuilders and in mobilizing voters for the referendum on independence in January 2011.

According to Anne Itto (2006) the roles women played as combatants, supporters of fighting forces and peacemakers qualify them to sit at the negotiating table and to assume an active role in execution and implementation. Sudanese women have worked very hard to keep families and communities together during conflicts through singing peace songs, persuading their husbands, sons and brothers to stop fighting, risking dangerous peace missions across enemy territories, or marrying across enemy lines to unite or reconcile warring communities. There were times when women stopped conflict from escalating by defying or opposing decisions by male members of the community to go to war.[1] In order to effectively address social, economic and general problems of war facing women, many women organized themselves into groups, networks and NGOs on both sides of the political divide. These activist networks (including the Sudanese Women's Voice for Peace, New Sudan Women's Federation, and New Sudan Women's Association) went all over the world advocating peace.

According to Edward (2011) the participation of women in political and representation in public affairs of South Sudan is a fairly recent phenomenon. Before this, no initiative and affirmative action was taken in this regard. In recently established South Sudan, women and men have occupied different and unequal positions in the society. For example, while women are usually relegated to their stereotypical roles of nurturing and caring, men assume political positions, conduct business, serve in the military and perform other roles deemed as male's. Such gender configurations and/or different positions of women and men are shaped and reinforced by societal cultural norms and practices, religion, customs, perceptions, socialization process, and colonial patriarchal practices and policies.

The changing perception about South Sudanese women is reflected in the statement given by Itto. According to Itto, who is one of the most senior women in South Sudan politics, Deputy Secretary General of the Sudan People's Liberation Movement and Agriculture Minister, "Those ones—education and early marriage, forced marriage—these are not things we change overnight. You can have the best of laws, but something when it becomes a habit, a practice, a tradition, it will take five, ten years to move people out of it. When something is a habit you can have the laws, but you have to change people's attitudes.

Political participation is based on actions on the part of individuals which either directly or indirectly affect the authoritative allocation of scarce resources, either material or symbolic, in their community or between communities either within or outside their society (Verba *et al.* 1978). Bourne (2010) explains political participation has been proven to take incredibly diverse forms such as being a member of a political party or community-based organizations, displaying an active role within a range of cultural or leisure interactions, contacting a politician to express ecological concerns, suggestions or ideas, signing a petition, setting public buildings on fire and even shooting at policemen during demonstrations and riots. Diemer (2012) referred to political participation as an "engagement with traditional mechanisms in the... political system, such as voting in elections and joining political organizations". Munroe (2002) defined political participation in terms of the degree to which citizens are exercising their right to engage in political activities (e.g., to protest, to speak freely, to vote, to influence or to get more energetically involved). Such definitions capitalize on the lawful nature of political praxis, in other words, they clearly establish a frame of reference with the available repertoire of political praxis within the conventional political norms, although these norms are not necessarily uniform across countries or across time.

Huntington and Nelson (1976:3) defined political participation as an "activity by private citizens designed to influence government decision-making" whereas Verba *et al.* (1995:38) characterized it as an "activity that has the intent or effect of influencing government action—either directly by affecting the making or implementation of public policy or indirectly by influencing the selection of people who make those policies." The praxis does not seem to be important enough in the context of these definitions in as much as they are mainly teleological in nature. Isaksson *et al.* (2012) observed political participation tends to be unequally distributed across citizens. Gender differences in political participation would reproduce gender inequalities in other areas of development also. With respect to the gender gap in political participation, it is not unreasonable to assume that resources relevant for political participation, e.g., education and information, are differentially available to men and women, that motivational forces stimulating engagement, e.g., participatory norms, differ between the genders, and that women and men have unequal access to recruitment networks.

Political participation is not static; it is a very dynamic and evolving social phenomenon. A number of factors have been identified as being related to political participation. Vecchione and Caprara (2009) found that gender, education and age are significant factors affecting participation levels. Jennings and Markus (1988) stress on the relationship between socio demographic variables (such as age, marital status and gender) and levels of political participation. Ross (1986) there is focus on variation in female political participation and a collection of theories. There are different parameters of female political participation which are as follows: political participation declines with complexity (i.e., women have more power in bands than in states); correlated with contribution to subsistence (female participation increases with contributions to the economy); Social structure: fraternal interest groups (patrilineages and age-grades); war: negatively correlated with female participation (male supremacist complex) psycho cultural dispositions (child rearing practices); father absence and protest masculinity.

Lovenduski (2000) writes that there are different arguments for increased female representation: normative arguments that says it is unfair for men to monopolize representation and pragmatic arguments which stress women's special interests and experiences that can only be represented by women. The normative and pragmatic arguments, Lovenduski states, do not say that getting more women into politics will affect the outcome of politics. On the other hand, which is based on the stance of difference means that getting more women in politics will lead to an improvement of the politics.

Sumbadze (2008) expresses gender in politics has two sides, and although separate it is associated with each other. One is women's representation and the other is concern for women's issues. Representation increases the likelihood for considering women's issues as well as brings in gender perspective; however representation on its own cannot guarantee the desired outcome. Gender refers to the roles, relationships, attitudes, behaviour and values, etc. that society ascribes to men and women. Much of the recent focus on gender relations has to do with the influence of feminism. Another thinker Waylen (1996) thinks feminists all over have come to characterize gender relations as matters of subordination and inequality. Different roles are given to women and men where women's supposed caring nature and men's aggressive nature provides clear roles.

Clark (1991) brings up a number of common theories on low representation within feminist theory. Women and men are taught different roles in life where the home is the women's area and politics and public life is seen as the man's world. Another point in this sex role problematic is the fact that house work and family responsibility hindrances women from participating in politics and public life. She mentions male conspiracy theory which derives from feminist ideology and is based on the idea that men are discriminating women therefore women have low representation in political office. She continues with institutional constraints that women are less likely than men to become incumbents and therefore have less chance to get into office. The power, prestige and desirability of political office, she concludes, has also been seen as a factor determining the level of representation of women since these characteristics are seen as male dominated where women have strong difficulties to compete with men.

Participation in electoral processes involves much more than just voting. Political participation derives from the freedom to speak out, assemble and associate; the ability to take part in the conduct of public affairs; and the opportunity to register as a candidate, to campaign, to be elected and to hold office at all levels of government. In African countries also men and women have an equal right to participate fully in all aspects of the political process. In practice, however, it is often harder for women to exercise this right. In post-conflict countries there are frequently extra barriers to women's participation, and special care is required to ensure their rights are respected in this regard. Women's participation in mainstream political activity has important implications for the broader arena of governance in any country. Governance relates to a set of rules, institutions, and values that are involved in the management of state and society. Governance institutions and processes include political parties, parliaments, government and their interactions with society. Although governance is a generic term which could mean good government or management, the governance values, types of government, the nature of political processes, the political parties and organizations, which/whose interests are represented and protected, and the extent of power that the masses have to challenge the state or in suggesting alternatives in methods of governance etc. may vary in different political systems. Women constitute half the population in a political system which supports equality and where both women and men are legally eligible for political office, women's participation should be equal to that of men. Representation is not only a means of ensuring individual participation. It is also the responsibility of the representatives to act on behalf of the constituents, including women, who elected them and reflect their ideas and aspirations. Women's disproportionate absence from the political process would mean that the concerns of half the population cannot be sufficiently attended to or acted upon as it denies their viewpoints sufficient opportunity to be integrated in the political system.

Political Participation of Women in Africa

The lone female voices one encounters in political circles, including in Africa, are insufficient to effect the changes that are so important to women. As a tiny minority in governance, women could be subjected to pressures, and their capacities as representatives, policy makers and decision takers are constrained by their numbers. In such low numbers, and with insufficient clout, women ministers tend to be relegated to and concentrated in, social areas rather than legal, economic, political and technical functions of government. It goes without saying that when women are represented in critical numbers in parliaments, as well as at the grassroots level, their perspectives and interests will be taken into account and their concerns given higher priority. Ndulo (2009) explores greater political participation will also allow women to make a meaningful impact on democracy, and to sustain the effort for the empowerment and representation of women. Globally, women's representation in parliaments stands at 18.2 per cent—the highest it has ever been, but still not high enough. Today only 22 countries have achieved a critical mass of 30 per cent or higher women representation in their national parliaments, mainly as a result of constitutional quotas written into law and requiring that a certain percentage of political positions be occupied by women. Six African countries i.e., Burundi, Mozambique, Rwanda, South Africa, Tanzania and Uganda were succeeded and recognized the importance of equity between women and men in decision-making and they instituted changes in their electoral and parliamentary processes.

Tripp (2001) explains the real fact that until the 1990s it was unheard of for women to run for the presidency in Africa. Yet in the 1990s, Charity Ngilu and Wangari Maathai ran in the 1998 Kenyan presidential election and Ngilu has announced plans to run again in 2002. Rose Rugendo of Tanzania's party Chama Cha Mapinduzi sought her party's nomination in the 1995 presidential primaries as did Sarah Jibril in Nigeria in 1989. Although unsuccessful in these bids for power, these women set an important precedent in their respective countries. Ruth Sando Fahnbulleh Perry was Chair woman of the Council of State of Liberia, she has been on the six-member collective presidency of Liberia, chairing this Council of State since September 1996. She is the first non-monarchical head of an African state. In 1994 Uganda's Wandera Specioza Kazibwe became the first female Vice President in Africa. Sylvie Kinigi served as Prime Minister of Burundi from 1993 to 1994, and during this same period, Agathe Uwilingiyimana was Prime Minister of Rwanda until she was assassinated in office. Senegal also claimed a woman vice president in 2001.

Tripp (2001) further explains that in several countries, the 1990s saw women's increased involvement in the constitution making process. Women were very active in the process of drafting the new South African Constitution, which guarantees women rights to equality, freedom and security of the person, freedom from violence, the right to make decisions concerning reproduction, and the right to security and control over one's own body. The Women's National Coalition lobbied hard to have the Women's Charter passed. The independent Women's National Coalition (WNC), South Africa had been formed in 1991 after much deliberation to unite women of all parties and political persuasions. The Coalition brought together 81 organizational affiliates and 13 regional alliances of women's organizations including organizations affiliated with the African National Congress, the Inkatha Freedom Party, the National Party, Pan Africanist Congress, Azanian Peoples Organization, and the Democratic Party. WNC also brought together interests as diverse as the Rural Women's Movement, Union of Jewish Women, and the South African Domestic Workers Union. By the end of the decade, the Ethiopian, Lesotho, and South African legislative bodies had female speakers of the house and Uganda, Zimbabwe and South Africa had female deputy speakers. African women were also demanding better representation at the ministerial level, especially where they had made gains in parliamentary representation. Zimbabwe, for example, had only two female cabinet ministers out of a 24 member cabinet and South Africa had only three out of 27.

According to Kemp *et al.* (1995) over three million women participated in focus groups organized by WNC to voice their opinions on women's concerns. Regional and national conferences were held and a Woman's Charter was drafted and endorsed by the national parliament and all nine regional parliaments in 1994. The Charter addressed a broad range of concerns, including equality, legal rights, economic issues, education, health, politics, and violence against women. The constitution allows for the Charter to be used as a basis for reforming government policy.

In Zambia the National Women's Lobby Group (NWLG) along with six other NGOs succeeded in getting the Constitutional Commission to incorporate into the draft Constitution a section on women's rights, focusing on discrimination, affirmative action, violence against women and the implementation of the UN Convention on the Elimination of All forms of Discrimination against Women. Similar measures were adopted in Malawi, where women's organizations involved in the Constitution making process had to be constantly on the alert so that women's concerns were not dropped from the agenda or reprioritized. Rwandan women are exceptions as they have proved themselves as the greatest achievers in political level. Rwanda ranks highest in the world in terms of female representation in Parliament with over 50 per cent representation. Recently Nkosazana Dlamini-Zuma, who has broken the glass ceiling by becoming the first elected woman head of the AU Commission. In Africa, as in the rest of the world, women are largely underrepresented in the political arena. However, 2011 and 2012 saw an unprecedented number of female presidential candidates vying for office. 2012 also ushered in the second female Head of State as well as a female Chairperson of the African Union Commission for the very first time.

Powley (2005) explores the female representation in Africa has seen the fastest growth in any region of the world. But gender disparity in political participation on the continent is also the most severe. UN Women reports that the average percentage of female parliamentarians in lower houses of sub-Saharan Africa is 20.8 per cent. According to the Inter-Parliamentary Union statistics, on 1 April 2013, the percentages of women participation in lower or single house in national parliament are as follows: Rwanda 56.3 per cent, South Africa 42.3 per cent, Mozambique 39.2 per cent, Angola 34.1 per cent, Uganda 35.0 per cent, Algeria 31.6 per cent, Burundi 30.5 per cent, Guyana 31.3 per cent, Tunisia 26.7 per cent, South Sudan 26.5 per cent, Lesotho 26.7 per cent, Sudan 24.6 per cent, Namibia 24.4 per cent, Senegal 22.7 per cent, Malawi 22.3 per cent, Mauritania 22.1 per cent, Liberia 11 per cent, Ghana 10.9 per cent, Botswana 7.9 per cent, Gambia 7.5 per cent, Congo 7.4 per cent, Nigeria 6.8 per cent, Egypt 2 per cent (The Inter-Parliamentary Union statistics 2012). According to estimates by the Inter-Parliamentary Union (IPU), an average 16.8 per cent of parliamentary seats are held by women in sub-Saharan Africa. No true democracy can be attained without being inclusive and participation of women. Hence, women are to be integrated into key decision-making positions that are strategic to access key resources critical to empowerment and participation.

Two African women, Ellen Johnson Sirleaf and Leymah Ghowee both from Liberia, Africa in 2011 were awarded Nobel Prize for their non-violent struggle during the revolution. Kenya also produced the first woman Nobel Peace prize laureate, the Honorable Waangari Maathai. Other rising women are President Joyce Banda of Malawi, Boussaina Kamel, the very first female presidential aspirant of Egypt (2012), Honorable Rebecca Kadaga, first female Speaker of the House in Uganda's Parliament, Honorable Rabiaa Nejlaoui, youngest Member of Parliament in Tunisia, and Honorable Hlobisile Ndlovu, Minister of Youth, Sports and Culture of Swaziland. In other African nations, women make up a significant part of their governments. Mozambique, one of the countries where quota systems have been implemented is ranked fifth in the world for female representation in Parliament. The presence of a significant proportion of female members of Parliament perhaps diverts attention from the substantive inequality experienced by grassroots women. It is, therefore, critical that discourse on gender rights continue beyond the political sphere and into the household. Equal participation in politics is imperative to the advancement of peace, stability, gender equity, human rights, good governance and ultimately the consolidation of democracy. Sub-Saharan Africa seems to be moving in the right direction, but fruitful and efficacious female, political participation is limited to individual cases.

Political Participation of Women in South Sudan

During the decades-long Sudanese Civil War, women played an integral part in the movement for independence and peace. On 9 July 2011, their dreams were realized and South Sudan became the world's newest democratic nation. Kuany (2010) shows the concern now shifts to ensuring that women are not marginalized in the decision-making bodies of the new government nor political life, where women's participation remains low. South Sudanese women constitute over 60 per cent of the population in Africa's newest state. South Sudan women seek 30 per cent representation in the new state. Despite these challenges, it seems that the transformations occurring in South Sudan are creating spaces and opportunities for women to mobilise and organise for more participation in the nation-building process.

The participation of women in political and public affairs of South Sudan is a fairly new concept for them. Till now women involvement in politics was not seen as a woman's prerogative. According to some observations and research studies South Sudan has revealed that women and men occupy different and unequal positions and power relations both within the family and society at large. The current political space that women enjoy came from the liberation struggle which was lead by the Sudan People's Liberation Movement. It was in 1994 that the movement decided to adopt an affirmative action policy that gave women 25 per cent representation in any decision-making (body) and they would be allowed also to participate in the remaining 75 percent. The major breakthrough for women's participation in politics came after the signing of the Comprehensive Peace Agreement (CPA) in 2005 which stipulated a 25 per cent for women's representation in all levels of government in recognition of their roles and contributions to the liberation struggle. The interim period (2005-2011) witnessed an increase in the number of women in decision-making positions of the former Government of Southern Sudan.

Batha (2011) explores that in political participation, out of the total of 90 ambassadors, nine were women. The Transitional Constitution of the Republic of South Sudan (TCRSS) stipulates that at least 25 per cent of seats and positions in each legislative and each executive organ of the state needs to be allocated to women as part of affirmative action designed to redress historical injustices. This also extends to judiciary, Council of Ministers, to Independent Institutions and Commissions. Currently, there are more than 95 female MPs in the recently reconstituted National Legislative Assembly, and five women in the newly formed Council of States. In the newly formed government of the Republic of South Sudan, there are five female ministers and nine deputy ministers. Similarly, there are women who serve as head of commissions, presidential advisors, and other higher positions in the national and states governments. However, women's involvement in politics is not free of contestations and challenges. Women still face numerous challenges some of which are socio-cultural, while others relate to different status of women—such as differential educational status, age, marital status, class, family background, ethnic and regional variations, economic, etc.

South Sudan has ten states and ten governors. But only one state has a female governor-Warrap State. Ms. Nyandeng Malek Deliech is successfully holding the position of the governor of Warrap State replacing male appointed Governor, Tor Deng Mawien. There are currently seven Presidential Advisors. Six are male and one is female. Out of 29 ministerial portfolios, five are occupied by women. There are 15 members on the Austerity Measures Committee established by the President. No woman sits on that committee. Three are currently ten Grade 1 Ambassadors. All ten positions have gone to male ambassadors and none to women. There are 27 undersecretaries and only four are women. Other organs of government show a similar pattern, all failing to reach the 25 per cent mark; most don't even attain half of the required quota. There is a wide discrepancy between the professed ideal, the constitutional mandate and the reality on the ground.

According to Inter-Union Parliamentary statistics 2011 South Sudan women participation status in lower house is 26.5 per cent and upper house is 10 per cent in the national parliament. On 6 May 2012, more than 50 female leaders from across South Sudan gathered in Juba for a workshop on women's rights under the transitional constitution, aiming to improve the future permanent constitution. South Sudanese women call for scratching out harmful customary laws and drafting new developing laws for women development (Inter-Union Parliamentary Statistic 2011). The South Sudan government ministries have taken some developing steps towards women's increased participation in Parliament and formulate laws that promote and protect women's rights. South Sudan's ruling party has said it intends to increase the mandatory percentage of women in the SPLM from 25 per cent to 35 per cent in order to empowering women so that in the future they will be able to compete with men on an equal basis. Women in South Sudan currently make up approximately 30 per cent of the legislature, with more than 25 per cent holding ministerial positions

According to Sudan Tribune (2013) Government statistics show that in the Northern Bahr el Ghazal State Legislative Assembly there are more women than men. The Northern Bahr el Ghazal State Minister of Information and Communication Jackline Nyibol Ajonga has announced great news for the women in South Sudan following the increase of women affirmative action in government to 35 per cent on 12 March 2013. Nyibol also appreciates the wise decision taken by the president to have given youth 20 per cent representation in his government which she says both two elements [youth and women] are of crucial importance in any government to deliver the services to the public.

Increased global efforts in gender equality, women's political participation, and human rights constitute another enabling factor for equality in South Sudan. The Millennium Development Goals (MDGs), which many world leaders have endorsed, include commitments to women's empowerment and gender equality, which are now considered essential to achieving all MDGs. Women's political participation and gender mainstreaming, including in postconflict societies, have also been on the global security agenda since 2000, with the adoption of Security Council Resolution 1325. The Security Council has since adopted several other resolutions that focus on sexual violence in conflict, set out institutional mechanisms to prevent sexual violence, ensure protection for women in conflict, and address impunity. It also has appointed a special representative on sexual and gender-based violence (GBV) in conflict situations; South Sudan is a priority country on the representative's agenda for 2011-12. Global commitments to encouraging women's participation, gender mainstreaming, and combating GBV are evident in United Nations Security Council Resolution 1996 (2011), which established the UN Mission of the Republic of South Sudan (UNMISS). Drawing on its resolutions on women, peace, and security, the Security Council affirmed the importance of appropriate gender expertise in the mission.

The desire of South Sudanese women to engage themselves is of the sign of development. South Sudanese women themselves have been organizing, leading, funding and participating in large conferences, meetings and projects on women's political participation. To speak of 'women' in South Sudan is both a challenging and strategic move.

According to Faria (2011) South Sudanese women come from a diverse range of ethnic-regional, religious, and linguistic communities these differences have made organizing as "Women" and around gender equality an ongoing struggle. And yet as we embark on South Sudanese independence, recognizing both the past and ongoing contributions of women to peace in the South, and the significant and ongoing challenges faced by them today, is a vital project. Women have also actively participated in the struggle for land, resources, greater autonomy and recognition—efforts that have reworked norms around political subjectivity and the acceptable role of women. The post-conflict period has thus seen a flourishing of civil society in South Sudan opening up many new spaces for women's political and social engagement and activism. Women thus represent a valuable resource for the Government of South Sudan and others seeking to build a strong and politically sustainable nation-state. Yet in South Sudan we see the promise of a more sustainable feminist nationalism. This is reflected in part by women's growing political voice, the important involvement of women in the referendum process, and the centering of women's empowerment in government and non-governmental development discourse. In this new moment, women will undoubtedly play an important role in directing the post-conflict direction of the new country.

Government Initiatives for Increasing Women Participation and Representation in South Sudan

In July 2010, the United Nations General Assembly created UN Women, the United Nations Entity for Gender Equality and the Empowerment of Women. In doing so, UN Member States took an historic step in accelerating the Organization's goals on gender equality and the empowerment of women. UN Women's South Sudan has developed a Strategic Note for the period 2012-2013 and is aligned with the South Sudan Development Plan and the United Nations Development Assistance Framework (UNDAF) (2011-2013). Targeted gender equality and women's empowerment interventions will be undertaken to increase development effectiveness. The three strategic priority areas for UN Women South Sudan focused on: Women's leadership and participation in gender-responsive governance, increase Women's economic empowerment and opportunities, improve security and protection for women and girls. Ali (2011) explores three main components for promoting women's economic security are: Mainstream women's economic empowerment across South Sudan government machineries and existing development programmes. This will be through enhancing technical capacity as well as by increasing the number of economic empowerment gender-sensitive initiatives, policies, strategies and programmes and UN agencies; and enhancing the economic livelihoods of women farmers by increasing access to agricultural markets for women farmers and diversifying their sources of income, enhance economic livelihoods and capital base of women by providing them with entrepreneurship skills training and development services to facilitate their access to markets and finance, increase access to functional numeracy and literacy for women and girls.

On 7 May 2013, UN-supported women's National Conference Constitutional Development held in the South Sudanese capital of Juba organized by the South Sudan Women General Association and the National Democratic Institute, with support from United Nations Mission in South Sudan (UNMISSION), brings together women representatives from all 10 states of South Sudan and they discussed and laid down recommendations for the drafting of the country's new constitution. South Sudan's National Constitutional Review Commission took "serious note" of concerns raised by organizations promoting the role and rights of women in society and emphasized that United Nations Mission in South Sudan would also support the participation of women in political and decision making through political, technical and logistical support. First national conference on South Sudan's National Action Planning on the UN Security Council Resolution 1325 on Women, Peace and Security held in Juba, South Sudan held in 29-31 January 2013. South Sudan in collaboration with Organization for Women Development, the Ministry of Gender and Social Welfare, and UN Women, conference focused on participation, protection, prevention and relief and recovery for women.

Sexual and gender-based violence, access to justice, access to education and women's political participation, particularly in constitution building, were some of the issues identified. The importance of the participation of rural women and traditional leaders was also highlighted throughout the conference (South Sudan: women call for greater representation in UNSC resolution 1325 National Action Plan, and for CEDAW ratification). South Sudanese Civil Society Organizations also participated in a National Action Plan strategy session facilitated by the Global Network of Women Peace builders (GNWP). They came up with additional issues such as protection for peace activists and women human rights defenders; and the need to integrate implementation of women's rights treaties such as the Convention on the Elimination of All Forms of Discrimination against Women (CEDAW) and other human rights norms into the National Action Plan NAP 1325.

The South Sudan Civil Society Organization (CSO) Working Group on the development and implementation of South Sudan National Action Plan (NAP) 1325: women, peace and security also held a consultative discussion to develop an advocacy strategy for the ratification of CEDAW in South Sudan. They agreed on the following next steps: integrate CEDAW in their respective organizations' capacity building initiatives; build partnership with the South Sudan Women Lawyers' Association, Constitutional Review Commission, Women's Parliamentary Caucus, Ministry of Justice, Ministry of Foreign Affairs, Ministry of Gender, National Human Rights Commission among others[2] (CEDAW SouthSudan.)

The Global Network of Women Peacebuilders (GNWP) in collaboration with EVE Organization for Women Development organized a consultation session among civil society organizations at the Juba Regency Hotel on 2 February 2013. The consultation had the objective of raising awareness on CEDAW as well as to identify advocacy strategies around the ratification of the Convention. The training started with a presentation on the introduction and background of CEDAW. Participants were able to gain an understanding of the basic elements of the CEDAW —rights and freedoms enshrined, the role of the Committee, the use of General Recommendations, the Optional Protocol among others. The presentation also included best practices in the use of CEDAW in stopping violence against women, promoting girls' education, improving health care for women, improving women's lives at work, and protecting women's legal rights (Tesfaye, 2013).

Ms. Ophelie Namiech is IsraAID's country director in South Sudan. IsraAID, an organization pioneers in the field of post-trauma assistance related to sexual violence. She has been working in South Sudan since 2011, supporting the efforts of local communities and institutions in the field of social development, in partnership with the State Ministry of Gender and Social Development, South Sudan Police Services, the NGO 'Confident Children out of Conflict' and other Community-Based Organizations.[3] IsraAID is developing a Gender Based Violence investigation course and is looking to bring a team of Israeli police officers to South Sudan. IsraAID in association with Rashi Foundation established the center of treatment for children who are victims of sexual abuse, fostering the development of a solid network of safe places and services.

Namiech (2013) explains the different initiatives have been taken by South Sudanese government for gender-sensitivity and protective techniques for women in the society. For bring out the change in the society south Sudanese government had conducted a Special training on gender and crime statistics for South Sudan National Police Service on 15 December 2012. In Juba, sixty police personnel from the ten states of the Republic of South Sudan and national headquarters completed a specialized training programme on crime statistics and gender crimes at Juba Raha Camp, Juba. The aim of the training programme was to increase the capacity of the police personnel with skills to efficiently and professionally respond to gender-based violence and improve its management system with a specific focus on gender related crimes. The week-long training programme upgraded the knowledge of the officers on gender-based violence and equipped them with practical tools to respond to such crimes in a more gender sensitive manner.

Challenges and Obstacles before South Sudanese Women

South Sudanese challenges affect men and women differently, and affect differently women from different ethnic and socioeconomic backgrounds, and from different states of South Sudan, in distinct ways. Edward (2011) has listed few causes which are as follows:

First, cultural practices and perceptions in South Sudan represent major obstacles to women's participation in politics and other public affairs. The existing customary laws make it still harder for women to escape the bondage of domestic roles which relegate them to the status of second class citizens. The high rate of illiteracy among women in South Sudan is another obstacle to women's political participation.

Secondly, women themselves can also act as hindrance to their own advancement and empowerment, especially when they internalize the long held assumptions and perceptions that politics and other public affairs are only for men while, women's place is at home. Internalizing such assumptions negatively affect women's attitudes toward politics.

Thirdly, the gendered division of labour, which puts heavy burden on women's shoulders further contributes to the marginalization of women in politics and public life. Fourthly, according to South Sudan's Deputy Minister Priscilla Joseph Kuch Gender, Child and Social Welfare Department said that, "Violence against Women is one of the major contributing obstacles to the country's development." Violence against women is the abuse of human rights. Both physical and psychological violence against women have profound implications for a woman's health and empowerment. A battered woman who has suffered bodily harm cannot participate in various activities.

Fifthly, perhaps one of the most challenging areas is women's education in South Sudan. Most women in South Sudan cannot read or write. One of the most significant "traditional" barriers to women's participation is lack of education.

Sixthly, despite the relative increase in the number of women in senior positions in the government, nonetheless, women are not yet fully incorporated as equal partners into the male-dominated political structure of South Sudan. Edward explains although the allocation of twenty five per cent of seats to women ensures women's political participation, it does not avail women with the same power to make decisions on issues of national importance as their male counterparts.

Seventhly, one of the biggest challenge facing women legislators is policy implementation.

Lastly, South Sudan is severely lacking in infrastructure and has some of the worst human development indicators worldwide. Social and cultural practices harmful to women compound the effects of conflict and marginalization. There are constant internal and external security threats, a limited understanding of gender equality, and a tendency within communities to view gender as an alien and illegitimate concern, given the acute problems that South Sudan faces.

For gender equality and sustainability, it is important for the government to have a more and more infrastructure facilities, women political participation and strong training programmes to provide necessary expertise in gender empowerment. Linkages among civil society organization working on issues of importance to women will result in improve women involvement in policies. To ensure that in the South Sudan of tomorrow, women will have full equality with men, special focus is being directed at educating, capacitating and empowering girls and young women who, despite certain gains, continue to lag behind the men in access to education, resources and opportunities. At the same time, South Sudan government and policy makers should emphasize on the important role that can be played by women in the informal sectors also. Literacy and skills training are must for women advancement. There is no doubt that women are the future of South Sudan, and its leaders must invest in women's development, if they want their country, and continent, to advance in the 21st century and beyond.

The political parties in South Sudan and civil society should collaborate to create a stronger platform to represent the voice of women at the national level and local level. Promotion of women to perform and participate in the issue facing society is not only the recognition of their rights, but it is for the encouragement of mutual understanding and respect of the dignity of the human kind within the biggest frame, whereby gender equality discourse has to be realized and incorporated to the political system and institutional instruments appropriately. To promote women's participation at all levels, South Sudan should set priorities for the new state through consultations and other democratic processes that involve wide participation by women. Ensure a quota of at least 30 per cent of seats at all levels of government for women in South Sudan's permanent constitution. The government also must ensure women's access to decision making in the national economy and remove obstacles to their participation in it, in the public and private sectors and in the informal economy. Although the United Nations Missions in Sudan (UNMIS) and United Nations Population Fund (UNFPA) have established units within the police that address GBV and trained the police on women's rights and the needs of female survivors of GBV. There is also a need for psychosocial support services for GBV victims and survivors. The government of South Sudan should continue to prioritize health and education in its public statements and in practice, and remove access barriers for women and girls (UN Mission in Sudan).

Conclusion

The deeply entrenched and highly complex political, social and economic challenges affect the lives of men and women in South Sudan on a daily basis. South Sudanese women face an additional and unique set of challenges. Despite efforts by the government of South Sudan and international organizations aimed at empowering women, including advocating for high levels of school enrolment of girls and introducing a quota system for women in government, this deeply patriarchal society is strongly resistant to changes aimed at empowering women. The long lasting struggle for South Sudanese women continues to be a challenge even in post conflict era. Wherein, women are trying to carve out a meaningful life in a tenuous peace. Twenty first century belongs to South Sudanese women. Now time has come for women to take the responsibility of building the world's newest nation, the South Sudan. After watching the changing realties for women in Africa, now it is for the South Sudanese women to stand up and take political participatory responsibility. When we talk of political participation here, we present some prominent landmarks for women's political participation in Africa. Under diversified roles women in African participated as legislators, cabinet ministers, Ambassadors, elected head of the AU commissions, policy makers, decision makers, constitution drafting committee members, president, prime ministers, influential leaders, party leaders, leaders of women organization, etc. Being a new born country, South Sudan has to cover a long run to achieve an adequate women political representation. So women in South Sudan should inspire themselves by observing the political representation of women in other African countries. The emerging and ever increasing women political participation can only be understood under struggling scenario for women in major parts of Africa. The struggle included insecurity and non recognition in social, economic and political spheres. The same circumstances prevailed in South Sudan and will encourage women emancipation. The new republic in the South Sudan cannot achieve its political, economic and social objectives without a successful integration of women into the nation-building project. Progress in the South Sudan to a larger extent will depend on how the state integrates the women power into the nation-building project. Women represent the majority of population in South Sudan. New democratic spaces are opening up, especially in the South Sudan. Women should mobilize effectively and must seize the opportunity for more political participation. It is an urgent need for South Sudanese women to enhance their efforts and representation at all levels i.e. executive, legislative and judiciary. Women do need to focus on social-economic, political and cultural empowerment at rural and urban levels. Political leaders must think to improve women's economic conditions by creating economic programs such as small-credit unions that cater for specific needs of women in urban and rural areas. An effective measure would be to frame transformation, inclusive policies to promote education at all levels. Women should strongly pursue a goal to empower themselves. They must join political parties, women's associations, and civil society groups for their contribution towards the society. A sustainable policy will also require the education of men in South Sudanese communities alongside their female counterparts. Without the incorporation of men, the reform can only be partially successful. It requires equal and integrated efforts for both men and women to make the South Sudan a stronger, healthy and prosperous place to be called home. Given that South Sudanese women are affected by both the political and economic forces, a constructive effort must engage women in building a new nation.

NOTES

1. Anne Itto, 'Guests at the table? The Role of Women in the Peace Process', Concilliation Resources, 2006, http://www.c-r.org Conciliation Resources is a peace building NGO supporting people at the heart of conflicts who are striving to find solutions. We work with them to deepen our collective understanding of the conflict, bring together divided communities and create opportunities for them to resolve their differences peacefully. We are there for as long as we're needed to provide advice, support and practical resources. We then take what we learn to government decision-makers, and others working to end conflict, to improve peace building policies and practice worldwide.
2. South Sudan: South Sudanese Women Call for Greater Participation in Constitutional Review. *Sudan Tribune*. 25 January 2012.
3. Namiech Ophelie. From Israel to the women of South Sudan. 6 March 2013. Ophelie Namiech is IsraAID's country director in South Sudan; IsraAID has been working in South Sudan since 2011, supporting the efforts of local communities and institutions in the field of social development, in partnership with the State Ministry of Gender and Social Development, South Sudan Police Services, the NGO 'Confident Children out of Conflict' and other Community-Based Organizations

REFERENCES

Ali, N. M. (2011). *Gender and State Building in South Sudan*. United States Institute of Peace.

Alvy, L. (2004). *Violence Against Women in Sudan Reveals Common Weapon of War*. National Organization for Women. www.now.org/issues/global/120304sudan.html. Retrieved on 22/11/2012.

Amnesty International. (2004). *Darfur: Rape as a Weapon of War: Sexual Violence and its Consequences*. http://web.amnesty.org/library/index/engafr540762004. Retrieved on 24/01/2013.

Anderson, G. N. (1999). *Sudan in Crisis: the Failure of Democracy*. Gainesville: University Press of Florida.

Batha E. (2011). *Question and answer with Anne Itto: Is women's position in South Sudan changing*? Trustlaw. www.vtopics.com/Women/news/?index=5440ý Retrieved on 19/07/2013.

Beswick, S. (2010). Women, war and leadership in South Sudan (1700-1994). In Spaulding, J. and Beswick, S. (eds.) *White Nile, black blood: war, leadership, and ethnicity from Khartoum to Kampala.* Asmara. London: Red Sea Press.

Bourne, P. A. (2010). Unconventional political participation in a middle-income developing country. *Current Research Journal of Social Sciences*. Maxwell Scientific Organization. maxwellsci.com/print/crjss/v2-196-203.pdf Retrieved on 28/10/2012.

Butegwa C. (2006). Women in Darfur Look to ICC. Institute for war and peace reporting IWPR. *International Justice ICC. iwpr.net/report-news/women-darfur-look-icc*. Retrieved on 30/12/2012.

Cain, Kenneth. (1999). The Rape of Dinah: Human Rights, Civil War in Liberia, and Evil Triumphant. *Human Rights Quarterly.*

Clark, J. (1991). Getting There: Women in Political Office. *The Annals of the American Academy of Political and Social Science.*

Diemer, M. A. (2012). Fostering marginalized youths' political participation: Longitudinal roles of parental political socialization and youth sociopolitical development. *American Journal of Community Psychology.*

Edward J. K. (2011). South Sudan: Women and political Participation in the Country. Sudan Tribune: Plural News and Views on Sudan. *allafrica.com/stories/201109081039.html*. Retrieved on 22/12/2012.

Faria, C. (2011). Gendering War and Peace in South Sudan: The Elision and Emergence of Women. Association of Concerned Africa Scholar. Analysis and Action on Polices Impacting Africa. www.*concernedafricascholars.org/bulletin/issue86/faria/*ý Retrieved on 22/05/2012.

Garang, N. A. (2010). Warrap Women Celebrate election of first female governor. Sudan Tribune *www.sudantribune.com/spip.php?article34923* Retrieved on 22/11/2012.

GOSS. Government of the Republic of South Sudan—Ministries. Government of the Republic of South Sudan, *http://www.goss.org/* Retrieved on 17/09/2012.

Hale, Sondra. (1996). Gender Politics in Sudan: Islamism, Socialism, and the State. Boulder, Colo.: Westview.

Hamilton, Rebecca. (2011). Sudan dispatch: What about the Women?', The New Republic. *http://www.tnr.com.*

Hamilton, Rebecca. (2011). Sudan Dispatch: What about the Women? The Pulitzer center and the New Republic, Juba and Bentiu. Sudan. *www.newrepublic.com/article/world/82070/south-sudan-change-women*ý Retrieved on 11/11/2012.

Huntington, S. P., and Nelson, J. M. (1976). *No Easy Choice: Political Participation in Developing Countries.* Cambridge: Harvard University Press.

Inter-Parliamentary Union. (2001). *United: Trends and Nations, World's Women Statistics*, 1970-1990. New York.

Isaksson, A. Kotsadam, A. and Nerman, M. (2012). *The Gender Gap in African Political Participation: Individual and Contextual Determinants*. Department of Economics. School of Business, Economics and Law at University of Göteborg, Sweden.

Jennings, M. K., and Markus, G. B. (1988). Political involvement in the later years: A longitudinal survey. *American Journal of Political Science. www.lsa.umich.edu/UMICH/polisci/Home/People/.../MarkusCV.pd* Retrieved on 24/12/2012.

Katherine, A. E. (2011). Election time in Sudan: Will it bring change for women?. Peace for women. *www.consultancyafrica.com* Retrieved on 31/11/2012

Human Rights Watch. (1996). Shattered Lives: Sexual Violence During the Rwandan Genocide and its Aftermath.

Kuany, M. A. (2010). Women and Culture: Role of Women in Development of Southern Sudan. USA. *www.borglobe.com/25.html?m7:post=women-and-culture-the*. Retrieved on 15/12/2012.

Lamprianou, Iasonas. (2013). Contemporary Political Participation Research: A Critical Assessment Lamprianou in Nicosia, Cyprus. K.N. Demetriou (ed.), *Democracy in Transition*. Springer-Verlag Berlin Heidelberg.

Lovenduski, J. (ed.). (2000). *Feminism and Politics*: Volume II. Ashgate. Dartmouth.

Munroe, T. (2002). *An Introduction to Politics. Lectures for first-year students*. Canoe: Kingston.

Ndulo, M. and Grieco, M. (2009). *Power, Gender and Social Change in Africa*. Cambridge Scholars Publishing. UK.

Patterson, Donald. (1999). *Inside Sudan: Political Islam, Conflict, and Catastrophe*. Boulder, Colo.: Westview Press.

Rai, R., Ramadhan, A. A. and Tulchinsky, T. (2012). Prioritizing maternal and child health in independent South Sudan. *Maternal and Child Health Journal. www.consultancyafrica.com* Retrieved on 25/10/2012.

Refugees International. (2004). Rape, Islam, and Darfur's Women Refugees and War-displaced. *http://www.refugeesinternational.org/content/*. Retrieved on 22/11/2012.

Refugees International. (2004). Sudan: For Raped Women in Darfur, Access to Reproductive Health Services Limited *http://www.refugeesinternational*. Retrieved on 08/02/2013.

Refugees International (2005). Sudan: Inform Rape Survivors of Right to Seek Life-saving Treatment. *http://www.refugeesinternational.org/content/*. Retrieved on 04/07/2013..

Refugees International. (2006). Sudan: Town in North Darfur Reflects Changing Nature of the Conflict. *http://www.refugeesinternational.org/content/*. Retrieved on 14/06/2013.

Riziq, Lula . (2011). Sudanese Advocacy Networks In solidarity. Juba, Sudan: South Sudan Women's Empowerment Network (SSWEN).

Ross, M. (1986). Female Political Participation: A Cross-Cultural Explanation. American Anthropologist. *www.unl.edu/rhames/courses/ppoint/polpar.pdfý* Retrieved on 16/03/2013.

South Sudan. (2012). Contraceptives give women the right to choose. IRIN. *http://www.irinnews.org*. Retrieved on 26/02/2013.

South Sudan (2012). The biggest threat to a woman's life. IRIN. *http://www.irinnews.org*. Retrieved on 15/03/2013.

South Sudan (2012). The Role of women in Nation-building in South Sudan. Pambazuka. Peace for women E-news. *www.pambazuka.org/en/category/features/80972*. Retrieved on 11/01/2013.

SPLM Women's Conference Convenes in Juba', Goss Mission. (2007). *http://www.gossmission.org*. Retrieved on 11/01/2013.

Statistics and Evaluation Southern Sudan Centre for Census. (2010). Key Indicators for Southern Sudan. Juba. Sudan: Southern Sudan Centre for Census, Statistics and Evaluation (SSCCSE).

Stewart, M. and Taylor, M. (1995). Empowerment and estate regeneration. Bristol Policy Press.

Sudan Tribune. (2013). South Sudan's women warriors suffer in peace. Sudan Tribune, *http://www.sudantribune.com/South-Sudan-s-women-warriors*.

Terror and Crisis in Sudan's Blue Nile State. Huff Post World. Sudan4Jesus run. (2013) *www.sudan4jesus.com/2013/...crisis-in-sudans-blue-nile.html*. Retrieved on 02/06/2013.

Tesfaye, Selamawit. (2013). Towards Ratification of CEDAW for South Sudan. Workshop in Juba Regency Hotel, Juba. South Sudan.

Thomas, D. Q. and Regan, E. R. (1994). *Rape in War: Challenging the Tradition of Impunity.* SAIS Review, Winter-Spring. The Johns Hopkins University Press.

Tripp, A. M. (2001). The new political activism in Africa. Extracted from Journal of Democracy. *academia.edu/.../Womens_Movements_in_Southern_African_Democrati...ý* Retrieved on 21/03/2013.

UNESCO. (2011). Why Education Will Foster Stability in an Independent South Sudan. Paris France—Buenos Aires Argentina: United Nations Educational, Scientific and Cultural Organization Report.

Vecchione, M. and Caprara, G. V. (2009). Personality determinants of political participation: The contribution of traits and self-efficacy beliefs. Personality and Individual Differences. *dippsi.psi.uniroma1.it/users/caprara-gian-vittorioý* Retrieved on 20/05/2013.

Verba, S. (1961). *Small Groups and Political Behavior.* Princeton: Princeton University Press.

Verba, S., Nie, N. H., and Kim, J.-O. (1978). *Participation and Political Equality: A Seven-Nation Comparison.* Cambridge: Cambridge University Press.

Women in South Sudan Mobilizing Through Political Parties. (2011). Juba, South Sudan. *www.wdn.org/.../women-south-sudan-mobilizing-through-political-parti...ý* Retrieved on 22/04/2013.

Women in Western Equatoria hail the success of southern referendum process. The Sudan Tribune. 2011. *http://www.sudantribune.com.* Retrieved on 06/02/2013.

Women's Democracy Network. (2010). Southern Sudan Legislative Assemblies: A Legislator's Guide to Gender Politics. Women's Democracy Network Training Materials. *http://www.wdn.org.* Retrieved on 17/06/2013.

Woods, A. (2012). Rape being used as tool of war in Sudanese conflict. Women's news views and current affairs. womensviewsonnews.org/...used...war-in-Sudanese-conflict Retrieved on 22/06/2013.

World Report (2013): South Sudan. Human Rights Watch from *www.hrw.org/world-report/2013/country-chapters/south-sudan.* Retrieved on 22/07/2013.

Zambakari, Christopher. (2012). South Sudan: Institutional Legacy of Colonialism and the Making of a New State. *The Journal of North African Studies. www.tandfonline.com* Retrieved on 02/05/2013.

Part II

Economy and Society

5
Regional Economic Governance in Africa

Ian Taylor

This chapter is an attempt to provide an overview of the diverse typologies of regional governance in sub-Saharan Africa (SSA), which are currently shaping the increasingly complex scales and space associated with regionalism on the continent. In order to understand how regional economic governance has played out in Africa, it is vital to grasp the extant political culture(s) dominating the processes as these inevitably and intimately shaped the diverse regionalist projects across SSA. It is argued that the particular political cultures in SSA have been decisive in shaping the character and nature of regional governance modalities and have wrought particular types of region-building on the continent that are not immediately recognisable as such from the perspective of most regionalist literature, focussed as it is on (formal) institutions and political (and legal) processes of regional integration. Equally, such realities have engendered diverse and often contradictory economic governance structures at the regional level. I argue that in fact the objective conditions in Africa demand a rethinking of what exactly constitutes "regional economic governance" in Africa and suggest that in fact three main types can be identified that, though not fitting the narrow institutionalism of most work on regionalism, explains and describes the day-to-day conditions encountered by most African citizens.

A discussion of the dominant features of national governance in Africa is a prerequisite for understanding regional economic governance in SSA. Certainly, to the extent that regional organizations exhibit shared approaches to economic governance, their central tenets and operational assumptions are unlikely to be immune from the broader political culture evident within their member states. Crucially, to analyse regional economic governance in Africa, an analysis of the dominant patterns of political culture among SSA's state elites is vital. Although there are significant differences across the continent's states, the dominant political culture can be characterised as neopatrimonial, that is, systems based on personalised structures of authority where patron-client relationships operate behind a façade of ostensibly rational state bureaucracy. For decades, this political culture has prioritised regime security over other projects, be they human security, economic co-operation or regional integration. As Claude Ake notes, 'the struggle for power has become so intense and so absorbing that it has overshadowed everything else, including the pursuit of development'(Ake, 1991).

Political Culture and Regionalism

As John S. Duffield has observed, the concept of '*political culture* has been used to denote the subjective orientations toward, and assumptions about, the political world that characterize the members of a particular society and that guide and inform their political behavior'. In his opinion, analysts 'have distinguished three basic components of political culture: the cognitive, which includes empirical and causal beliefs; the evaluative, which consists of values, norms, and moral judgments; and the expressive or affective, which encompasses emotional attachments, patterns of identity and loyalty, and feelings of affinity, aversion, or indifference' (Duffield, 1994:774). The evaluative category is of importance not least because of the recent shift in the way various state elites in SSA have defined the official norms and values that are said to guide the diverse array of regional economic communities (RECs) on the continent.

The study of political culture is based on the assumption that autonomous and reasonably enduring cross-cultural differences exist and that they can have important political consequences. As noted by Ronald Ingelhart, one of those consequences is the effect political culture can have on the prospects for the success and sustainability of governance. In particular, 'The political culture literature argues that the evolution and persistence of mass-based democracy requires the emergence of certain supportive habits and attitudes among the general public. One of the most basic of these attitudes is a sense of interpersonal trust' (Inglehart, 1989:1204). This is understood as a prerequisite for the formation of secondary associations, which, in turn, are thought to be essential to political participation and economic participation.

In our opinion, the central characteristics of the political culture held by most of Africa's state elites stem from the neopatrimonial basis of their regimes and the subsequent inability of the ruling classes to construct a hegemonic order. These factors have significant implications for how these elites operate and what commitments are likely to inform their shared beliefs about regional economic governance and how to manage and promote (or not as the case might be) various RECs. As numerous analysts have argued, the political story of most African states can be interpreted as revolving around a struggle for power and survival that marginalized all other concerns, including national development[1]. This struggle has witnessed the emergence of what are often called neopatrimonial regimes. Such regimes are said to exhibit four characteristics. First, they display 'the more or less systematic resort to clientelism to gain and maintain political support'. In other words, political authority is often 'based on the giving and gaining of favours in an endless series of dyadic exchanges that go from the village level to the highest reaches of the central state (van de Walle, 2001:51). Second, this clientelism is 'largely based on privileged access to state resources, rationed by leaders following a strict political logic'. As a result, the boundary between the public and private spheres is extremely blurred. Within this context, the third characteristic is the centralization of power usually around the presidency, which, in turn, is usually located within the capital city. Finally, neopatrimonial states house hybrid regimes wherein the informal mechanisms of political authority described above 'coexist with the formal trappings of the modern state' such as a bureaucracy, written laws and the institutions of a Weberian legal-rational system. These regimes are hybrids because the governing elites rely upon the trappings of a rational-legal order even as they consistently subvert it for their own advantage. Daily government in a neopatrimonial regime thus resembles a balancing act to maintain a degree of political stability by satisfying the regime's supporters and weakening its opponents.

One of the fundamental problems with such systems is that they breed great resentment in individuals and groups that are excluded from the governing regime and hence are denied access to the state's resources[2]. It is in this sense that the ruling classes in many African states lack hegemony over society, at least in the Gramscian understanding of the concept[3]. By the ruling class, we mean the senior political elites and bureaucrats, the leading members of the liberal professions, the nascent bourgeoisie and the top members of the security arms of the state (Markovitz, 1987:8). The early years of post-colonial nationalism in Africa were, broadly speaking, an attempt to build an hegemonic project which bound society together around more issues than simply discontent with the imperial powers. This project quickly collapsed into autocracy and failure, however, as most graphically—but not exclusively—typified by the career of Kwame Nkrumah. Moral and political modes that rise above notions of economic-corporate interests and instead reflect broader ethico-political ones remain missing in many parts of Africa even today. Consequently, because the ruling classes have been unable to preside over a hegemonic project that is viewed as legitimate by the majority of domestic society, they have been forced to revert to modalities of governance that seek to dominate opponents. These are commonly expressed through both the threat and actual use of violence and the immediate disbursal of material benefits to supporters within the context of neopatrimonial regimes. Without these twin strategies—both unfavourable to long-term development and political stability—the ruling elites in much of Africa cannot maintain order. In the worst cases, Bonapartism develops, where the nascent bourgeoisie finds itself compelled to tolerate (in order to preserve its position) the rule of a military and police apparatus as a means to prevent its overthrow—as the military coups in Nigeria repeatedly have attested.

This sort of political culture has had important consequences for Africa, not least a deeply negative impact on the overall standards of regional economic governance. The modes of governance in Africa have encouraged despotism and unpredictability—the latter of course being anathema to the construction of a stable legal order and development. As a result, for most of the post-colonial period, much of Africa has been trapped in a circle of under-development, which has stimulated societal conflict, both at the extreme level of wars and at the more mundane juncture where numerous states stagger from one crisis to another.

In the absence of hegemony, Africa's leaders have relied on effected control and patronage rather than through building what Max Weber called rational, technical states where authority is vested in a public office (rather than a charismatic individual) and state tasks are administered by an effective bureaucratic apparatus. Indeed, although Africa's elites undoubtedly command the state apparatus, with varying levels of intensity their own practices often undermine and subvert the state's institutions and the effectiveness of its bureaucracy on a daily basis. This is then mirrored at the regional level in a variety of ways.

Because most African elites exercise power in circumstances that lack hegemony (as per Gramsci), the relative autonomy of the state is absent and their rule is intrinsically unstable. This means that there is very little political space to allow reform and autocracy is relied on as a means of control. Such a milieu necessarily breeds a deep reluctance to give up state power (cast in Africa as "sovereignty"), which is an intrinsic ingredient to region-building and regional economic governance. Instead of a stable hegemonic project that binds different levels of society together, what exist in much of West Africa are intrinsically *unstable* personalised systems of domination. Absolutism reigns and power is upheld through patrimonial practices by means of the commandeering of state resources. Corruption, not hegemonic rule, is the cement that binds the system together and links the patron and their predatory ruling class together (Markovitz, 1987:36). Consequently, capturing the state—or at least being linked favourably to those who command its apparatus—is usually a precondition for acquisition and self-enrichment and regional questions are deemed abstract and unimportant unless they either directly threaten the incumbents' positions or can be utilised to garner increased resource flows. Regional cooperation for the sake of region building is not high on the list of any political agenda that most African elites may possess.

Within neopatrimonial regimes, the personalisation of political power—either at the low or high social levels—has constructed well-defined roles that are understood by all participants. They are much less well understood by external actors, however. In fact, Western donors and institutions have often turned a blind eye to this situation (Lockwood, 2006). They also blithely assume that Western concepts and institutions exist in Africa *in toto* (or at least can be transplanted to the continent with only minimal fine-tuning). Indeed, much NGO work within SSA on regionalism focuses on the (often self-proclaimed) importance of actors within 'civil society'. Part of the problem, however, is that the states within the region generally lack the 'autonomous agentic individual' and a significant degree of political space distinct from, and beyond, state power that is a prerequisite for developing the sort of civil society and civic associations popular in the Western imagination[4]. 'Autonomous individuals', free from communal, ethnic, and class loyalties are a rarity in most parts of Africa. Instead, what is arguably more common is what Jordan Smith characterised as the 'Patronage, Per Diems and the "Workshop Mentality"' (Smith, 2003). The amount of donor-funded workshops on regionalisms bears testament to this.

Varieties of Regional Economic Governance in Africa

The above perspective on politics in Africa results in the possibility of a variety of modes of regional economic governance. We draw attention to three particular modes of regional governance in Africa, namely neoliberal regional governance; sovereignty-boosting regional governance; and regional shadow governance. Our analysis aims to help explain the origins, the main actors, and the purposes of these three varieties of regional economic governance. We assert that regionalism in SSA is more complex (and sometimes also more detrimental) than simply being an instrument to enhance an ambiguous "national interest" (the realist view) or the procurement of the "public good" or "trade" (which underpins liberal explanations). Potentially, state actors create regionalization in order to achieve private goals and promote particular (vested) interests rather than broader societal interests. As a result, regionalization will not necessarily be harmonious or beneficial to all participants, contradicting the liberal assumptions about the inherent worthiness of commerce. On the contrary, regionalization may well be exclusionary, exploitative, and also reinforce asymmetries and imbalances within society and within and across geographic spaces.

As we have suggested in the discussion on political culture in SSA, governance in Africa is both more pluralistic and complex than commonly believed. The weakening of the "state" does not necessarily imply an equivalent weakening of governance, which instead may be stronger at other levels than the national, involve new actors, and be both informal and private—typically neopatrimonial in other words. We put forward the idea that in fact there are three broad modes of regional governance in contemporary Africa. By abstracting from various concrete cases it is possible to identify more general modes of governance, which in many cases overlap. Although the three modes of regional governance emerge within a particular Africa context, it is important to point out that similar structures can be discerned in other parts of the world (albeit these are usually referred to with different terminologies).

Neoliberal Regional Governance

The great majority of formal present-day regionalist schemes in Africa are founded on the notion that the regional economic integration project should be market-driven, outward-looking, and remove obstacles to the free movement of goods, services, capital and investment within the regions as well as to the rest of the world. The overall intention is to ensure a closer integration into the world economy. The main justification of this strategy is that it contributes more to the process of (global) liberalization than it detracts from it. According to this line of thinking, which is often labelled "open regionalism" or "adjustment-adapted market integration",[5] there is no contradiction in the great number of co-existing regional trading and economic integration schemes in Africa since they are all perceived to contribute to the same goal of liberalization, reduced protectionism, and downsizing of the role of the state in the economy. In Southern and Eastern Africa there is a number of co-existing regional interstate frameworks, such as the Southern African Customs Union (SACU), the Southern African Development Community (SADC), the Common Market for Eastern and Southern Africa (COMESA), the Cross-Border Initiative/Regional Integration Facilitation Forum (CBI/RIFF), and the Indian Ocean Rim Trade Bloc (IORTB). A similar pattern exists in most other macro-regions in Africa, West Africa being particularly apposite in this regard. Although each regional project can be seen as a mode of governance in its own right, it is striking how the various projects conform to the same overall neoliberal belief system and broader "system of rule".

The external and "global" dimension is crucial. The International Financial Institutions (IFIs) and American and European donor agencies strongly promote, enforce, and support neoliberal regional governance. However, although the African regional organizations and African states often claim to be supportive of neoliberal regional governance, there is also resistance. In this sense it is sometimes more of a model than the real existing mode of regional governance on the African continent.

Hand in hand with neoliberal governance at the macro-regional level, there is a simultaneous and perhaps even stronger logic at play on the micro-regional level. Southern Africa is a good illustration of such trends. The Southern African region is reconfigured by the implementation of a number of spatial development initiatives (SDIs)[6]. These are targeted, short-term interventions with the main purpose to crowd-in private investment in order to unlock economic potential, to enhance regional economic integration, and to become integrated into the global economy. It is a bold neoliberal market paradigm that rules investment decisions. As stated by one of the main architects: "In order to be selected for inclusion in the SDI process, a project must offer a commercially viable return on investment, i.e. it must be a bankable project— a project which a commercial financial institution would be willing to back" (Jourdan, 1998:20). The SDIs are governance mechanisms designed to quickly change legislation, change the role of the public/state, broaden the ownership base of the economy, and enhance market "competition". As such they are designed to be part of a broader pattern of neoliberal regional governance in Southern Africa.

Considering the size of the SDI projects, they are weakly institutionalized. There is an intention to be informal and nonbureaucratic, as this allows for flexibility and adjustability to private and contextual demands. This mode of regional governance represents a radical shift from "older" formal and ambitious public modes of governance in favour of a notion that conforms to neoliberal globalization, whereby "too much government" is considered a systemic fault. According to the official view, there is only a need for minimal formal organizations and institutions since these are seen as rent seeking and bureaucratic anyway. The result is a narrow and exclusivist governance mechanism, geared only or primarily toward enhancing privatization and private investment projects and public-private partnerships (PPPs). This implies a loss of public participation and democratic control in the decision-making and implementation process. Again informality serves the interests of the powerful and wealthy, especially a small ruling political elite and transnational capitalist interests (Soderbaum & Taylor, 2003).

Through the two-track model of open regionalism and SDIs, an informal but nevertheless strong coalition of economic and political elite interests, led by South African actors create and sustain neoliberal regional governance in Southern Africa, which also draws in (outward-oriented) economic and political elites in the neighbouring countries. As indicated above, to a significant extent this mode of governance is also actively promoted from the outside through external actors, such as the IFIs and the European and American donor community.

According to neoliberal regional governance, "good governance" is thus defined as "less government" and "getting the prices right", rather than providing public goods and intervening in the economy and ensuring poverty reduction (Thompson, 2000). It indicates the commodification of basic material needs and everyday life, which only results in a retreat of the conventional welfare and development ambitions of the state. Poverty reduction is reduced to economic growth, and development projects must be "bankable" and "profitable". The public is needed mainly to ensure an enabling environment for the private. In other words, the public has been subsumed under the private. It is a systemic fault in this type of governance to accommodate the interests of the poor, the disadvantaged, and the unemployed who lack the means to participate, much less "compete" on a global market (Mittelman, 2000).

In accepting this ideology, the government/state becomes the disciplining spokesperson of global economic forces—a "transmission belt for transnational capital" in Coxian terminology—rather than the protector against these forces, which is the classical task of mercantilist nation building and public governance[7]. Although all strategies are surrounded by rhetoric of people-centred development, the role of public institutions has been reduced to implement trade and investment liberalization or boost new bankable and commercially viable investment projects, often of gigantic proportions. Even public roads are commercialized. In this process the main function of the state has been reduced to a gigantic investment promotion agency. Although neo-patrimonailism is obviously not absent in Southern Africa, it remains true that the region is home to most of Africa's "functioning" (to use a Western understanding of the term) states. Thus their ability, capacity and willingness to yield to private actors are perhaps stronger than in any part of the continent.

Sovereignty-boosting Governance

Having noted the above, it should be noted that it is a widespread belief in the research field that "regional integration" requires a ceding of state sovereignty and national decision-making authority to supranational institutions[8]. Although this dichotomy between sovereignty and functioning regional integration is first and foremost a remnant from neofunctional theory, it continues to plague the debate. The notion that sovereignty constitutes an "obstacle" is to misunderstand ways through which state actors and political leaders are able to use regionalism and regional governance to bolster their regimes and governments. There is widespread evidence in Africa how state elites pool or rather boost their sovereignty through various types of regional cooperation and regional governance structures. This may or may not promote the "interests" of the citizenry and the broader public.

According to intergovernmentalist and neorealist logic, such state-steered regional governance can possibly be portrayed as a means to promote the "national interest". Indeed, regional governance in order to pool or boost sovereignty equals the national interest. However, there are at least two main reasons why conventional state-centric and intergovernmental analysis is not enough, or is even misleading, and why it is necessary to make inquiries for whom and for what purposes such sovereignty-boosting emerges. First, due to their inherent "weakness", most of the post-colonial states in Africa tend to be obsessed with absolute sovereignty and the formal status of their governments, rather than the promotion of "national" or "public" interest in a more comprehensive sense. Second, in many cases the so-called state is much less than what it pretends to be: the type of regional governance designed to boost the government is exclusivist and centralized, "reflecting the perceptions of government leaders, small groups of civil servants and perhaps also key bilateral and multilateral donors" (Simon, 2003:71). In fact, as we have noted, often the "state" is not much more than an (neopatrimonial) interest group, and in the worst instances it has degenerated into a post-modern mafia syndicate (consider for instance Liberia under Charles Taylor or Zimbabwe under Robert Mugabe).

To understand how certain governments use regional economic governance to boost the official status and sovereignty of their governments, one has to consider the nature of statehood in Africa. It is widely agreed that the states in Africa are "weak". However, these states enjoy international recognition even though they often lack substantial and credible "statehood" by the criteria of international law. The result is that in their international relations weak states tend to place heavy emphasis on formal and absolute sovereignty—that is, the maintenance of existing borders and the principle of nonintervention in domestic affairs—because it enhances the power of the governing political elite and its ability to stay in power (Clapham, 1996). In fact, the institution of formal sovereignty is the justification for their continuation and survival as states. The principle of formal sovereignty has clearly been successful in Africa. While many African states are extremely "weak", the state system and the old colonial boundaries have, with a few exceptions, remained intact—seemingly everlasting. The result is a somewhat paradoxical situation with "weak" states and rather "strong" or at least "stable regimes" (Boas & Dokken, 2002:136).

The argument raised here is that that there are many instances whereby political leaders and regimes are using regional governance to promote rather than to reduce absolute state sovereignty and its legitimacy. In many places around Africa ruling political leaders engage in a rather intense diplomatic game, whereby they praise regionalism and sign treaties, such as free trade agreements. West Africa is a fruitful example. Ever since the foundation of ECOWAS, an increasing number of members and sectors have been added. In this way ECOWAS's political leaders have been able to create an image that the organization is constantly developing. This has enabled them to be perceived as promoters of the goals and values of regionalism, which in turn has enabled them to raise the profile and status of their (often) authoritarian governments.

The problem is that this has not been to serve public interest but rather a more myopic objective to raise the formal status of their crumbling governments. To implement policies is not the first priority. Instead, ECOWAS decision-making is highly formalized, and to some extent even ritualized. This social practice is then repeated and institutionalized at a large number of ministerial and summit meetings, which in reality involves no real debate and no wider consultation within (or between) member states. Many other regional organizations in Africa function in a similar fashion, including SADC. For the political leaders, it is a matter of constructing an image of state building and of promoting important values. As Sidaway and Gibb note, discussing SADC:

> [F]ormal participation in SADC is another way whereby the states seek to confirm, fix and secure the appearance and power of "sovereignty". Rather like the boundaries and colour schemes of political maps, participation in fora such as SADC is a way in which the state is actively represented as a real, solid, omnipresent authority. In doing so, the fact that it is a contested, socially constructed (not simply natural) object is obscured, and states would have us take them for granted as the natural objects of governance and politics (Sideway & Gibb, 1998: 179).

From the point of view of governments and political leaders, this type of regional diplomacy is often "successful". The problem is that many post-colonial states in Africa are to an overwhelming extent ruled by personal leaders, who are often portrayed as embodying the idea of the state. The personal rulers often use the coercive instruments of the state to monopolize power and to further their own interests, including to deny or restrict the political rights and opportunities of other groups (Clapham, 1996). Whether this type of regional governance also promotes broader public interests, such as democratization and human security, remains an open question. Its viability, strength, legitimacy, and desirability rests with how the ruling regime is interpreted.

Regional Shadow Governance

It is widely recognized that there are many vibrant and dynamic processes of *de facto* and informal market activities all over the African continent. Although these may sometimes be understood as "survival strategies" created by the poor, the excluded, and other non-state actors, it is important to recognize that many researchers draw attention to the fact that "state/ regime" actors are deeply entrenched in informal market activities with the purpose to promote patronage networks and (hidden) private self-interests. For instance, it is widely agreed that the parallel economy in the Democratic Republic of the Congo, which exceeds the official economy in size, has expanded as a consequence of the systematic corruption, the theft of state revenues, and the personal rule of successive presidents. In the case of Sierra Leone this type of state was referred to by William Reno as the "Shadow State"; a state where the formal façade of political power based upon informal markets sheltered corrupt politicians (Reno, 1995).

It is often shown that these types of activities extend beyond the borders of the Shadow State as such. Stephen Ellis and Janet MacGaffey elucidate the crucial relationship between politics and economics and between the domestic and the international level:

> International trade in Africa, and inter-continental trade particularly, occupies a crucial strategic position chiefly because of the scarcity of foreign exchange which is necessary to import manufactured goods and which can play a vital role in the construction of a political power-base. Government ministers and officials regulate access to hard currency either by their control of the state, or by going into business themselves or through nominees including members of their own family, or indirectly, by forming alliances with traders. The interplay of the resulting trade and clientist networks is an ingredient in most successful political careers in Africa (Ellis & Mac Gaffey, 1996: 31).

Although the international dimension is mentioned in the literature, the regional dimension seldom receives enough attention. The argument raised here is that we can increase our understanding of what is going on by analysing shadow networks as a particular mode of regional governance, that is, as a particular (but) malign "system of rule" for goal achievement.

The viability of informal shadow activities depends on states' lack of transparency, declining financial capacities, and territorial control. It also depends on the exploitation of boundary disparities, and demands their preservation in order to prosper. For instance, dominant rentier-elite factions in the BLSN-countries (Botswana, Lesotho, Swaziland, Namibia) were reluctant to renegotiate the Southern African Customs Union and were 'dragging their feet because the old formula [was] advantageous to them' (Sideway & Gibb, 1998: 178). It is a feature of regional economic governance in many parts of SSA that certain state elites and rentier classes actively seek to preserve existing boundary disparities and also seek the continued failure of regional organizations and policy-frameworks in order to further their own private interests. Sometimes the strategy is less subtle. For instance, in Central Africa, 'a number of state elites in the Great Lakes and southern African regimes have ceased to use the mantle of sovereignty to promote the collective good. Instead, they have used it to help bolster their own patronage networks and weaken those of potential challengers' (Taylor & Williams, 2001: 281). This mode of regional shadow governance grows from below, and it is designed for personal accumulation and not for the regulation of formal regional economic interaction nor for the encouragement of formal-public modes of regional governance.

It needs to be recognized that these activities and networks are inherently inequitable and extremely uneven. They accumulate power and resources at the top, to the rich and powerful, and to those with jobs, including the urban poor and the rural producers. Small-scale cross-border traders have a disadvantage since the economies of scale are "only for those who can pay the necessary bribes" (Bach, 1999: 162). The only "popular" dimension of these networks can be found in their capacity to adjust to market demands and in the ruthless exploitation of populations that are confronted with a diminishing of alternatives to satisfy their needs (*Ibid*: 62).

The attempts to restrict these activities have been counterproductive. In the new (neoliberal and post-Cold War) context where the state apparatus itself offers fewer opportunities for private accumulation and where formal barriers between countries have been reduced, shadow states have gone regional. In the process of going regional they have expanded to more criminal activities, such as new trades in illicit drugs (including heroin, mandrax, and cocaine), arms, light weapons, and other merchandise of war. In fact, these economic networks can even be actively involved in the creation and promotion of war, conflict, and destruction, as seen for instance in Angola, the Democratic Republic of Congo (DRC) and Zimbabwe (Maclean, 2002). The DRC is a prime example of this for here:

> Far from being a humanitarian and developmental disaster which sabotages the nascent [African] Renaissance, for well-placed elites and businessmen the wars in the Great Lakes region … offer potentially substantial resources for those able to exploit them. This explains much of the foreign interventions in the DRC:

> it is not only about preserving national security and defeating enemies, it is also about securing access to resource-rich areas and establishing privatised accumulation networks that can emerge and prosper under conditions of war and anarchy. In this sense, war assumes the characteristics of a business venture, the beneficiaries of which are unlikely to abandon the venture easily (Taylor & Williams, 2001: 273).

Through regional shadow governance state and nonstate actors come together in diffuse and volatile economic networks in order to profit from violence and from underground economies. It is a devilishly well-calculated terror war and obviously has little to contribute to human development and security, or for that matter the broader national interest.

Conclusion

Three particular modes of regional economic governance are highlighted in this chapter: neoliberal regional governance; sovereignty-boosting governance; and regional shadow governance. The first is perhaps the dominating mode of regional governance in contemporary Africa. It emerges in many corners of Africa and in different guises. It is pushed under continental African frameworks, such as the New Partnership for Africa's Development (NEPAD), various macro- and sub-regional economic integration schemes as well as cross-border micro-regional initiatives, such as the development corridors and SDIs in Southern Africa. Neoliberal regional governance is created by coalitions and networks of governments, big business, IFIs and donors, albeit with national governments formally determining policies. Moreover, although neoliberal regional governance is built on a certain degree of formality, its overarching strategy and direction is broader and more important than intergovernmental regional organizations, such as SADC, CBI and COMESA.

Neoliberal regional governance seeks to promote the public interest, so the official discourse goes. However, the fundamental problem is that the public is subsumed under the private. Neoliberal regional governance reinforces a process of neoliberal globalization, which lacks ethical content and contains a drastically reduced role for public interests since this governance depends on global market demands and on access to international capital, and does not focus on poverty reduction and public goods. In its detrimental form neoliberal regional governance implies a diffuse and turbulent system of competing and changing authority structures, with the consequence of "exclusion" as well as a drastically reduced role for the state/government as we know it. Nevertheless, under the right conditions this mode of regional governance has the potential to be transformed into more inclusive, democratic, and just governance structures, primarily through the mobilization of local business and the involvement of civil society.

The second mode of regional governance highlighted is designed to boost sovereignty and national government. It represents a system of rule with the regime largely in control, assuming the privilege of intervention by reference to a value system focused on political order, state stability, and national sovereignty. It is created and promoted by those actors pushing such an agenda, mainly political leaders, governments, and securocrats. It is based on a certain degree of formality in order to obtain legitimacy, or to make informal competitors (including rebels and quite often political opposition) illegitimate. Sometimes it emerges as a direct result of neoliberal regional governance, since the latter may actually undermine both national sovereignty and a functioning government. The desirability of sovereignty-boosting regional governance depends to a large extent on the interpretation of whether the involved regime/government is considered to be ruling for or against the people and the public interest (that is what sovereignty is used for). For instance, when figures such as Robert Mugabe or Charles Taylor are in control, there are good reasons to be sceptical. Questionable political figures such as Charles Taylor and Robert Mugabe may at the same time be actively involved in the third type of regional governance, that is, regional shadow governance.

In this chapter I suggest that sometimes the Shadow State has gone "regional", which is partly a consequence of neoliberalism and the fact that there is not much left to plunder of state resources. In regional shadow governance, a small number of regime actors use the formal state apparatus as a façade and join forces with a limited number of informal or criminal private actors, private security companies, and/or military leaders to bolster their own private interests. This mode of regional governance occurs in many parts of Africa, first and foremost where the Shadow State exists. One of the most tragic examples is the regional intervention by ECOWAS Cease-fire Monitoring Group (ECOMOG) in West Africa. Although often referred to as a success story in the literature, it is clear that ECOMOG became part of the political economy of violence that kept the conflicts going in the West African war zone. Important sections of the ECOMOG troops actively took part in the crimes committed against civilians and became heavily involved in warlord politics and plunder. The questionable role of the ECOMOG force is perhaps best illustrated by how it came to be known in Liberia as "Every Commodity and Movable Object Gone". A similar type of logic prevails in the wars in the Great Lakes region.

One general assertion I wish to emphasise is that there is a pluralism of modes of regional economic governance in Africa. Sometimes the three modes may be distinct and not closely related. Sometimes only one or two prevail within a given region. At other times they may co-exist without much interaction. Yet, at certain times the three different modes of regional governance overlap and stand in a rather complex (and sometimes dialectic) relationship with one another. As a result they may persist in spite of their sometimes detrimental and contradictory effects.

Neoliberal regional governance is perhaps the dominating mode of regional governance, at least as a discourse, in most regions of Africa. The fact that the regional dimensions are an integral part and fit the broader neoliberal strategy is what makes it rather pervasive. Sometimes it constitutes more of a model (promoted from the outside) rather than the reality of regional governance in Africa. Sovereignty-boosting regional governance may occur for many different reasons. As indicated previously, during the last decade it has often emerged in response to the challenge posed by neoliberalism and globalization to the sovereignty and legitimacy of the state/regime. Hence, sovereignty-boosting regional governance may emerge as a strategy to rescue what neoliberalism challenges. Regional shadow governance may also be related to the two other forms of governance and may be explained as a consequence of neoliberalism and structural adjustments, which have left little to plunder of state assets. As a result certain corrupt regime actors (and certain businessmen) go regional. And since they need the state and formal regionalism as a façade to continue with their rent-seeking and plunder, they also need to pursue sovereignty-boosting regional governance as a shelter.

Taken together, this picture of partly overlapping and often informal and private modes of governance is what makes Africa an intriguing and heterogeneous continent with more complexity compared to what can be detected through the dominating approaches in the research field. Since the cases of this study are taken from the current empirical scene in Africa, there is a possibility that this scene may look very different tomorrow. On the other hand, according to the more pessimistic view, it looks as if these modes of economic governance, perhaps in combination, give a good clue to the current political and economic system in Africa, and perhaps also what will become its future.

NOTES

1. See, for example, Michael Bratton and Nicholas van de Walle 'Neopatrimonial Regimes and Political Transitions in Africa', *World Politics*, Vol. 46, No. 4 (1994), pp. 453-89; Thomas Callaghy 'The State as Lame Leviathan: The Patrimonial Administrative State in Africa' in Zaki Ergas (ed.) *The African State in Transition* (London: Macmillan, 1987); Victor LeVine 'African Patrimonial Regimes in Comparative Perspective', *Journal of Modern African Studies*, Vol. 18, No. 4 (1980), pp. 657-73; and Roger Tangri *The Politics of Patronage in Africa: Parastatals, Privatization and Private Enterprise* (Trenton: Africa World Press, 1999). This summary draws upon Nicolas van de Walle, *African Economies and the Politics of Permanent Crisis, 1979-1999* (Cambridge: Cambridge University Press, 2001), esp. pp. 115-29.
2. A second problem is that because of the way they discourage graft and the development of expertise in the long-term, neopatrimonial systems that are dependent on external resources are liable to experience a crisis if those outside sources are reduced.
3. In Gramsci's framework hegemony referred to the way in which an entire system of values, beliefs, attitudes and morality permeated throughout society to the extent that this system achieved the status of common sense and thereby had the political effect of supporting the status quo of power relations. See Antonio Gramsci, *Selections from the Prison Notebooks* (London: Lawrence and Wishart, 1971).
4. See Robert Fatton, 'Civil Society Revisited: Africa in the New Millennium', *West Africa Review*, Vol. 1, No. 1 (1999), p. 3 and Chabal and Daloz, *Africa Works*, pp. 17-30.
5. Cross-Border Initiative, *Volume 2: Country Papers and Progress Reports for the Initiative to Facilitate Cross-Border Trade, Investment and Payments in Eastern and Southern Africa and the Indian Ocean* (Harare: CBI, 1995); World Bank, Sub-*Saharan Africa: From Crisis to Sustainable Growth* (Washington, D.C.: World Bank, 1989); Jens Haarløv, *Regional Cooperation and Integration within Industry and Trade in Southern Africa* (Avebury, 1997).
6. See "Spatial Development Initiative (SDI) in Southern Africa," available online at www.africansdi.com; Fredrik Söderbaum and Ian Taylor, eds., *Regionalism and Uneven Development in Southern Africa: The Case of the Maputo Development Corridor* (Aldershot: Ashgate, 2003).
7. See Robert Cox, "Global Perestroika," in Robert Cox, ed., *Approaches to World Order* (Cambridge: Cambridge University Press, 1996); Fredrik Söderbaum and Ian Taylor, "Transmission Belt for Transnational Capital or Facilitator for Development—Problematising the Role of the State in the Maputo Development Corridor," *Journal of Modern African Studies* 39, no. 4 (2001): 675–695.
8. Ernst B. Haas, *Beyond the Nation-State* (Stanford: Stanford University Press, 1964): Heribert Dieter, Guy Lamb and Henning Melber, "Prospects for Regional Cooperation in Southern Africa," in *Regionalism and Regional Integration in Africa: A Debate of Current Aspects and Issues*, discussion paper 11, (Uppsala: Nordic African Institute, 2001), p. 63.

REFERENCES

Ake, Claude. (1991). How Politics Underdevelops Africa in A. Adedeji, O. Teriba and P. Bugembe (eds.) *The Challenge of African Economic Recovery and Development.* London: Frank Cass. pp. 316-329.

Bach, Daniel. (1999). Regionalism versus regional integration: the emergence of a new paradigm in Africa. in Jean Grugel and Wil Hout. (eds.). *Regionalism Across the North-South Divide. State Strategies and Globalization.* London: Routledge. p. 162.

Bøås, Morten and Dokken, Karin. (2002). *Internasjonal Politikk og Utenrikspolitikk i Afrika sør for Sahara.* International Politics and Foreign Policy in Africa, South of the Sahara. Oslo: Universitetsforlaget. p. 138.

Clapham, Christopher. (1996). *Africa and the International System. The Politics of State Survival.* Cambridge: Cambridge University Press.

Duffield, John S. (1994). Political Culture and State Behavior: Why Germany confounds Neorealism. *International Organization*, Vol. 53. (4). p. 774.

Ellis, Stephen and MacGaffey, Janet. (1996). Research on Sub-Sahara's Unrecorded International Trade: Some Methodological and Conceptual Problems. *African Studies Review*, Vol. 39(2). p. 31.

Inglehart, Ronald. (1988). The Renaissance of Political Culture. *American Political Science Review*, Vol. 82. p. 1204.

Jourdan, Paul. (1998). Spatial Development Initiatives (SDIs)—the official view. *Development Southern Africa*, Vol. 15(5). p. 20.

Lockwood, Mathews. (2006). *The State They're* In: An Agenda for International Action on Poverty in Africa. London: ITDG Publishing.

MacLean, Sandra. (2002). Mugabe at war: the political economy of conflict in Zimbabwe. *Third World Quarterly.* 23(3) pp. 513-528.

Markovitz, Irving. (ed.). (1987). *Studies in Power and Class in Africa.* Oxford: Oxford University Press. p. 8.

Mittelman, James H. (2000). *The Globalization Syndrome. Transformation and Resistance.* Princeton: Princeton University Press.

Niemann, Michael. (2000). *A Spatial Approach to Regionalisms in the Global Economy.* Basingstoke: Macmillan.

Reno, William. (1995). *Corruption and State Politics in Sierra Leone.* Cambridge: Cambridge University Press.

Sidaway, James and Gibb, Richard. (1998). SADC, COMESA, SACU: Contradictory Formats for Regional Integration in Southern Africa. in David Simon. (ed.). *Reconfiguring the Region. South Africa in Southern Africa.* London: James Currey. p. 179.

Simon, David. (2003). Regional Development-Environment Discourses, Policies and Practices in Post-Apartheid Southern Africa. in Andrew Grant and Fredrik Söderbaum (eds.). *The New Regionalism in Africa.* Aldershot: Ashgate. p. 71.

Smith, Jordan. (2003). Patronage, Per Diems and the "Workshop Mentality": The Practice of Family Planning Programs in Southeastern Nigeria. *World Development*, Vol. 31 (4). p. 703-715.

Söderbaum, F. and Taylor, I. (2003). *Regionalism and Uneven Development in Southern Africa: The case of the Maputo Development Corridor*. Aldershot: Ashgate.

Taylor, Ian and Williams, Paul. (2001). South African Foreign Policy and the Great Lakes Crisis: African Renaissance Meets Vagabonde Politique. *African Affairs* 100. p. 281.

Thompson, Carol B. (2000). Regional Challenges to Globalisation: Perspectives from Southern Africa. *New Political Economy,* Vol. 5(1). p. 41-58.

Van de, Walle N. (2001). *African Economies and the Politics of Permanent Crisis, 1979-1999*. Cambridge: Cambridge University Press. p. 51.

6

Growth and Poverty Reduction in Africa

Political Economy Challenges

Alemayehu Geda and *Addis Yimer*

Notwithstanding the recent optimism about African economies, the performance of these economies since the time of political 'independence' can only be described as dismal. There has been a secular deterioration in their terms of trade (particularly from the mid-1970s); the level of external debt has grown enormously, leading to near insolvency; dependency on foreign aid has grown at an alarming rate (and this has been exacerbated by stagnation in exports); and, finally, levels of investment have been extremely low. Partly as a result of the latter, physical and social infrastructures have also deteriorated. Political instability, frequent wars, and natural disasters have further aggravated this situation. The major question to be asked then is 'why?' In fact it might be relevant to ask whether there are special features specific to Africa that can help explain the massive poverty and inequality that engulfed the continent. What is interesting in this regard, which is the focus of this study, is that what is the macroeconomic policy direction pursued with regard to the challenge of growth and poverty reduction. The policy approach pursued to address these challenges has also implications on whether appropriate policy has been carried out and it's political underpinning.

It is instructive to note that macro policy is not made in a political vacuum. The political economy context, both internal and external, in which macro policy is formulated. has a strong bearing on the resultant macro policy and, hence, the macroeconomic environment for growth and poverty reduction. In the last three decades (since the early 1980s), macro policy making in Africa has been primarily driven by the influence of the World Bank and the IMF (International Financial Institutions, IFS, hence forth). This can be traced back to what is called the Berg Report - The World Bank's *Agenda for Action* (1981) and the World Banks comprehensive report on sub-Saharan Africa in 1989. This is complemented by the political as well as analytical support of the IMF to the bank in the latter's aggressive push for conservative monetary and fiscal policy through aid conditionality. Although the aid from the IMF (and to some degree from the WB) may not be that significant, their seal of approval of a country's obedience to their prescribed macro policy is the only way to get aid from OECD donors - and hence their importance. The IFS assistance to the region even today is conditional on this macro stance.

Thus, the financial, political or ideological (notice the neoliberal policy prescription with policy conditionality) as well as intellectual (notice the RMSMX and IMF financial programming models) dominance of the Bank and IMF on Africa has made macro policy making in Africa basically a strict implementation of the Bank's and Fund's prescribed macro policy—conservative monetary and fiscal policy combined with unguarded liberalization—summarized in short as the Structural Adjustment and Stabilization Policies (SAPs). Interestingly, these policies are implemented across the developing world without due consideration to variation among developing countries in the world.

The IFS arrived at this policy prescription for African countries based on their understanding of the African economic crisis (*see* World Bank, 1981; 1989). In this understanding, the Bank in particular argued that the *main* factor for African economic crisis lies in policy mistake; which is said to be biased against agricultural and export production; highly regulated, strong intervention of the government in the economy and lax monetary and fiscal policies. The logical conclusion drawn from this diagnosis is to implement what they considered appropriate policy—the SAPs (*see* World Bank, 1981, 1989; 1994).

In this article, an attempt to critically examine how the African economic crisis is understood by mainstream neoclassical economics and its implications for macro policy making in Africa is made. This is contrasted with an alternative way of looking at the same crisis from another angle of the economic profession, which can loosely be termed as the heterodox approach or the political economy approach to economic analysis. These two approaches are different not only in the diagnosis and application of economic tools to understand the African economic crisis, but also on the philosophical basis or methodology of how to conduct economic policy research.

The rest of the article is organized as follows. In the next section, we will examine how the African economic crisis is understood by neoclassical and an alternative heterodox schools in economics. This is followed by section three where we examined the political economy of policy making internally. This is followed by section four where we have attempted to draw lesson from the political economy of policy making in fast growing Asian economies. Section five concludes the chapter.

Africa's Economic Crisis: What Caused It?

There are three sets of contending explanations for Africa's economic crisis. The first is set originally out in World Bank (1981)—also known as 'the Berg Report'—and a number of subsequent World Bank publications. An alternative explanation for Africa's economic problems, associated with the United Nations' 'Economic Commission for Africa' (ECA) is outlined in *African Alternative Framework to Structural Adjustment Programmes,* AAF-SAP (ECA 1989a). Finally, there exists a third view, which is less clearly associated with any particular institution and largely held by academics of a Marxist orientation. This latter position is often offered as a critique to the other two explanations. The scope of all three sets of explanations is general, encompassing every aspect of the African economic crisis.

The World Bank's *Agenda for Action* (1981) argues that Africa's problems relate to underdeveloped human resources, political fragility, problems of restructuring colonial institutions, inheritance of poorly shaped economies, climate, and geography and population growth. The Bank's insistence that policy failure represents the *main* explanation for Africa's economic crisis, and consequent emphasis on the need for reforms, has continued with the publication of its long-term perspective study (World Bank 1989). The Bank argued in the 1990s that orthodox macroeconomic management represents the road to economic recovery in Africa and, hence, more adjustment, not less, is required (World Bank 1994). This assertion has been the subject of various criticisms, coming from a host of different angles (*see*, among others, ECA, 1989; Adam, 1995; Mosley, Subasat, and Weeks, 1995; Lall, 1995; White, 1996; Alemayehu, 2002).

In contrast, the ECA, almost twenty years ago (1989), prefers to explain Africa's problems in terms of deficiencies in basic economic and social infrastructure (especially physical capital), research capability, technological know-how and human resource development, compounded by problems of socio-political organization. The ECA sees inflation, balance of payments deficit, a rising debt burden and instability of exports as resulting from a lack of structural transformation, unfavourable physical and socio-political environment, as well as an excessive outward orientation and dependence. The ECA study suggests that weaknesses in Africa's productive base, the predominant subsistence and exchange nature of the economy and its openness (to international trade and finance) have all conspired to perpetuate the external dependence of the continent. Hence, one of the striking features of the African economy is the dominance of the external sector. This has the effect of rendering African countries quite vulnerable to exogenous shocks. Consequently, according to the ECA viewpoint, perceiving African problems in terms of internal and external balance problems and seeking a solution within that framework (most notably, through the implementation of structural adjustment programmes) implies not only the wrong diagnosis, but also the wrong treatment. The ECA study argues that '...both on theoretical and empirical grounds, the conventional SAPs are inadequate in addressing the real causes of economic, financial and social problems facing African countries that are of a structural nature' (ECA 1989: 25).

Based on this alternative diagnosis, and the major objectives of the '*Lagos Plan of Action*' (OAU 1981), the ECA (1989) formulated an African alternative framework to the Bank/Fund's policy recommendations. The ECA framework focuses on three dynamically interrelated aspects, which need to be taken into account. First, the operative forces (political, economic, scientific and technological, environmental, cultural and sociological), second the available resources (human and natural resources, domestic saving and external financial resources) and third the needs to be catered for (i.e., focusing on vital goods and services as opposed to luxuries and semi-luxuries). The adoption of this general framework would allow the different categories of operative force to influence not only the level and structure of what is produced, but also the distribution of wealth. Moreover, these forces may then influence the nature of needs to be catered for and the degree of their satisfaction. At a concrete level, this is envisaged as taking a number of policy directions. Firstly, improving production capacity and productivity, mobilization and efficient use of resources, human resource development, strengthening the scientific and technological base and vertical and horizontal diversification. Secondly, improving the level and distribution of income, adopting a pragmatic balance between the public and private sectors, putting in place 'enabling conditions' for sustainable development (particularly economic incentives and political stability), shifting of (non-productive) resources, and improving income distribution among various groups. And, finally, focusing on the required needs, particularly in relation to food self-sufficiency, reducing import dependence, re-alignment of consumption and production patterns and managing of debt and debt servicing (*see* Alemayehu, 2002 for detail).

Thus, the core of the disagreement between the bank and ECA views centres on 'the role of the market' mechanism (Oskawe quoted in Asante, 1991: 179). While the Bank believes in the market mechanism as representing the fundamental instrument of resource allocation and income distribution, the ECA questions this viewpoint. Thus, while the bank focuses mainly on financial balances, the ECA considers a much broader transformation as an enabling condition for the former. While the Bank emphasizes the export sector, the ECA strategy advocates selectivity (*see* also Asante, 1991: 180). While the Bank expresses concern about anti-export bias and population policy, the ECA prefers to emphasize the need to ensure total structural transformation and food self-sufficiency. While the Bank places more emphasis on short-term policies than on Africa's long-term needs, the ECA strategy, as defined in the Lagos plan of action, stresses the importance of also addressing issues of long-term transformation, alongside these short-term policies. However, these institutions do agree on some major issues, such as the need for human resource development, improving the efficiency of parastatals, and sound debt management.

The ECA analysis was quite comprehensive in addressing the causes of the crisis and in suggesting not only short-run solutions, but also a framework for long-term transformations. From ECA's (1989) analysis and recent events, it could be argued that some of the elements that may help explicate Africa's severe under-development include: (1) weak initial conditions (such as ailing institutions, human capital and an extractive and lingering colonial history) at the time of independence; (2) the dependence of almost all African countries on primary commodity production and trade; (3) the lack of non-aid financial capital and the alarming level of aid-dependency; (4) the lack of ownership of policies because they are invariably imposed on Africa by donors; and (5) the prevalence of conflict and poor governance.

It is unfortunate that this deeper insight and a heterodox/structural approach to economic analysis of the ECA in the late 1980s has been completely replaced by the World Bank and the IMF policy diagnosis and prescription. Notwithstanding a systematic rejection of this analysis and prescription by a number of African and Africanist scholars (*see, inter alia* Adam, 1995; Mosley, *et al.* 1995; Lall, 1995; Ngwenya and Bugembe, 1987; Fantu, 1992; Adedeji, 1993; Stefanski, 1990; Ali, 1984; Wheeler 1984; Mamdani, 1994; Stein 1977; Fosu, 1991—all cited in Alemayehu, 2002), and even African institutions, such as ECA through its 1989 compressive critique, the macroeconomic policy prescription has been imposed in the continent until today. In fact, at the time of writing this article, despite the IFS's engagement with countries in the continent mediated through the Poverty Reduction Strategy Papers (PRPs), the macroeconomic policy contents of the PRSPs remains fundamentally unchanged from that of the SAPs. In fact, with the benefit of hindsight, we realize that the ECA 1989 analysis foresaw in what is to be realized in the 1990s and early 21st century for it has argued that "...Both on theoretical and empirical grounds, the conventional SAPs are inadequate in addressing the real causes of economic, financial and social problems facing African countries that are of a structural nature (ECA, 1989a: 25)[1].

This debilitating externally imposed macroeconomic policy making by IFIs and major donors (such as the OECD countries) in Africa, which is largely political, is compounded by the political economy of policy making internally.

The Internal Dimension of the Political Economy of Macro Policy Making in Africa: The Recent Evidence

A recent comprehensive study of the political economy of growth in Africa using over 27 countries as case study by the African Economic Research Consortium (AERC) noted that, during the period where SAPs remain the blue print for the continent (in the last three decades), there were about four political regimes that characterized the political and policy landscape of post-independence Africa (*see* AERC growth research, 2008). These are governments characterized by State Controls (SC) where the state's role in the economy is strong, Adverse Redistribution (AR) where there is a bias in distribution of income to some regions or communities, those governments characterized by Inter-temporally Unsustainable Spending (IUS), and those that has shown State Breakdown (SB) as that of Somalia; also presented is the complementary Syndrome-free (SF) category—a category free of the above adverse charaterstics (*see* Fosu, 2008 and Table 6.1). Each of these categories that characterize the policy regimes in Africa are given in columns 2 to 6 of Table 6.1. Reading Table 6.1, for instance, we note that in 33.8 per cent [37.15 using the AERC sampe of 26 countries] of the cases since independence (or 26.3 per cent if this occurrence is weighted by population size of countries where it occurred) the syndrome of strong state control is observed in the continent.

Table 6.1: Anti-growth Syndromes—Relative frequencies of occurrence from independence to year 2000, 46 [26] SSA countries (per cent)

	State Controls	*Adverse Redistribution*	*Intertemporal*	*State Breakdown*	*Syndrome Free*
Unweighted	33.8 [37.1]	21.9 [18.2]	8.8 [11.5]	10.2 [8.8]	25.4 [24.4]
Population-weighted	26.3	31.6	13.1	10.2	18.9

Notes: The first row comprises the set of non-weighted relative frequencies, with figures for the 26-country case-study sample in square brackets.

Source: Fosu (2008)

Having this classification, the AERC study noted that the quality of economic policy pursued by each of these regimes noted above and shown in Table 6.1 has a powerful effect on whether countries seize the growth opportunities implied by global technologies and markets and by their own initial conditions (Fosu, 2008). According to Fosu's summary, this syndrome based classification aggregates multi-dimensional policy into broad patterns that occurred repeatedly in African countries. The evidence that the syndromes reduce growth is strong in the AERC studies: Fosu and O'Connell, 2005) find, for example, that avoiding the syndromes is simultaneously a necessary condition for attaining sustainable growth in SSA and a nearly-sufficient condition for preventing growth collapse. Indeed, being syndrome-free may add as much as 2.5 per cent points per year to per capita growth (*See* Fosu, 2008.)

The AERC study underlined that at the time of independence in many African countries, strong central governments were perceived as the optimal mechanism for nation building. In many instances, these efforts appear to have actually succeeded in preventing state breakdown in terms of open rebellion. Unfortunately, however, the strategies adopted then also resulted in various anti-growth syndromes of controls, adverse redistribution and inter-temporally unsustainable spending (Fosu, 2008). According to Fosu's summary from these studies, without the appropriate checks and balances, the executive was free to carry out policies unencumbered, a process that seems to have spawned many of the syndromes. Meanwhile, the military became the only real credible agent for changing governments through coups d'état. This situation resulted in elite political instability (EPI), which has been deleterious to growth in Africa (Fosu, 1992, 2001 cited in Fosu, 2008). In its severe form, furthermore, EPI could constitute state failure, a phenomenon that tends to be the most growth-inhibiting syndrome (Fosu and O'Connell, 2005; cited in Fosu, 2008).

What is also transpired in this AERC study is that the relationship between type of political system and the choice of policy regime is found to be empirically significant (*See* Bates, 2008a). According to Bates, based on AERC 27 countries case studies, the political forces that underpin the choice of control regimes seem to appear to arise from three sources. One of them is ideology. High levels of government intervention occur when governments find principled reasons for overriding thc allocations generated by markets. A second is the power of organized interests— interest groups constitute the primary means by which political preferences shape policy choices. Regional inequality constitutes the third—it generates incentives to adopt policies designed to overcome the economic impact of disparate endowments and to create political institutions with the power to elicit the transfer of resources (Bates, 2008a). In short, these forces, according to Bates, have shaped the political conduct and economic performance of governments in post-independence Africa. This is compounded by tendencies of state failures with their associated cost for growth and poverty reduction in some conflict prone African countries (Bates, 2000 8b).

What is the implication of such pattern of political process and policy making for the growth of African economies and poverty reduction? In short, as Bates (2008c) noted, the poverty of the state, the prospects of wealth from predation, and the prospect of losing office from the conditions under which growth and development could be undermined were major problems. In a situation where these tendencies are avoided and yet competitive democracy and democratic institutions are missing, private sector operators may suffer from risk and uncertainty related to the political order. According to Gunning (2008), again based on the 27 case studies, African economies may well face more risk than other countries. In addition, the scope for risk-coping is often lower than elsewhere: low population density makes it difficult to rely on insurance or credit. Governments have increased the risk exposure of private agents, while at the same time undermining institutions, which support risk-coping (*see* Gunning, 2008).

According to Bates (2008c), recent political reforms seem to have less impact upon the management of the macro-economy either. In the face of prospective political defeat, the evidence suggests, Bates (2008) noted, governments in competitive systems tend to spend more, to borrow more, to print money, and to postpone needed revaluations of their currencies than do those not facing political competition. The relationship between political competition and macroeconomic mismanagement appears to have weakened over time. This will compound the micro level risk private agent's face in Africa, which we noted above. As aptly remarked by Bates (2008c) the empirical results, nonetheless, pose a challenge to those, who seek in political reform the remedy for Africa's economic malaise (Bates, 2008c). In general, however, as noted by Gunning (2008), one needs to know to what extent growth is reduced by governance-based risk or by governance-related restrictions on risk-coping by private agents.

From the AERC study as well as the analysis carried by Bates, Fosu and Gunning briefly noted above, we can infer that the nature of policy matters a lot for growth and poverty reduction. In addition, we also infer that policy making is invariably informed by the struggle for power and control of interest groups or the political elite in Africa. This underscores the need to understand the centrality of the political economy of policy making in the design and implementation of programs for poverty reduction in Africa. However, on these questions, there is, as yet, no evidence and further research is in order.

Another strand of the political economy of Africa, which is relevant for private sector development/underdevelopment is what Emery (2003) has rightly termed 'from road blocks to red tape'. In short, the African political system is stifling for private economic agents not only for the simple financial gain, but most importantly and primarily, the political elite wants to control the private sector for its potential political imperative. This stifling regulation and red tape on the private sector is a legacy of the colonial system where the colonial masters were imposing similar institutional set-up of regulation and control and structured the economy for extraction of resource and stifle potential political resistance in all places except in settler colonies (*see* Geda, 1998, 2002; Acemuglu, 2001, Emery, 2003 for detail). The post-independence political elite basically inherited this system and are using it to date to further its interest. Relating this to current reality, Emery (2003) noted that the businessmen in Africa are subjected to a maze of administrative control as this serves an important political function, albeit indirectly. This function is to subject any business to arbitrary and punitive enforcement at times entirely by legal means at virtually any time, so that even a successful business in an unregulated sector is always exposed to political action, by subtle and indirect means. African governments are reluctant to do away with them because they have proven politically useful (*see* Emery, 2003: 11-14). In short, as Emery noted "A successful businessman, who is not somehow beholden to the political establishment for his success, is a potential political threat. If he's an active member of the opposition or developing his own power base by virtue of his economic clout, then he is perhaps a real political threat". This is not a major problem for foreign based private sector operators, however. Given the political clout of their source government (a case in point being the Chinese government in many fragile and undemocratic states) they would actually serve the African state as a patronage, whether willingly or unknowingly (*see* Emery, 2003). Thus, a true and fundamental change on African investment climate and politically environment for growth requires changing such deep political parameters in such a way that African firms are free of such control and all have legally and politically binding level playing ground.

In general, however, the existence of economic and political stability, avoidance or scaling down of bureaucratic obstacles and interventions, prudent investment regulations and availability of infrastructure are usually regarded as conducive environments for development. Recent events show that sub-Saharan African countries have made considerable efforts over the past decade to improve their policy and investment climate. Regardless of such improvements, it is evident that the African economic environments still have serious shortcomings compared with their international competitors (Eifert and Ramachandran, 2004). Thus, good policies are central in improving the economic environment. It is perhaps for this reason that the first message of *Africa Competitiveness Report 2007* (World Economic Forum, 2007) is that good policies matter more for the investment climate than resource abundance or sea access—'for improving the investment climate, geography and geology count less than good policies'. Good policies, however, require, *inter alia*, agreeable political landscape and good economic research that is politically informed.

In sum, it is imperative to see the amalgamation of these internal and external factors in seeking to understand the implication of the political economy of [macro] policy making on growth and poverty reduction. The amalgamation of these two impetus for policy making (the external, IFS, and the internal) has led the macro stance of African countries to be quite complex. Thus, it is instructive to ask what is the implication of such political economy pattern for growth and poverty reduction in the continent. Before highlighting this issue in the conclusion section, we will briefly describe the experience of newly developed Asian economies in the next section so as to draw lesson for Africa.

Lesson from the Political Economy of Policy Making in the Fast Growing Asian Countries

It is worth briefly noting the political economy of policy making process in the fast growing East Asian countries (in particular in Taiwan and South Korea), which have confronted similar problems in their drive for fast growth and poverty reduction, without which the registered success in those countries was unthinkable. One distinguishing feature of this process in Taiwan and Korea was the tradition of research, planning, implementation and monitoring of proposed policies based on an in-depth study and accurate information by the best and the brightest brains in each of these countries. The Council for Economic Planning and Development (CEPD) of Taiwan is the case in point (and the Koreans had similar institutions, such as Korea Institute for Economics and Technology and the Economic Planning Board). CEPD had over three hundred professional and non-professional staff. Of these, 250 were with university qualification, of which engineers make up 20 per cent, economists about 40 per cent, the rest being accounting, finance and statistics graduates. The staff is divided into seven departments: over all planning, sectoral planning, economic research, urban development, performance evaluation, financial administration, manpower planning, personnel and financial administration. The Economic Research Department had 50 professionals each of which monitors one sector in addition to other duties. As an advisory body of the cabinet, the CEPD is outside the ordinary machinery of the government that allowed it to pay higher than normal civil service salary to its staff, and can recruit higher-quality talent by offering relatively better terms. Not only CEPD was staffed by the best and the brightest in the country, but also it was chaired by the powerful political figures, such as the premier himself (and latter the president of the country). The story was also similar in South Korea as the president used to chair such policy forums including the public-private sector forum almost every month. Such policy formulating process is extremely necessary to ensure the development of evidence based policy, which is invariably missing in African countries.

There was also an explicit political-economy dimension to the success story of both Taiwan and Korea. The private firms in Korea (the *Chaebols*) were led by Koreans, who had close ties with the government and, over time, came to be the major supporters and financiers of the governing party and its president. This was not the case in Taiwan, however. Rather, the government (which was mainly mainlander Chinese) expanded its economic power through the formation and expansion of state enterprises (Hsueh *et al.*, 2001).

In both Taiwan and Korea, the role of the state in the industrial economy and promotion of exports was very large, and this included protecting the domestic market. One factor that is apparent in Taiwan, in particular, is that the leading sectors after the 1960s were also major exporters, and most of them were privately-owned. Government policy played a critical role in helping attain the boom in export manufactures (Hsueh *et al.*, 2001). In the 1980s, the emphasis in industrial policy shifted from heavy to technology intensive industries, and the issue became how to upgrade Taiwan's industries so that they remain internationally competitive. Scientific research was also geared from basic academic research towards applied scientific research that included the establishment of Taiwan's Science-based Industrial Park, reversal of brain drain by introducing appropriate incentive schemes, and a science and technology research plan, including the required budget that the government demanded from each relevant ministry. This process was basically similar in Korea too (Hsueh *et al.*, 2001).

In sum, as noted by Amsden (2001), the developmental state in the Asian countries was crucial for its industrialization and export expansion. The state set four functions for itself: (i) development banking, (ii) local-content management, (iii) selective seclusion (opening some markets for foreign transactions and closing others), and (iv) national firms formation. Two principles guided this effort: (a) to make manufacturing profitable enough to attract private entrepreneurs, and (b) induce enterprise to be result-oriented and to redistribute their monopoly profit to the population at large (Amsden, 2001:125). Similarly, judicious targeting and organization to ensure the efficacy of public policy to encourage primary product diversification and process, exportation and domestic capacity creation (through training, infrastructure provision including research, subsidies, credit provision, etc.) was made by governments of Southeast Asian countries (Jomo and Rock, 2003). In addition, an interesting political-economy factor that was crucial in most of the newly industrialized countries of Asia was the success in attaining growth with equity that accompanied their openness, which was not the case in Africa (Alemayehu, 2006).

It is instructive to look at the gap between this best practice of the East Asian experience briefly noted above and the condition in Africa. Identification of the gap between these successful Asian economies and Africa is crucial to draw appropriate lesson for an effective policy making and implementation in Africa as well as to examine the SAPs policies critically.

To begin with, we note that any lesson that we may draw from the Asian (in particular Taiwan and Korea's) experience need to take into account the difference between Africa and the successful Asian countries in terms of (a) variation in initial conditions, (b) the institutional and political difference between the two, as well as (c) the global environment, such as the cold war, which shaped the foreign relation of Taiwan and Korea and its impact on their success story. Notwithstanding such differences, we can draw the following lesson that may help the design and implementation of appropriate development policy for Africa.

The broader lesson is the importance of participatory development both in making of policies and at implementation stage in the success story of Asian countries. This participatory development effort was spearheaded by none other than the presidents of the countries. This is, in turn, mediated by able technocrats with the best capacity available. More specifically, first, there is a need to note that the macro policy and industrial strategy cannot be developed in isolation and need to be set in the context of a country's development strategy and the role of different economic agents (such as the state and the private sector) in that context.

However, except for a limited countries such as Egypt, Tunisia, Morocco, South Africa, Mauritius, the industrial sector and a development strategy for it in Africa is extremely limited. In fact, many countries in Africa are dependent on primary commodity export (as opposed to manufacture exports of Asia), which has become a booming sector in the last decade owing to a surge in demand for such commodities from the emerging economies. Thus, the task of industrialization in Africa is complicated by the need to transit from the commodity exporting economy to manufacture exporting economy-diversification. This requires first an appropriate management of the resource from the booming sector with a strategic direction of diversification. These require good institutions that will avoid rent seeking, and could manage to adopt good policies, which will promote rapid accumulation, investment and a socially efficient exploitation of resource rents. Participatory development and good governance is crucial in this process as the Asian experience shows.

Second, related to this, it seems crucial that agricultural development is a pre-requisite for success in growth and industrialization. Both in the growth process and once embarked on industrialization and exporting, the government needs also a labour market policy compatible with the stipulated growth. It also needs to keep the price of food and housing provision at subsidized price to keep labour cost for the private sectors low and make them competitive as well as ensuring political stability, as was the case in Korea.

Third, the role of government in ensuring success may need to go beyond policy making. The government not only needs to create the enabling condition (such as good economic policies: stable macro and optimal labour policies), but also may need to alter the incentive structure for public and private firms in the operation of the free market so as to ensure the success of exporting and industrialization. This is particularly required in the design and implementation of growth strategy that may include the development of export processing zones (EPZ) as well as industrial zones. Its intervention is also required to make firms and companies forward looking in diversification of exports, in building productive capacity though enhancing competitiveness and attraction of foreign investment. The hall mark of such role of government should be informed by an effective public-private sector partnership based on the principles of participatory development. The incentive schemes, however, need to be result-oriented and with the principle of graduation from an initial support system as firms develop in time.

Fourth, partnership with foreign firms and countries is central for successful industrialization and export development strategy. This will help not only to get access to the markets of the developed countries, but also as a tool in facilitating technology transfers for countries in Africa that have a brief industrial history and limited technological capability. Such markets could also serve as sources of growth, provided that export rents from such preferential arrangements are not disproportionately taken by firms from the preference offering countries. Thus, the role of the public sector is not only to ensure public-private partnership, but also support and guide domestic-foreign private sector partnership.

Fifth, the experience in Asia shows that Taiwan took up export-promotion of labour intensive manufacturing products, just as Korea did, but the choice of technologies for Taiwan was not similar to that of Korea's. Taiwan took the dominant role of its small firms into account in the design of its policy. Thus, export and industrialization development strategies need to depend on the structural and institutional context of the country in question and the nature of its private firms—in short there is no one-size fits all policy for all countries.

Finally, the institutions of private property, good policy and the competence of the government in economic governance are also found to be central in the growth and development process of countries in the East Asian success and need to be adopted by African countries. This, however, needs capacity building primarily in the public sector (and latter in the private sector). We note in passing, however, that this is quite a contrast to SAPs (the WB and IMF's) view of the role of the government in a developing economy.

Conclusion: The Current Macro Policy Discourse and its Prospects

Notwithstanding the ECA's intellectual challenge to the SAPs in the late 1980s, SAPs have been the (macroeconomic) policy framework informing policy making in Africa for the last three decades. According to Mkandawire and Soludo (ECA, 1999), SAPs in Africa have made significant progress on economic fundamentals but poverty remains widespread and the institutional requirements for sustaining growth and equitably extending its benefits to the population remain onerous (ECA, 1999). Mkandawire and Soludo noted that poverty in adjusting countries is comparable to the regional average, if not worse. Initially, there were attempts to address the negative social impacts of SAPs by ad hoc 'social safety net' measures, but this has changed over time. The recent emphasis of the World Bank and the IMF is to link SAPs with poverty reduction through Poverty Reduction Strategy Papers (PRSPs).

The PRSPs and realization of the Millennium Development Goals (MDGs) are key elements of current public policy discourse in Africa. The PRSPs are essentially extensions of the SAPs, where the major macroeconomic policy direction in SAPs cannot be questioned in the new PRSPs and sponsored by the Breton Wood Institutions. PRSPs suggest that there are opportunities to scale up participatory learning strategies from grassroots to national levels, while also offering new possibilities to budget for these activities and increase public interest and participation in poverty monitoring (UNDP, 2002). Success in PRSPs requires, among other things, realization of sustainable growth.

The last five to seven years saw a significant improvement in growth and growth prospects of Africa. However, this optimistic scenario has been clouded by the impact of the global economic crisis and by the fact that it is largely related to the recent commodity price boom in the continent. Though the impact of the global crisis was mild by world standard, the task of coping with the global crisis was daunting, especially when seen in the context of limited fiscal and monetary space that the countries in Africa have.

It is interesting to see if this growth has been translated in poverty reduction. Some country experiences show that growth is the most powerful weapon in the fight against poverty. It creates jobs that use labor, the main asset of the poor in developing economies like that of Africa. According to recent estimates, growth accounts for approximately 80 per cent of the poverty reduction that has occurred over the last 15 years, lifting 500 million people around the world above the poverty line (Ministry of Finance, Japan, 2008). Growth among emerging and developing economies has been generally strong with activity driven by a robust global growth, sound economic reforms, and strong domestic private demand in recent years. Thus, growth is definitely linked with poverty reduction, but this needs to be looked at in the context of the political economy of growth and policy making. In particular, it is instructive to ask what is the implication of this for formulating conducive macro policy that could enhance growth and poverty reduction at the same time.

However, macro policy is generally informed by the political economy of policy making. In Africa, as we noted in this article, in the last four decades macro policy was generally imposed by IFS on African countries through aid conditionality. Thus, Africans hardly own such policies. This debilitating imposition of macroeconomic policy by IFS and major donors on Africa is compounded by the political economy of policy making internally. The amalgamation of these internal and external political economy factors need to be understood so as to come up with an appropriate macro policy for growth and development in general and poverty reduction in particular.

As it stands now, in terms of macro policy, however, the PRSP and even the MDGs macro policy frameworks are the continuation of the SAPs because the essential ingredients of the macro policy prescriptions remained unchanged. The post global crisis situation, however, is creating a macro policy vacuum, which, if left unchecked may lead to lax monetary and fiscal policy, which will threaten macroeconomic stability. Thus, there is a need to have an appropriate macro policy, which is informed by a pro-poor growth, macroeconomic stability and pays due attention to role of the political-economy landscape of a country in question. Lack of sensible alternative macro policy framework for poverty reduction[2] that could replace or substantially change the hitherto framework is a challenge for policy makers and their partners in the continent. In particular, maintaining the delicate balance between prudent macro policy and the developmental role of the state to support the weak private sector needs rigorous analytical approach informed by the lesson from the East Asian economies. The issue deserves the attention of not only governments in Africa, but also international and regional institutions responsible for development and poverty reduction policies.

Such analytical framework need to take the political economy of policy making and its implications on board too. In this regard, first regional institutions, such as the ECA, AERC, etc. may need to come up with a realistic analytical framework, which reflects the structure of African economies and its political-economy set-up. This will contribute towards having an informed policy making, democratic-developmental state and intelligent engagement with the private sector through innovative institutions. Second, it seems that different regimes in the continents (those with competitive democracy, fragile states as well as those in the middle) have problems in getting development friendly [macro] policy, as the latter could be overridden by their interest for power and control of resources by the political elite. Although a prescription across the board is not possible, macro policy making in each country need to be informed by the specific country's political economy and structural conditions. The overall focus of governments and their development partners need to be encouraging the setting up of functional institutions that would be in a position to make development and investment friendly policies and regulations. International and continental organizations could be important in realizing this by acting as agents of restraint in this process.

NOTES

1. While there are areas where the first two approaches both converge and diverge, the third explanation for Africa's economic crisis stands firmly in opposition to both. Thus, the core of the disagreement between the bank and ECA views centres on 'the role of the market' mechanism. While the Bank believes in the market mechanism as representing the fundamental instrument of resource allocation and income distribution, the ECA questions this viewpoint (*see* Alemayehu, 2002 for detail).
2. The UNDP's Bureau for Development Policy under the directorship of Terry McKinley has been attempting to develop such alternative macro policy framework in Asian countries. It has also attempted to do the same in Africa making Zambia its pilot country (see McKinley, 2003; Chisala *et al.,* 2006).

REFERENCES

Acemoglu, Daron, Simon Johnson, and James A. Robinson. (2001). The Colonial Origins of Comparative Development: An Empirical Investigation. *The American Economic Review*, Vol. 91(5): 1369-1401.

Adam, Christopher. (1995). Review Article: Adjustment in Africa: Reforms, Results and the Road Ahead. *World Economy*, Vol. 18(5): 729-35.

Adedeji, Adebayo. (1993). Introduction: Governance, Aid and Africa. in Douglas Rimmer (ed.). *Action in Africa: The Experience of People Involved in Government, Business and Aid*. London: James Currey and The Royal African Society.

Ali, Liaqat. (1984). Africa's Commodity Trade and Structure of Marketing and Distribution of Primary Commodities. *Foreign Trade Review*, Vol. 19(3): 367-389.

Amsden, Alice H. (2001). *The Rise of the Rest: Challenges to the West from Late-Industrializing Economies*. Oxford: Oxford University Press.

Asante, S. K. B. (1991). *African Development: Adebayo Adedeji's Alternative Strategies*. London: Hans Zell Publishers.

Bates, Robert. (2008). Political Reform. in Benno Ndulu, S. O'Connell, R. Bates, P. Collier, and C. Soludo. *The Political Economy of Economic Growth in Africa: 1960-2000*. Cambridge: Cambridge University Press.

Bates, Robert. (2008a), Domestic Interest and Control Regimes. in Benno Ndulu, S. O'Connell, R. Bates, P. Collier, and C. Soludo. *The Political Economy of Economic Growth in Africa: 1960-2000*. Cambridge: Cambridge University Press.

Bates, Robert (2008b). Political Conflict and State Failure. in Benno Ndulu, S. O'Connell, R. Bates, P. Collier, and C. Soludo. *The Political Economy of Economic Growth in Africa: 1960-2000*. Cambridge: Cambridge University Press.

Collier, P. and S. O'Connell. (2008). Opportunities and Choices. in Benno Ndulu, S. OConnell, R. Bates, P. Collier, and C. Soludo. *The Political Economy of Economic Growth in Africa: 1960-2000*. Cambridge: Cambridge University Press.

ECA (1989a). *African AlternativeFramework to Structural Adjustment Programs for Socioeconomic Recovery and Transformation (AAF-SAP)*. Addis Ababa: ECA.

ECA (1989b). *Statistics and Policies: ECA Preliminary Observation on the World Bank Report: Africa's Adjustment and Growth in the 1980s*. Addis Ababa: ECA

Eifert, B. and Ramachandran, S. (2004). Competitiveness and Private Sector Development in Africa: Cross-Country Evidence from the World Bank's Investment Climate Data. the World Bank, Washington, DC.

Emery, James J. (2003) Governance, Transparency, and Private Investment in Africa. Paper presented at OECD Global Forum on International Investment. Johannesburg, 17-18 November.

Fantu, Cheru. (1992). Structural Adjustment, Primary Resource Trade and Sustainable Development in Sub-Saharan Africa. *World Development*, Vol. 20(4): 497-512.

Fosu, Augustin and Stephen O'Connel. (2005). Explaining African Economic Growth: The Role of Anti-Growth Syndromes (AERC Growth Project, Revised: August 4, 2005)

Fosu, Augustin. (2008). Anti-growth syndromes in Africa: A Synthesis of Case Studies. in Benno Ndulu, S. OConnell, R. Bates, P. Collier, and C. Soludo. *The Political Economy of Economic Growth in Africa: 1960-2000*. Cambridge: Cambridge University Press.

Geda, Alemayehu. (2006). Export Development Strategy, Export Success Stories and Lessons for Africa: The Challenge for Afreximbank. (Distinguished Lecture offered at the occasion of the 11th Meeting of the African Export- Import Bank (Afreximbank) Advisory Group.

Geda, Alemayehu. (2011). Economies and Relevant Economic Analysis: A Heterodox Approach Economic Research in Africa. (Paper Presented at CODESRIA Conference, Senegal, Dakar, September 28, 2011).

Geda, Alemayehu. (2012). *Fundamental of International Economics for Developing Countries*. Nairobi: AERC/Moran Publishing.

Geda, Alemayehu. 2002. *Finance and trade in Africa: Macroeconomic response in the world economy context.* Basingstoke: Palgrave-McMillan.

Gunning, Jan Willem. (2008). Shocks, Risks and African Growth. in Benno Ndulu, S. O'Connell, R. Bates, P. Collier, and C. Soludo. *The Political Economy of Economic Growth in Africa: 1960-2000*. Cambridge: Cambridge University Press.

Haggard, Stephan. (1990). *Pathways form the Periphery: The Politics of Growth in the Newly Industrialised Countries*. Ithaca: Cornell University Press.

Hsueh, Limin, Chen-kuo Hsu, and Dwight H. Perkins. (2001). *Industrialization and the State: the Changing Role of the Taiwan Government in the Economy, 1945-1998*. Cambridge, Mass.: Harvard Institute for International Development

Jomo, K.S. and Michael Rock. (2003). Resource Exports and Resource Processing for Export in Southeast Asia. in Ernest Aryeetey, Julius Court, Machiko Nissanke and Beatrice Weder (eds.). *Asia and Africa in the Global Economy*. Tokyo: United Nations University Press.

Krueger, Anne O. (1990). Asian Growth and Trade Lessons. *The American Economic Review* Vol. 80(2): 108-112.

Lall, Sanjaya. (1995). Structural Adjustment and African Industry. *World Development* Vol. 23(12): 2019-31.

Lin, Yifu Justin. (2011). New Structural Economics: A Framework for Rethinking Development. *The World Bank Research Observer* Vol. 26(2): 193-221.

Mamdani, Mohammed. (1994). A Critical Analysis of the IMF Program in Uganda. in Ulf Himmelstrand, Kabiru Kinyanjui and Edward Mburugu (eds.) *African Perspective on Development*. London: James Currey Ltd.

Mkandawire, Tandika, and Charles Soludo. (1999). *Our Continent, Our Future: African Perspectives on Structural Adjustment.* Trinton, NJ: African World Press.

Mosley, Paul, Turan Subasat, and John Weeks. (1995). Assessing Adjustment in Africa. *World Development,* Vol. 23(9): 1459-1473.

Ndulu, Benno, S. O'Connell, R. Bates, P. Collier, and C. Soludo. (2008). *The Political Economy of Economic Growth in Africa: 1960-2000*. Cambridge: Cambridge University Press.

Ngwenya, A. R., and P. K. Bugembe. (1987). The Origins and Causes of the African Social and Economic Crisis. In International Conference on Africa: The Challenge of Economic Recovery and Accelerated Development (Abuja, Nigeria 15-19 June).Series title: ECA/CERAD/87/11. Addis Ababa, Ethiopia: UNECA.

OAU (Organization of African Unity). (1981). Lagos Plan of Action for the Economic Development of Africa: 1980-2000. Addis Ababa: OAU.

Okey, Mawussé K. N. (2011). Institutional Reforms, Private Sector, and Economic Growth in Africa, UNU-WIDER Working Paper No. 2011/40.

Stein, Leslie. (1977). Export Trends in East Africa. *Development and Change*, Vol. 8(1): 103-116.

Taylor, Lance. (1983). *Structuralist macroeconomics: Applicable models for the Third World.* New York: Basic Books.

Taylor, Lance. (1991). I*ncome distribution, inflation and growth: Lectures on structuralist macroeconomic theory.* Cambridge, Mass: The MIT Press.

Wade, Robert. (2004). *Governing the Market: Economic Theory and the Role of Government in East Asian Industrialization.* Princeton: Princeton University Press.

Weeks, John. (2011, forthcoming). *A Critique of Neoclassical Macroeconomics*. London: Edward Egar.

Wheeler, David. (1984). Source of Stagnation in Sub-Saharan Africa. *World Development*, Vol. 12(1): 1-23.

White, Howard. (1996a). Adjustment in Africa: A Review Article. *Development and Change*, Vol. 27(4): 786-815.

White, Howard. (1996b). Zambia in 1990s as the Case of Adjustment in Africa. Economic *Research Seminar*. The Hague: Institute of Social Studies.

Word Bank. (1994). *Adjustment in Africa: Reforms, Results, and the Road Ahead.* Washington DC: The World Bank.

World Bank. (1981). *Accelerated Development in Sub-Saharan Africa: An Agenda for Action.* Washington DC: The World Bank.

World Bank. (1989). *Sub-Saharan Africa: From Crisis to Sustainable Growth: A Long-term Perspective Study.* Washington DC: The World Bank.

7

Occupational Health and Safety Framework in the Global Era

A Study of Labour Brokers in the City of Durban

Ivan Niranjan and *Sultan Khan*

Trade liberalization, privatization and deregulation in South Africa were given impetus by the signing of various international agreements. The ratification of these agreements inevitably led to the globalization of the economy. The most significant agreements are the free trade agreements with the European Union and with the Southern African Development Community (Theron, Godfrey and Visser, 2007:3). Globalization has hastened the restructuring of work and work modes through the introduction of flexible forms of production, such as casualisation, outsourcing, subcontracting and temporary employment. Flexible employment has emerged as a threat to labour rights, which invariably threaten human rights (Mathekga, 2009:30). The right to a safe and healthy workplace is under threat in the globalized economy, which places downward pressure on occupational health and safety legislation and enforcement. The global race for markets affects both developing and developed economies as transnational corporations travel the world in search of lowest wage amongst most vulnerable workforces, and the least regulated in respect of occupational health and safety (Brown, 2002:12).

South Africa, given its economic isolation in the dark days of apartheid has now entered the global economy and has become an important economic actor in the region, continent and the world. Many multi-national co-operations are now participating in the South African economy and the state is creating the necessary infrastructure and policy frameworks for mutual economic benefits. However, an important issue of concern is the laxity in implementing regulatory frameworks that protect workers health and safety, which is contested by trade union movements, who are active actors in partnership with the state sometimes resulting in a compromising relationship in its attempts to help reduce rising unemployment rates given the historical legacy of apartheid. Such a compromise has often led to low levels of monitoring of workers health status in the production sector as a trade-off for foreign investments, job creation and workers health. Labour brokers have partly contributed to this precarious position despite the fact that South Africa has a comprehensive Labour Act and regulations. This study examines the role of labour brokers in the context of globalization and the compromise of workers' health and safety needs in rubber industry in the city of Durban. The chapter commences with an conceptual overview of globalization and its effect on the compromise of workers' health and safety followed by a scan of the South African labor market and policy context regulating it followed by a section that deals with the key findings of the study.

Internatioanal Labour Agents Failure to Promote Promises of a Decent Work Agenda in the Context of Challenges imposed by Globalisation on the Labour Market

During the re-integration of South Africa into the international economic arena, President Nelson Mandela in his address to the International Labour Conference aptly had the following to say on the plight of workers worldwide:

> Decent work is based on the efforts of personal dignity, on democracies that deliver for people, and economic growth that expands opportunities for productive jobs and enterprise development. Decent work is about the right not only to survive but to prosper and to have a dignified and fulfilling quality of life. This right must be availableto all human beings (Rodgers, Lee, Swepston and Daele, 2009:205).

The concept "work" is qualified by Rodgers *et al.* (2009:224) as transcending labour or employment issues, but reflects the variety of ways in which people provide to the economy and society. The premise covers both formal and informal economies. The word "decent" however, signifies the idea of a realistic ambition, which meets social norms of income, of conditions of work and security, of rights and dignity. Decent work requires government departments to regulate and enforce conditions of service and workers' rights and security.

The same authors (Rodgers *et al.*, 2009:208) assert that the divide between the law and the economy is not easy to bridge and results in the economic sector dominating. Economics is about trade-offs as they consider adverse economic effects of higher standards as well as the social impacts of economic policies and develop flexible policy response. The legal approach involves a framework of fixed principles and rights to which economic relationships are seen as less significant. In response to such trade-offs, the ILO has provided protective rights to workers in member nation states. As a consequence, its main focus is to promote opportunities for women and men to obtain decent and productive work, in conditions of freedom, equity, security and human dignity (Rodgers *et al.* (2009:222). To quote Jukka Takala, the former Director in the International Labour Organization, 'Progress requires a safe and healthy labour force; no country can achieve a high level of competitiveness and productivity without taking, care of the safety, health and well-being of its workers' (Rodgers *et al.*, 2009: 124).

In so far as globalisation is concerned, Holkeri (2001:55) the president of the 55th General Assembly of the United Nations, points out that new technologies and expansion of trade regimes have hastened the speed of global movement of goods, services, labour and markets. Markets have become more open and inclusive. In the Northern hemisphere, health and safety of workers are primarily related to their age, gender and type of profession, whilst in the Southern hemisphere, poverty forces people to work in the informal economy without supervision and work safety assurances. Poor nutrition, long working hours and exposure to chemicals and work-related accidents make workers in developing countries unequal compared to their counterparts in richer nation states. In the formal sector, globalization leads to sub-contracting and flexibilization, which compromises the health and safety standards of the poor (Holkeri, 2001:55). In the informal sector, un-employment trends have increased phenomenally and are actively supported by government policy but are deficient in terms of occupational health and safety regulations and resources (Ryan, 2009:13).

Goldstein, Helmer and Fingerhut (2001:56) reiterate that more flexible labour policies lead to weakened commitment to occupational health and safety regulations within nation states. Global competition leads to employers viewing the prevention of occupational injuries and diseases not as part of the quality management system, but as a barrier to trade (Goldstein, *et al.,* 2001:56). Globalization creates the potential for the movement of hazardous products and substances to countries with less stringent regulatory systems (Ryan, 2009:7).

The Presidential Economic Joint Working Group (2009:2) comprising Labour, Business and Government states that the global financial crises was caused by diverse factors including gross imbalances and equities in the global economic system, the financialisation of economies, ineffectual regulation in several of the major world economies and poor business practices has resulted in significant asset depreciation, closures of companies, rising unemployment and a slowing down of economic growth. South Africa is now integrated into the world economy and is also affected by the fall in demand for its export products and the fall in prices of key export commodities. Low income workers, the unemployed and vulnerable groups are at a greater risk from such an economic shock. The potential for the economic crises to destabilize the welfare of the vulnerable, including their jobs, health, and education and to increase inequality and poverty is, however, recognized internationally (Presidential Economic Joint Working Group, 2009:4). Ntshalintshali (2010:6) cautions that the financial crises should not make government compromise the decent work agenda by acceding to pressure of not banning labour brokers, who have emerged as middle persons in the economy and have become agents that help compromise worker rights, allowing for cheap, low paid labour to thc capitalist classes.

Loewenson (2001:863) argues that globalization under liberalized markets has benefited the strong industrialized economies and marginalized the weak. Liberalized trade has been guided by the transfer of obsolete and hazardous technologies, chemicals, processes and waste, including asbestos and pesticides no longer produced or used in industrialized countries. Occupational health under liberalized tax and trade system can be seen in Export Processing Zones (EPZ). EPZs have been associated with high levels of machine-related accidents dusts, noise, poor ventilation, and exposure to toxic chemicals.

Jauch (2002:102) points out that in Mexico, employment in the EPZ (maquiladoras) grew by 10.4 per cent in 1995, however it was accompanied by job losses of nine per cent in Mexico's manufacturing sector outside the zone. Employment in the manufacturing sector shifted towards the EPZ sector without increasing the total number of jobs. This process was described as the "maquiladorization" of the Mexican economy. In Africa, Zimbabwe and Namibia, national labour laws are suspended as an incentive to accommodate investors when they passed their national EPZ laws in 1994 and 1995, respectively (Jauch (2002:104). The Zimbabwe Congress of Trade Unions (ZCTU) argued that Zimbabwe's Labour Relations Act should apply because:

- It is no longer viable to compete on the basis of cheap labour as the global emphasis is shifting to technological-capacity, which requires skilled workers;
- Cheap unskilled labour produces poor-quality products, while high-value-added products from skilled workers are more competitive;
- Poor working conditions provoke dissatisfaction and labour unrest as well as lower productivity and poorer product quality; and
- It is morally unacceptable to remove the gains Zimbabwean workers have made since independence (Jauch, 2002:104).

The National Union of Metalworkers in South Africa (NUMSA) passed a resolution not to reject EPZs on the proviso that compliance with South African labour legislation is mandatory (Jauch, 2002:112). The Congress of South African Trade Unions (COSATU) opposes EPZs on the basis that they are not a workable industrial development strategy for South Africa (Jauch, 2002:112). The views of NUMSA and COSATU are understandable in view of potential human rights infringements and worker exploitation in the IDZs.

Overview of South Africa's Labour Markets

Standing (1997) states that the South African manufacturing sector in the context of globalisation is turning towards greater use of flexi-workers through casual labour, contract labour, sub-contracting to smaller organizations, home workers and other "out workers", and agency workers. Horton and Langhinnerich (2002:8) attribute the growth in these non-standard forms of labour to demand and supply factors in the labour market. Supply of labour in South Africa with high levels of unemployment makes job seekers willing to accept any form of employment as an alternative to unemployment and consequently poverty. The changing demographic character of the labour market with more elderly people and women entering the labour market makes workers more vulnerable. Women prefer part-time work as it enables them to balance their work and family life (Horton and Langhinnerich, 2002:8).

Internationally, there is a move towards greater flexibility, decentralization and specialization of production and South Africa as an emerging economy is no different in following suit. The focus on making profits and increasing shareholder value pushes employers to reduce the cost of production and more specifically labour with the consequent shift to non-standard patterns of employment (Horton and Langhinnerich, 2002:9). Labour brokering has emerged rapidly in the country in response to increasing demands by the manufacturing sector for a cheap supply of workers.

Riet (2010:2) points out that labour brokering or temporary employment services (TES) as referred to in the Labour Relations Act, 1995 (Act 66 of 1995) and the Basic Conditions of Employment Act, 1997 (Act 75 of 1997) is an activity concerned with the placement of workers in the labour market. The concept of labour brokering serves as a middle employment agency between the worker and the employer (Ndunge, 2009:35). The labour broker remunerates the worker for services rendered to the client. Labour brokers provide workers to clients, who are not limited to a temporary employment, but cover a wide range of labour contracts. Notwithstanding the term "temporary" in the Labour Relations Act, 1995 (Act 66 of 1995), there is an absence of legal provision on the duration of labour brokerage involvement in engaging workers. Consequently, the duration of brokering is indefinite, ranging from days, weeks, and months to years. The relationship between the labour broker and the client is regulated by a commercial contract, which is not subject to the provision of labour laws that are currently in place.

Ndunge (2009:36) explains that employing workers with the aim of making them available to a third party has created discontent amongst the major role players in South Africa, which includes organized labour movements and the chamber of business. In this contract, the broker employs the worker but makes him or her available to a third party (the client) to carry out services. The client has an employment contract with the labour broker, who determines the tasks to be performed and performance outcomes. The labour broker as a middle agent becomes the legal employer of the worker and absolves compliance to the condition of employment from the employer. Technically, it is not the true employer as the labour broker has nothing to do with the daily responsibilities of the employee.

Ndunge (2009:36) points out that the worker has an employment relationship with the labour broker, who is the legal but nominal employer. An uncertain work relationship with the real employer exists, who is the broker's client, who neither employs nor pays the worker, but is the dominant entity in this employment arrangement. Workers in South Africa are protected by the Occupational Health and Safety Act, the Compensation for Occupational Injuries and Diseases Act and the Unemployment Insurance Act. The legal fiction that the broker is the real employer means that workers are powerless to enforce the rights enshrined in the Constitution of the country and other pieces of legislation that protect their rights. The worker cannot take action against the "real" employer, which the lawover looks as not the employer, but only against the labour broker should there be contraventions of different forms of labour legislations. The labour broker is not required to be present at the workplace and neither determines the tasks to be performed nor supervises the performance of such tasks (Ndunge, 2009:38).

Notwithstanding such a precarious employment arrangement, Benjamin (2009:4) provides clarity that labour brokers placing workers with a client for an indefinite period or for a period of three months or longer are considered being an employee of the client. Consequently, the client is considered to be the employer for the purposes of compliance with health and safety legislations in the workplace. This is enshrined in both the Occupational Health and Safety Act (1993) and the Mine Health and Safety Act (1996) (Benjamin, 2009:4). Hence, the joint legal obligations of the labour broker and the client embody the different facets of the occupational health and safety standards. The client has the day-to-day obligation to provide a healthy and safe workplace and the labour broker is required to observe the health and safety conditions in the work environment (Benjamin, 2009:9).

Crush, Ulicki, Tseane and Van Veuren (2001:7) cite Rees who argues that South African employers use sub-contracting to cheapen costs, increase flexibility, disallow unions and avoid protective regulatory measures and conformity to labour legislation. The pattern of employment of contract workers is often highly unpredictable, irregular, insecure and unstable (Crush, *et al.,* 2001:14). Given such a workplace environment, workers and trade unions in South Africa are united in pursuit of removing labour brokers as middle agents in the labour markets, if not the labour broker system needs to be redressed by changing the unfair features endemic in this labour procurement system. The labour brokering system has come under the political spotlight for a while, which requires workers to engage in productive activity for longer hours and under very dangerous conditions. Majority of these workers are not provided with the standard industry non-wage benefits, such as medical schemes, sick leave or compensation in the event of injury and/or death (Crush, *et al.*, 2001:14).

At a labour solidarity level, brokering and retrenchments contributed to a decline in union membership and worker assertiveness in protecting their rights for fair labour practice. The system has resulted in the emergence of hostility and conflict amongst workers employed by the principal employer and the labour broker on account of discrepancy in the conditions of service since the principal employer uses labour brokers as a means to avoiding trade union intervention in preserving worker rights in pursuit of increasing profits (Crush, *et al.,* 2001:30).

Labour Brokers and the Enslavement of Workers due to Low Levels of Implementing Occupational Health and Safety Policy Frameworks

Kenny and Bezuidenhout (1999:190) assert that workers employed by labour brokers are seldom unionized and are discouraged from joining trade unions. They cite a quote from their study on a worker's comments that highlights the concerns of workers under such a vicious system of employment practice:

> "The contractors (labour broker) do not allow contract workers to join the union. If a worker joins the union, he is fired. Contract labour is not unionized. They are using them to fight us (the union), because we cause strikes."

On the contrary, labour brokers argue that most of their workforce under their tutelage is not unionized because it is difficult to organize them due to the labour force being moved around to different clients over short periods of time (Kenny and Bezuidenhout, 1999:190). They argue that workers falling under the tutelage of the labour brokering system are considered different to workers engaged by the principal employer and, consequently, physically separated from each other and are prevented from building a common worker solidarity (Kenny and Bezuidenhout, 1999:190) in order to evade health and safety legislation. To illustrate this practice, the study by Klerck (1994:32) highlights the violation of occupational health and safety regulations amongst workers originating through labour brokers. It was found that factories in the petro-chemical industry use sub-contracted workers for the most dangerous aspects of work. These subcontracted workers are not organized by trade unions and neither do they have knowledge of the provision of health and safety legislations.

Labour Minister, Membathisi Mdladlana stated that the exploitation of workers by labour brokers will cease once new legislation is promulgated to redress this practice. The minister describes labour broking as a form of human trafficking in the context that such practice involves selling workers' labour to the highest bidder. Mdladlana points out that this is an extreme form of free market capitalism, which reduces workers to commodities that can be traded for profit similar to retailing meat or vegetable commodities. The minister reiterated that labour brokers are pro-employer and anti-trade unionism. Such a statement resonates with the manifesto of the ruling party, the African National Congress (ANC), which professes the avoidance of worker exploitation and makes a political commitment for decent work for all workers in the country. The manifesto affords protection to the terms of employment relationship by proposing legislation to regulate contract work.

In pursuit of such a manifesto, it seeks to amend legislations to regulate labour brokers as contained in the Basic Conditions of Employment Act (1997), the Employment Equity Act (1998) and the Labour Relations Act (1995). The planned amendment however, omits the Occupational Health and Safety Act (1993), which is the primary legislation that safeguards the health and safety of workers.

Despite some political commitment to reform in terms of regulating the labour market, Horton and Langhinnerich (2002:9) are skeptical that workers employed by labour brokers will not have the desired effect in protecting worker rights in terms of this system of employment. They argue that workers are part of a commercial relationship within the system of labour brokerage and, consequently, will not receive the protection intended by labour law reforms. Laws that provide anti-discrimination, employment equity, wage and hour protections are largely ineffective for such vulnerable workers. The contracting out of production and services to another organization undermines the position of existing employees in respect of job security and bargaining power. Plant level rights that workers have enjoyed such as breaks, work schedule control, consistency of job responsibilities are removed as workers engaged by labour brokers are deprived of basic benefits. The shifting of production to smaller and less viable organizations results in lower wages, fewer benefits and less job security. The presence in organizations of workers with fewer rights and less power to defend the rights has a disciplining effect on the workforce as whole. Outsourcing has the effect of fragmenting conditions, as workers within the same work organization are covered by differing bargaining councils.

Methodological Approach to the Study and Research Findings

The study was undertaken in a rubber processing company that employed 440 workers of which 298 workers participated in the study. The sample population was split into four segments. The first segment of the sample population were workers only exposed to physical noise, the second population were workers only exposed to chemicals and the third population were workers exposed to both physical noise and chemicals and the fourth segment of the population was neither exposed to chemicals nor noise. The workers comprised of four categories of which three originated from three separate labour brokers and the fourth category are those employed by the principal employer on a permanent basis as depicted in Table 7.1.

Table 7.1: Breakdown of Employers in Categories

Employer organization	*Total number of workers in employment*	*Study population*	*%*
Principal Employer	40	31	10.5
Labour Broker A	150	67	22.4
Labour Broker B	180	141	47.4
Labour Broker C	70	59	19.8
TOTAL	**440**	**298**	**100**

It will be noted from the distribution in Table 7.1 that very small percentages (10.4%) of research subjects were in full time permanent employment in the study locality. The remaining comprised outsourced labor to the principal employer through the services of three labour brokers of which Labour Broker B provided almost half (47.4%) of the workforce in the study locality. Cumulatively, 89.5 per cent of the research subjects in the study were on temporary work contracts with no permanent job benefits accruing to them. Hence, this trend suggests that an overwhelmingly large percentage of research subjects were not assured of legal protection in terms of occupational health safety benefits, neither did they enjoy any long term work benefits.

The fact that an overwhelming large percentage of research subjects were being sourced by the principal employer in the study through labour brokers, it is not atypical to trends in the South African labour market landscape. Labour markets in the South African context are characterized by high levels of unemployment, thereby compelling job seekers to accept any form of employment as an alternative to unemployment. This finding confirms the assertion made by Standing (1997), who states that South African companies are turning towards greater use of flexi-workers, through casual labour, contract labour, sub-contracting to smaller organizations, home workers and other 'out workers', and agency workers. The issue of labour broking in South Africa is a highly politically contested one. Ndunge (2009:36) explains that this has created discontent amongst the major role players in South Africa, which includes organized labour and the chamber of business. In light of the legal context that the broker is the real employer means that workers are powerless to enforce the rights enshrined in the Constitution of the Republic of South Africa and the provisions of different Labour Legislations. One finds according to Crush, Ulicki, Tseane and Van Veuren (2001:7), who quote Rees arguing that South African, employers using sub-contracting to cheapen costs through increased flexibility often disallow unions and avoid protective regulation and legislation. It is in this context that this study confirms the nature and extent of labour brokering in the South African manufacturing sector and the implications and compromise of occupational and health safety regulations.

In the study, half of the research subjects as depicted in Graph 7.1 reported that they were exposed to some form of chemical in the workplace. Within this category, a small sample of research subjects were tested for exposure to Volatile Organic Chemical (VOC) exposure.

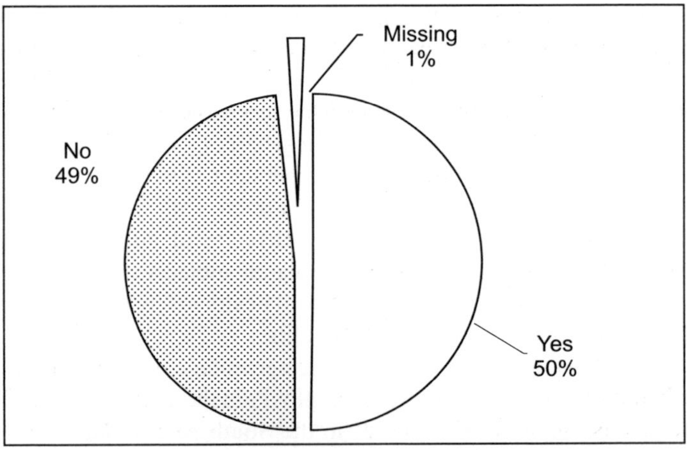

Graph 7.1: Distribution of Research Subjects Exposure to Volatile Organic Chemicals (VOCs)

A total of six workers were randomly tested for VOC in the study, which is tabulated in Table 7.2. The reason for selecting such a small sample of respondents to be tested for VOC was largely due to the costs involved in undertaking these tests and not to disrupt the workflow process as requested by the principal employer. Consequently, two were employed in the occupational category of Ripping Operator, i.e., those, who apply adhesive solvents to bond rubber treads, two in the category of Buffing Operator, i.e., those who remove excess rubber after moulding, one in the category of Painter, i.e., those who apply solvents to the rubber treads and one as laboratory technician, i.e., those who test the quality of the processed rubber.

Table 7.2: Sample Distribution of Workers Tested for Volatile Organic Chemicals (VOCs)

Sample Taken	*Area*	*Job Title*	*Sample Type*	*Time On*	*Time Off*	*Date*
Worker **A**	Treadline	Buffing Operator	VOC's	12H51	14H33	08/12/08
Worker **B**	Treadline	Ripping Operator	VOC's	12H54	14H36	08/12/08
Worker **C**	Treadline	Ripping Operator	VOC's	12H59	14H29	08/12/08
Worker **D**	Treadline	Buffing Operator	VOC's	13H01	14H38	08/12/08
Worker **E**	Treadline	Painter	VOC's	13H07	14H37	08/12/08
Worker **F**	Laboratory	Laboratory Technican	VOC's	09H24	13H30	10/12/08

It will be noted from Table 7.2 that all six employees tested for VOC's showed very low exposure to high priority ototoxins in keeping with the typology formulated by Morata and Little (2002:75) and Rawool (2012:13). This is largely due to the short term employment of workers, who although have exposure to VOCs whose full impact can only be ascertained after a long duration of exposure. Nonetheless, what is significant is the prevalence of three VOCs out of the eight categories defined by Morata and Little as high priority toxins as depicted in Table 7.3. The prevalence of Ethylbenzene, which is classified as additional ototoxins resulting in long term hearing impairment was significantly noted in this sample study. Although one cannot make a strong generalization from these separate tests undertaken on research subjects, due to restrictions placed by the research locality on the study to have all of its employees tested for VOCs, what is significant is the presence of VOCs in the work environment. Despite this, one may conclude that the prevalence of such ototoxins, in terms of the OHS Act (1993) may appear at face value that the research locality is in conformity with the South African occupational health and safety norms.

However, what this study highlights is the prevalence of two of the chemicals, Toluene and Ethylbenzene, which are internationally known to predispose workers to hearing impairment. In this respect, Morata (2003:677) argues that recent animal experiments confirmed that chemicals, such as toluene and ethylbenzene amongst other VOCs listed

Table 7.3: Results of Test for VOC Exposure

Chemical VOC's	*Worker A*	*Worker B*	*Worker C*	*Worker D*	*Worker E*	*Worker F*	*OHS Act 1993*
Acetone	0.245 mg/m³	0.354 mg/m³	0.716 mg/m³	0.008 mg/m³	0.008 mg/m³	0.008 mg/m³	1780 mg/m³
n-Pentane	0.5 mg/m³	0.413 mg/m³	0.008 mg/m³	0.008 mg/m³	0.45 mg/m³	0.008 mg/m³	1800 mg/m³
n-Hexane*	158.833 mg/m³	134.458 mg/m³	10.458 mg/m³	2.279 mg/m³	135.5 mg/m³	0.304 mg/m³	70 mg/m³
Toluene*	1.263 mg/m³	1.325 mg/m³	1.417 mg/m³	0.013 mg/m³	0.983 mg/m³	0.075 mg/m³	188 mg/m³
Ethyl benzene*	0.01 mg/m³	0.00056 mg/m³	0.01 mg/m³	0.01 mg/m³	0.01 mg/m³	0.01 mg/m³	435 mg/m³
Xylene*	0.01 mg/m³	0.00056 mg/m³	0.01 mg/m³	0.01 mg/m³	0.01 mg/m³	0.04 mg/m³	435 mg/m³

* Denotes presence of VOCs in the workplace.

in Table 7.3 interact synergistically with noise resulting in damage to the auditory system. Exposures to these chemicals in sufficiently high concentrations may affect hearing even in the absence of noise. Such chemicals inhaled or absorbed through the skin are known to enter the blood stream and affect the cochlear structures and the central auditory system (Odkvist, *et al.,* 1982; Morata, *et al.,* 2002 and Teixeira, *et al.,* 2002).

In the study half (50%) of the research subjects reported that they were exposed to noise levels about 85dBA in the workplace as depicted in Graph 7.2. This finding suggests that almost half of the research subjects risked ototoxic exposure due to the prevalence of high levels of noise in the workplace. What is significant is that they were exposed to noise at higher levels than the legal limits prescribed by the Occupational Health Safety Act (1993).

Interestingly, when the population means (μ) exposure to sound (84.5 dBA) in this study is compared to the South African Health and Occupational Safety norms, it would appear at face value to be within acceptable safety limits. However, a closer analysis of the findings to the noise range exposures for research subjects, one finds that it is between 70 to 97 dBA. This finding is significant as there is wide evidence provided by Gelfand (2001:157), Lustig *et al.* (2003:67), Ackley *et al.* (2007:101), Berger *et al.* (2003:484) and Pillay (2009), who assert that those, who are exposed to noise levels ranging between 71-90 dBA, are at risk of

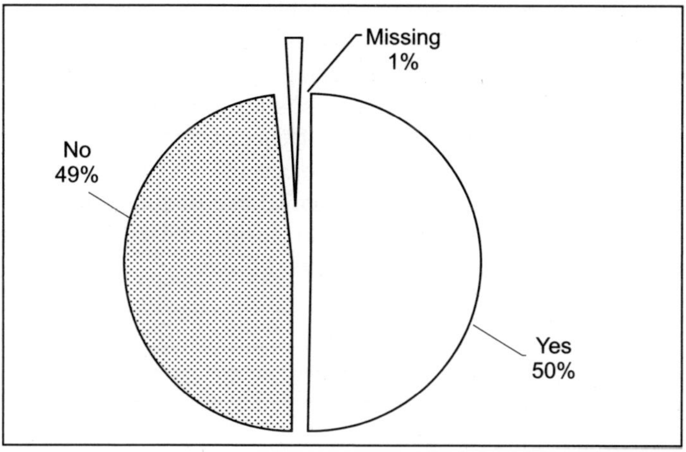

Graph 7.2: Exposure of Research Subjects to Noise to 85 dBA

severe hearing loss and those above 90 dBA are exposed to profound hearing loss. Considering that the research subjects in this study are employed under labour broking conditions, the system of labour broking involves a high turnover of staff over short employment periods. Hence, it may be argued that the longer employees are exposed to noise thresholds beyond the legal limit, they are more than likely to be exposed to serious hearing loss.

However, when comparing the severity of hearing loss based on an audiogram test, one finds a very small percent of research subjects in the severe to profound categories as defined in the audiogram. Nonetheless, the situation for research subjects appear serious in terms of long term hearing loss risk factors when analysing the audiogram for frequency range 4000Hz, 6000Hz and 8000Hz. Within this range, just more than 60 per cent of the research subjects are at risk of suffering permanent hearing loss should they continue to have exposure to noise at such a frequency range. It must be noted, considering that a vast majority of the research subjects are in the employment of labour brokers, who engage temporary staff with a high turnover over short duration, such long term detection may not be identified and protected for in terms of Compensation for Occupational Illnesses and Diseases Act (1993) may hardly surface considering the short frequency of employment.

Given that the workplace for research subjects is predominantly noise zones and the use of hearing protective devices is mandatory, the study highlights that 83.8 per cent of the research subjects use no such devices. Only 2 per cent of the research subjects reported using some form of hearing protective device. In this category of research subjects, the provision of hearing protective devices is made at the personal cost of the employee and not for the company. Hence, it comes as no surprise as to why the vast majority of research subjects (83.8%) do not use hearing protective devices as depicted in Graph 7.3 exposing themselves to the risk of hearing impairment or loss due to the unaffordability in acquiring such hearing protective devices in the workplace.

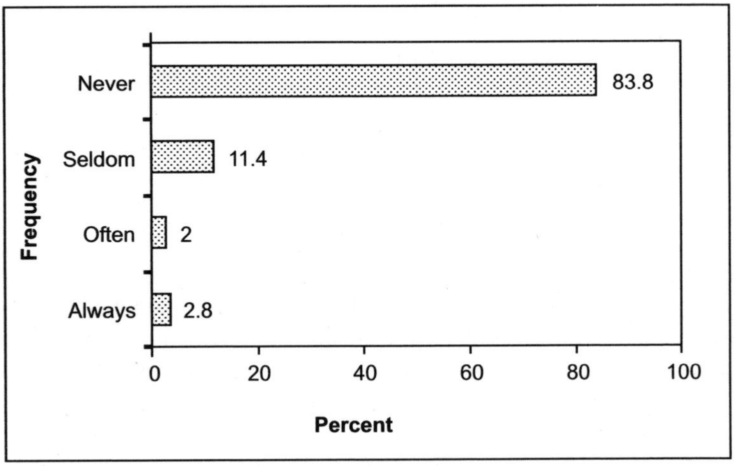

Graph 7.3: Use of Hearing Protective Devices amongst Research Subjects in the Workplace

Conclusion

Globalization has contributed to the restructuring of work and the introduction of flexible forms of work, such as outsourcing of employment through labour brokers. This type of employment does not receive the protection intended by labour law and are not allowed to join unions. Labour brokers argue that it is not possible for workers to organize themselves because their work location changes often. The Nambian Government banned Labour Brokers in 2008, however, this ban was overturned in 2010 by the Namibian Supreme Court. In South Africa, the Department of Labour was considering banning labour brokers, however, since the failed Namibian attempt, it is unlikely that South Africa will move to ban labour brokers. The financial crises made workers more vulnerable, consequently, occupational health and safety is compromised. The study has undertaken preliminary tests to ascertain whether exposure to VOCs and noise levels have any bearing on the auditory impairment amongst research subjects engaged in the workplace through labour brokers. Although there is some indication that such exposure is prevalent and has potential for long term compromise on the health and safety of workers originating from labour brokers, the study could not confirm at a significant level such a correlation for the simple reason that workers on labour brokering contract are employed on short term contracts and the full impact cannot be ascertained. However, what this study significantly highlights is the exposure of workers on labour brokering contracts to volatile chemical and unacceptably high levels of noise that can predispose them to serious hearing loss impairment should they continue working in such an environment for a longer duration of time. It also highlights that as a result of high levels of turnover of employees through the labour brokerage system exonerates the principal employer from the regulatory framework of the national Occupational and Health and Safety policy framework. Even though workers may suffer long term health consequences having being exposed to hazardous work conditions for short durations of time, they have little or no legal protection from their principal and labour broker employer should they sustain long term damages to their health. The system of labour brokerage compromises worker health status, evades Occupational Health and Safety prescriptions, reduces international labour frameworks to abuse by multi-natioanal co-operations in pursuit of capital and leaves behind a burgeoning national health care responsibility to cash strapped economies amongst and between developing nations. The system of labour brokerage can be dubbed tantamount to a sophisticated system of labour exploitation and slavery through legalized forms of cheating on the national states legal frameworks purported to protect the health and safety of its citizens in pursuit of economic growth.

REFERENCES

Ackley, R. S., Decker, T. N. and Limb, C. J. (2007). *An Essential Guide to Hearing and Balance Disorders.* New Jersey, USA: Lawrence Erlbaum Associates, Inc.

Benjamin, P. (2009). Untangling the triangle: The regulatory challenges of triangular employment. Preliminary draft for presentation to "Regulating Decent Work" Conference, Geneva 6-8 July 2009.

Berger, E. H., Royster, J. D., Driscoll, D. P. and Layne, M. (2003). *The Noise Manual.* Revised Fifth edition. Fairfax, USA: American Industrial Hygiene Association.

Brown, R. B. (2006). *Doing your dissertation in business and management—the reality of researching and writing.* Chennai, India: Sage Publication Ltd.

Crush, J., Ulicki, T., Tseane, T. and Van Veuren, E. J. (2001). Undermining Labour: the Rise of Sub-contracting in South African Gold Mines. *Journal of Southern African Studies,* Vol. 27(1).

Gelfand, S. A. (2001). *Essentials of Audiology*. Second Edition. New York, USA: Thieme Medical Publishers, Inc.

Goldstein, G., Helmer, R. and Fingerhut, M. (2001). Mobilizing to protect worker's health: The WHO global strategy on occupational health and safety. *African Newsletter on Occupational Health and Safety*, Vol. 1(3).

Holkeri, H. (2001). Globalization and its effects on Occupational Health and Safety. *African Newsletter on Occupational Health and Safety*. Vol. 1(3). December 2001.

Horton, C. and Langhinnerich, W. (2002). Research Report: Flexible labour markets in the auto-component and auto-assembly industries in South Africa. PRU Conference 2002.

Jauch, H. (2002). Export processing zones and the quest for sustainable development: A Southern African Perspective. *Environment and Urbanization.* Vol. 14; 101-113.

Klerck, G. (1994). Industrial restructuring and the casualisation of labour: A case study of subcontracted labour in the process industries. *South African Sociological Review,* Vol. 7(1): 32-62.

Kenny, B. and Bezuidenhout. (1999). Contracting, complexity and control: an overview of the changing nature of subcontracting in the South African Mining industry. *Journal of the South African Institute of Mining and Metallurgy.* July/August 1999.

Loewenson, R. (2001). Globalization and Occupational Health: A Perspective from Southern Africa. *Bulletin of the World Health Organization*, Vol. 79(9).

Lustig, L. R., Niparko, J. K., Minor, L. B. and Zee, D.S. (2003). *Clinical Neurotology Diagnosing and Managing Disorders of Hearing, Balance and the facial Nerve*. Ontario, Canada: Taylor & Francis.

Mathekga, M. J. (2009). The political economy of labour market flexibility in South Africa. Masters in Philsophy Dissertation: Stellenbosch University.

Mdladlana, Membathisi, www.labour.gov.za 05/08/09.

Minister to accelerate campaign on labour brokers [online] Available: http://www.labour.gov.za viewed 05/08/09.

Morata, T. C. and Little, M. B. (2002). Suggested guidelines for studying the combined effects of occupational exposure to noise and chemical on hearing. *Noise and Health*, Vol.4(14) pp. 73-87.

Morata, T. C. (2003). Chemical Exposure as a Risk Factor for Hearing Loss. *Occupational Environmental medicine*. Vol. 45: 676-682.

Ndunge, K. (2009). Labour Brokers—Should they be banned or regulated? *New Agenda*, Third Quarter 2009.

Ntshalintshali, B. (2010). The social economy: Africa's response to the global crises. [Online] Available: http://ilo.org/public/english/regionafpro/addisbaba.pdf/se_speechcosatu_enpdf viewed 05/12/2010.

Odkvist, L. M., Berghltz, L. M., Ahfeldt, H., Andersson, B., Edling, C. and Strand, E. (1982). Otoneurological and audiological findings in workers exposed to industrial solvents. *Acta Otolarungol.* Vol. 386: 249-241.

Pillay, M. (2009). Interviewed by Niranjan, I. Crompton Hospital, Pinetown, KwaZulu Natal, RSA. 25 May 2009, 11H00.

Presidential Economic Joint Working Group. (2009). Framwork for South Africa's Response to the International Economic Crises, 19 February 2009. [Online] available: http://www.info.gov.za/issues/economic_crises/index.html viewed 05/12/2010.

Rawool, V. W. (2012). Hearing Conservation in Occupational, Recreational, Educational, and Home Settings. New York, USA: Thieme Medical Publishers, Inc.

Republic of South Africa (1993). Mine Health and Safety Act 29 of 1996. Pretoria. Government Printers.

Republic of South Africa (1993). Occupational Health and Safety Act 85 of 1993. Pretoria. Government Printers.

Republic of South Africa (1995). Labour Relations Act 66 of 1995. Pretoria. Government Printers.

Republic of South Africa (1997). Basic Conditions of Employment Act 75 of 1997. Pretoria. Government Printers.

Republic of South Africa (2001). The Unemployment Insurance Act 63 of 2001. Pretoria. Government Printers.

Republic of South Africa (1993). Compensation for Occupational Injuries and Diseases Act, No 130 of 1993. Pretoria. Government Printers.

Republic of South Africa (1998). Employment Equity Act 55 of 1998. Pretoria. Government Printers.

Rodger, G., Lee, E., Swepston, L. and Daele, J. (2009). The ILO and the quest for social justice, 1919-2009. International Labour Office, Geneva, Switzerland.

Ryan, A. (2009). Profiling occupational health and safety in Southern Africa. *Occupational Health Southern Africa.* Volume 15, WAHSA Special Issue, 7-15.

Riet, H. V. D. (2010). Labour brokers—the future [online] Available: *www.saslaw.org.za* viewed 15/05/2010.

Standing, G. (1997). Labour market dynamics in South African industrial firms: The South African labour flexibility survey. Unpublished paper presented at conference on labour markets and enterprise performance in South Africa. Reserve Bank, Pretoria, Republic of South Africa.

Theron, J., Godfrey, Y. S. and Visser, M. (2007). Globalization the impact of trade liberalization and labour law: The case of South Africa. International Labour Organization. International Institute for Labour Studies.

Teixeira, C. F., Giraldo da Silva, L. and Morata, T. C. (2002). Occupational exposure to insecticides and their effects on the auditory system. *Noise Health*. Vol. 4: 31-39.

Working together we can do more. [online] Available: http://www.anc.org.za/elections/2009/manifesto/manifesto.html,viewed 17/02/09.

8
Financial Constraints to Small and Medium Enterprises in Africa

Sudhir Kapoor

The last century witnessed decolonization of African countries and their independence gave them opportunity to take charge of their own future. The hope was that post-independence period for Africa will alleviate Africa out of its miseries and reduce its marginalization. This hope and nostalgia changed into despair when Africa could not catch the global bus, and was left behind the rest of the world. Its economic and geo political situation was affected adversely when its share of international trade fell from about four per cent of the world trade in the 1960s to about less than two per cent in the early 1990s. The great socio-economic decline confirmed the fears of afro-pessimist that Africa faces enormously grave development challenges that included high population growth, high poverty levels, development lag, lower per capita income than before, corruption, HIV/AIDS, conflicts, environmental hazards and high unemployment levels. Although the support by international organizations like the International Monetary Fund (IMF), the World Bank (WB) and G8 countries was of much benefit, most countries of Africa still had to grapple with the problems of high levels of external debt. The revenue collected from the export of goods and services was being used to settle the debts. This had grave consequences on the economic performance of the countries leaving them economically dependent. Most independent African countries still depended for trade on former colonizers. Africa that was aid dependent, rather than milking their economy, was benefitting the concerns of the donors. At the same time, East Asian countries embarking on the alternative strategy of investing, focused on the ways to attract foreign investment. They tried to create environment that was conducive for foreign investors, which Africa clearly lacked. Neither could it generate domestic savings sufficient for capital formation for business. Despite all these ills affecting most of the continent, Africa turned the tides to its favor by the beginning of the new century.

The option Africa had was to rethink its growth strategies and redesign its development process. The New Partnership for Africa's Development (NEPAD) ushered in a new course of development. NEPAD's objective to enhance Africa's growth and development so as to have effective participation in the global economy was welcomed by all. The stress on Africa-initiated and Africa-owned policy gave new light and new hope to the Africans. There was a paradigm shift in addressing the challenges for sustainable development. It meant to re-establish human dignity and honor of Africans. The hollow developmental processes not suitable for African situations, often described as growth without development were reconsidered. Africa steered in the processes that were suitable for Africans, home grown and controlled by the Africans themselves. Africa undertook structural changes tailor made for them. African countries embarked on economic reforms, restructured macro-economic policies, allocated larger investments in the education and health sectors, brought about liberalization in markets and trade, encouraged democratization processes, reduced its aid dependence, diversified economy, strengthened trade and embraced positive changes in governance. The African countries that could sustain these reforms have raised their level of growth and are seeing development in real terms. These countries have given a hope to the whole African continent. They talk confidently and optimistically of 'African Renaissance' or 'African revival'. Some of these countries are now included by the World Bank and the United Nations Industrial Development Organization in the list of top economic gainers. These countries include South Africa, Kenya, Nigeria, Ghana, Angola, Rwanda and even Burundi. But Africa is not a monolithic entity and different countries of Africa have adopted different strategies for its development and, hence, are following different trajectories of growth.

For the first time in African history, Africa is showing signs of development and growth due to changes in policies and institutional frame work. Africa's collective GDP, at US$ 1.6 trillion in 2008, is now roughly equal to Brazil's or Russia's. While Africa's increased economic momentum is widely recognized, less known are its sources and likely staying power (Roxburgh, *et al.,* 2010). But it is sure that the future economic growth will be supported by Africa's increasing integration with the global economy. Africa is gaining greater access to international capital; total foreign capital flows into Africa rose from US$ 15 billion in

2000 to a peak of US$ 87 billion in 2007 (Roxburgh, *et al.,* 2010). It is estimated that Africa will be generating US$ 2.6 Trillion revenue annually by 2020, about $1 trillion more than today (Ramachandran, 2010). Radelet (2010) says that transformation brought about by emerging Africa and its continued resurgence can be sustained because of five deep and fundamental changes at work that includes the rise of democracy and more accountable government; introduction of stronger economic management and responsible economic policies; the end of the debt crisis and strengthening relations with the international community; the spread of new technologies; and the emergence of a new generation of public and private leaders, policy makers and activists. For faster and deepening economic growth, it has to provide space and scope for the development of private sector. Most countries of Africa have private sector that includes mostly state owned large scale enterprises, Small and Medium Enterprises (SMEs) and micro enterprises. Large scale enterprises could not significantly accelerate the economic growth. Most informal micro enterprises have a limited contribution. SMEs have the potential to play a central role in promoting economic growth and also can be a beachhead for industrializing economy. Thus, SMEs are the emerging private sector in most countries of Africa and are fast becoming drivers of private sector growth. Implementing right policies and providing adequate support can make SME sector most vibrant arm of the private sector.

Large enterprises entail large scale production and are capital intensive. They do provide benefits of economies of scale, but may require higher capital outlays that may be out of reach of most businesses in developing economies. Large scale industries have been found to fail in fulfilling their promise to alleviate poverty and reduce unemployment. Due to financial constraints and being densely populated, developing countries can explore the option of promoting SMEs for achieving faster economic growth. SMEs are labor-intensive and boost economy by creating more employment. It is seen that the major portion of private sector of most least developed and developing countries is constituted of SMEs and they have special characteristics and potentials that differentiate them from large scale enterprises. Hence, in the development process, they have a specific role to play. Many studies have shown that besides being the largest employers in both developed and developing world, SMEs play a dynamic role in development of markets and innovations; building of managerial and entrepreneurial skills; and promoting formation of domestic capital. Ayyagari, *et al.,* (2007) study indicates that SMEs contribute, on average, 60 per cent of total formal employment in the manufacturing sector in both developed and developing countries. Merchant (2012) found that in fact, every US$ 1 invested in an SME generates an additional US$ 10 in the local community. Not ignoring these advantages, governments have started to focus in a large way on the development and the central role of SMEs. Also, SMEs have flexible nature, so they can adapt more easily to varying market conditions and are able to bear adverse economic conditions better than the large scale enterprises. Besides these, there is also a belief that small scale enterprises should be promoted in developing countries so as to achieve industrial development, because most of the underdeveloped and developing economies have less developed institutions and establishments, therefore, setting up of large scale enterprises may not be a viable option from an economic stand point. SMEs also provide foundations for the development of industrialization in developing countries. The dynamic role of SMEs in developing countries positions SMEs as engines through which their economic growth and social development can be attained—the aim that has long been cherished.

Definition of SMEs

Since the classification of business into small and large depends on country's own criteria, it becomes difficult to find a universal definition of SMEs. Different definitions of SMEs have been given stressing different aspects. Some definitions are based on the type of raw material being used, some define by using the size of capital assets, some use skill of labour and value of annual turnover level and some by the number of paid employees. Ojowo (1989) distinguished small scale industries based on the type of raw materials used, source and technology used. His classification is: (i) Small scale industries based on indigenous technology, and local raw materials. (ii) Small scale industries based on foreign technology but local raw materials; and (iii) Small scale industries based on foreign technology and foreign raw materials. Stanley and Morse (cited by Osotimehin, *et al.,* 2012) classified industries into eight categories by size emphasizing the difference between small and medium sized industries and large industries based on varying characteristics, which include little specialization, close personal contact of management with production workers and lack of access to capital. They argued that establishments employing not less than 100 workers should be defined as medium sized whereas those with less than 100 employees be defined as small sized. Bachama (2010) says that the International Development Centre of Stanford Research Institute defines small scale industries as that segment of manufacturing industry, which are carried on a relatively small establishment having not necessarily all but some of the following characteristics; little or no specialization in management; close contact between the manager and those involved in the enterprise; lack of access to capital through organized security market, close integration with the local community in which it depends for both market and labour; and no dominant position in major markets. The UNIDO defines SMEs by using the criteria of number of employee. Its classifications for industrialized and developing countries were different.

The classification given for developing countries is as follows:

- Large-firms with 100 or more workers;
- Medium-firms with 20-99 workers;
- Small-firms with 5-19 workers;
- Micro-firms with less than 5 workers.

According to Abor and Quartey (2010), the characteristics of SMEs in developing countries can be understood under three broad headings: labour characteristics, sectors of activity, gender of owner and efficiency.

Labour characteristics

- Most SMEs are one-person businesses, the largest employment category is working proprietors. Their families, who tend to be unpaid, but active in the enterprise, make up roughly another quarter. The remaining portion of the workforce is split between hired workers and trainees or apprentices.
- SMEs are more labour intensive than larger firms
- Lower capital costs associated with job creation

In terms of activity

- They are mostly engaged in retailing, trading, or manufacturing.
- Retailing is mostly found in urban regions, while manufacturing can be found in either rural or urban centres.

Gender of owner

- Majority of SMEs are female-owned businesses,
- They are operated from home and are mostly not considered in official statistics.
- This clearly affects their chances of gaining access to financing schemes, since such programmes are designed without sufficient consideration of the needs of businesses owned by females.

SMEs and Economic Growth

There is a consensus among policy makers, economists and business experts that SMEs are drivers of economic growth as has been reported in the Literature Review on Small and Medium Enterprises' Access to Credit and Support in South Africa (2011). A healthy SME sector contributes prominently to the economy through creating more employment opportunities, generating higher production volumes, increasing exports and introducing innovation and entrepreneurship skills. It also stresses that the dynamic role of SMEs in developing countries insures them as engines through which the growth objectives of developing countries can be achieved. Even in the developed industrial economies, it is the SME sector rather than the multinationals or large enterprises that is the largest employer of workers. Another most important contribution of SMEs is that they try to promote economic diversification through the development of non-traditional and burgeoning sectors of the economy. The Global Entrepreneurship Monitor conducted a study on 37 countries in 2002 on entrepreneurship and economic growth and found that the economic growth of a country is directly correlated to its level of entrepreneurial activity strengthening the observation that SMEs are indispensable component of any economy. Irrespective of the stage of development of an economy, the importance of the small and medium businesses has been accepted by the economies world over. Due to their effective contribution towards economic growth, small businesses are considered to be a critical element for a successful *mantra* for an economy to achieve reasonable industrialization and growth.

As seen above, small scale enterprises play an important role in the provisioning of immediate large scale employment and, thus, help to limit the unemployment in the region. At the same time, SMEs require lesser capital costs for job creation in comparison to large enterprises, which are capital intensive. Also, SMEs contribute to value addition in the manufacturing sector. Quite often value addition activities promote the transition of economies from predominantly agricultural to industrial, that provide for more sustainable livelihoods. Thus, contribution to value chain of SMEs brings forth more desired structural changes with transformative result. They also help to achieve better growth objectives as compared to large scale enterprises.

Micro and small scale enterprises play intermediate and transitional role in the formation of large scale enterprises. SMEs provide a base for promoting consistent and gradual industrialization, which can be a more realistic design for achieving industrialization in most African countries. At the same time, by creating employment opportunities locally, they reduce regional disparities especially in the rural areas. Thus, SMEs assume a critical role in more equitable distribution of income than the larger enterprises. Uzor (2004) pointed that they helped in the distribution of income both in functional terms as wages and profits in nominal terms. Being labour intensive, they have a better chance of success in rural areas and semi-urban areas where SMEs help to contain out-migration by providing people with an alternative source of income. Tadesse (2009) says that, SMEs not only satisfy local needs by making differentiated varieties of products, by being spread all over the country, they also help ensure some form of equitable distribution of income-earning opportunities. SMEs are also usually locally-owned and controlled and, therefore, they can strengthen the extended family as well as other social networks and cultural traditions. More than large scale enterprises, SMEs have the ability to utilize local resources and, therefore, SMEs have primacy in rural areas. Thus, SMEs involve wider participation of rural and marginalized population in the development process. It enables not only more even distribution of incomes, but also of income earning opportunities especially in rural areas. By providing opportunities for employment, they discourage migration of the people to urban areas and lessen the consequent problem of congestion in the cities.

SMEs in Africa

According to IMF, more investment, both domestic and foreign is one of the main explanations behind stronger growth in Africa. Private sector investment in Sub-Saharan Africa is growing impressively and is setting a stage for enhancing potential for long-term growth. SMEs are becoming an important segment of private sector and are increasingly being recognised as productive drivers of economic growth and development for African countries. Banks, financial institutions, private equity firms and NGOs across Africa are encouraging entrepreneurs to come up with innovative business ideas and explore opportunities in initiating a business start up. SMEs are, thus, proving to be a lifeline for Africa by creating job opportunities and skilled workforce that, in return, is helping boost the productivity of this region (*SME Africa 2012*). In African countries, SME/SMIs have received attention because of their labour absorptive capacity in terms of both shrinking the public-sector and private-formal economy, and for increasing the number of new entrants in industries, thereby, promoting competition in various sectors of the economy (Kesper,

2000 cited in *Financing Small and Medium Scale Industries in Africa*). Increasing importance of the SMEs can be judged by the fact that in Africa, SME/SMIs and the informal sector represent over 90 per cent of businesses, contribute over 50 per cent of GDP, and account for about 63 per cent of employment in low income countries (United Nations Economic Commission for Africa, 2005). Small enterprises employing less than 50 employees constitute the greater part of industrial work force in most African countries (Liendholm and Mead, 1999). A study by the Competition Commission (2004) cited in the Literature Review on Small and Medium Enterprises' Access to Credit and Support in South Africa (2011) estimated that 99.3 per cent of South African businesses were SMEs and that these SMEs accounted for 53.9 per cent of total employment and contributed 34.8 per cent to GDP. This data shows that contribution of SMEs in African economy is significant, especially in employment generation. Tadesse (2009) stresses the fact that African women entrepreneurs own more than half of African SMEs and up to 70 per cent of Africa's vast rural population is active in formal and informal SME sectors. Despite this, in most African countries, SMEs contribute less than 20 per cent to gross GDP whereas the figure can reach up to 60 per cent in high-income countries (*ibid.*). But SMEs, which are innovative and experience good growth, can expand outside their country, and enter into regional as well as global networks.

Due to adverse government policies, wars, conflicts, political instability, red tape or dependence of economy on primary sector, SMEs could not establish themselves as veritable sector of economy earlier in Africa. Acknowledging its important role in economy, most African governments are more than eager to promote SMEs. In countries like South Africa, Ghana and Mauritius, SMEs are quite vibrant due to clear rules and regulations and favorable financial systems supporting private sector. Some countries like Gabon and Chad, with economy dependent on oil revenues, saw the sluggish development of non-oil sectors of economy including SMEs. With all the attendant problems, economies such as Kenya and Ghana have shown its determination for introducing and sustaining private-sector growth. According to Ayyagari, *et al.* (2007) the SME share of employment in select African countries shows that in some countries like South Africa, its share of employment is as high as 81.53 per cent using official country definition of SME, but it can be as low as 15.20 per cent and 16.72 per cent in Zimbabwe and Nigeria respectively. There is no definite pattern that emerges from the given data, but it can be said that SMEs in these countries provide substantial employment.

SMEs sector is sluggish in many African countries, the reason being that they have small local markets, fragile regional integration and very difficult business conditions, which include cumbersome official procedures, poor infrastructure, inefficient legal systems, inadequate financial systems and unattractive tax regimes. Many firms stay small and informal and use simple technology that does not require much use of national infrastructure. Apart from these factors, a massive shortage of skills and educational deficiencies, complicated regulatory challenges, restrictive labor practices, lack of recognition of the importance of stakeholders, failing to avail the opportunities created by e-commerce, aging infrastructure, access to new international markets are very crucial for the success of SMEs. Governments have even placed several barriers, like excessive regulation and red-tape to the detriment of SME development. Countries like Chad, Nigeria, Eritrea, the Republic of Congo and Guinea are considered as less attractive to new businesses due to high cost involved in starting business, high taxes and difficult credit access. Despite these problems, the World Bank Doing Business Report 2013, a co-publication of the World Bank and the International Finance Corporation shows that among the 50 economies with the biggest improvement since 2005, the largest share, 1/3rd are in Sub Saharan Africa. Though African countries do not feature in the top 20 overall for ease of doing business, they still offer aspects that make attractive startups. For example, countries like Mauritius, Ghana, Rwanda, South Africa, Botswana and Tanzania have made significant improvements in easing the cost of doing business in their countries.

Doing Business Report 2013 ranks Mauritius first on the continent for ease of doing business and ranks South Africa second on the continent. Likewise, Tunisia, Rwanda, Botswana and Ghana all have taken significant steps to provide an enabling environment for private business to thrive and expand. Botswana is amongst the top ten economies improving the most across three or more areas measured by Doing Business in 2011/2012. The same source reports that economies in Middle East and North Africa and Sub Saharan Africa have implemented more than nine institutional and regulatory reforms on average, in comparison to East Asia and the Pacific, Latin America and the Caribbean and South Asia have done about eight whereas Eastern Europe and Central Asia have done 17 such reforms per economy since 2005. Amongst the economies, which have consistently improved the business regulations since 2005 include Rwanda. It is number two improver globally and top improver in Sub Saharan Africa. Doing Business Database 2013 also shows that most

Sub Saharan Africa has weaker legal institutions and more complex and expensive regulatory processes. Thus, the pace of economic reforms and enabling business regulatory practices in Africa is a mixed one in the continent. But there is a momentum towards achieving enabling environment for business and easing the cost of doing business.

Encouraging government policies have led to a noticeable increase in the widespread emergence of entrepreneurial activity in sub-Saharan Africa. The highest average Total Entrepreneurial Activity (TEA is a key indicator of Global Entrepreneurship Monitor. It measures the percentage of adults (aged 18-64) in an economy, who are nascent and new entrepreneurs) rates were analysed in sub-Saharan Africa and Latin America/Caribbean. Zambia (41%) and Ecuador (27%) reported the highest rates in these regions (Xavier, *et al.* 2012). This implies that 41 out of 100 Zambians and 27 out of 100 Ecuadorians are engaged in some kind of entrepreneurial activity. When viewed geographically, non-EU and MENA regions have low rates of both TEA and established business ownership while Sub-Saharan Africa has high rates of both, although TEA rates are much higher—twice as high on average compared with established business ownership (*ibid.*). This indicates that formal business ownership is relatively high for some African countries and even higher than in many other regions of the world. But as far as North Africa is considered, business ownership is low may be because many of these states are rentier states. Thus, in most African countries, there is a confusing situation. On the one hand, there are several constraints hindering the growth of SMEs, at the same time, there is zeal and enthusiasm to improve the environment for the SMEs to flourish.

Access to Finance as a Major Constraint

Most studies highlight that in Africa, the most important constraint in the development, growth and performance of SMEs is the element of finance because their financial systems are still not adequate and lack sufficient development. Even for starting business or for its growth and its planned development, they find it difficult to acquire finance. The conditions set by financial institutions for obtaining finance are complicated and not SME friendly in Africa. These institutions often see SMEs as a risk because of poor guarantees and lack of information about their ability to repay loans. On the supply side, the financial sector tends to be highly oligopolistic and offer accessible finances primarily to large-scale industries. Banks provide finances to large enterprises and the micro-finance institutions focus on micro-enterprises. The requirements of middle-level enterprises remain neglected. Most SMEs in African countries are found in this middle gap between large and small firms. This middle space is known as "the missing middle" by the Africa Commission's Report. It is the credit gap. The crucial issue for most of the African countries is how to fill this finance gap. This gap can be bridged through institutional development and linking different agencies facilitating finances to SMEs. Most managers of SME usually do not prefer shareholding, but go for debt financing, which predominantly consists of bank financing. The banking system in Africa provides mostly short-term credit facilities to enterprises in the form of overdraft facilities. The availability of long term finances for SMEs is difficult. Micro credits are available to only smaller SMEs. In Africa, leasing and factoring as an option for financing are rarely used. Small micro credit banks, co-operatives banks and rural banks are not well established to provide required funds. The other sources of credits like personal loans and money lending are more limited for the SMEs in Africa. Unavailability of funds needed may result in reduced entrepreneurial activity and eventually leading to lowering of innovation and the growth of the economy.

Calice, *et al.* (2012) conducted a survey of SME financing in four East African countries, namely Kenya, Tanzania, Uganda and Zambia and found that according to enterprise-level data collected by the World Bank (various years), SMEs in Sub-Saharan Africa are more financially constrained than in any other developing region. Only 20 per cent of SMEs in Sub-Saharan Africa have a line of credit from a financial institution compared, for example, with 44 per cent in Latin America and Caribbean, and only nine per cent of their investments are funded by banks versus 23 per cent in Eastern Europe and Central Asia. They also noted that not all interviewed banks had gone as far as to set up separate SME departments at the time of the study. But the findings show that all the banks in Kenya and Zambia had separate units managing SMEs, whilst 75 per cent of the banks in Tanzania reported having dedicated SME units. Uganda had the lowest number of banks (25%) with separate units managing SMEs. Only those SME owners, who have a credit history and have significant capital, are preferred by banks. A large majority of banks in the region (88%) consider the lack of adequate information the most important deterrent to their involvement with the SME segment. Thus, the facilities, which are being provided by the banking sector to the SMEs, are limited and not so SME friendly. It has been seen that in rural areas, the network of banking system is not very efficient and is sparse, therefore, access to the financial services becomes very difficult and the transaction cost increases even more. Besides, concentration of banking systems in urban areas results in the neglect of the rural population. Also, in the absence of financial resources, governments of many African countries depend on domestic sources, such as bank credit to finance government budgets, thereby siphoning off huge funds, which otherwise would have been made available to the private sectors. Foreign investors also do not express interest in Africa due to micro economic and political instability, under-developed markets, slow privatization, staggering economic growth, over regulation, lack of liquidity and incoherent credit policies.

The other reasons for the lack of availability of finance in Africa are that most African countries are characterized by weak capital markets, low levels of financial intermediation and low private capital. For these reasons, they cannot effectively provide financial support much needed by the SMEs, as they often lack the scale and collateral. Sometimes, financial markets are unable to function optimally due to weak political and economic policies and lack of supporting networks. Along with this, the legal system is sometimes inadequate or archaic and may not provide adequate confidence to the investors to invest their money in the SMEs. Economic indicators in Africa are also not very healthy for promoting investment in the private sector, especially in SMEs. Allen, *et al.* (2009) observe that in the pre-crisis 2007, the liquid liabilities (scaled by GDP) stood at about 30 per cent for sub-Saharan Africa (SSA), whereas the minimum for the other developing economies was about 4 per cent. When it comes to provision of private credit and financial intermediation, the news is even worse. The average ratio for private credit (scaled by GDP) was only 17 per cent for SSA, whereas the average for the other developing countries ranged from 32-43 per cent.

Access to formal credit is generally oriented towards large scale enterprises and several perceptual barriers and risks are associated with loans to SMEs. This limits SMEs access to credit from formal financial institution. Improvements in the capital market in African countries, Oteh (2010) says are essential because they facilitate the diversification of their economies. He also insists that Africa must strive hard to provide the enabling environment to allow capital markets to grow and become a viable source of finance for all types of businesses.

There are several programs dedicated for facilitating SMEs, but availability of funds is small, segmented and require co-ordination of different agencies. But the fundamental problem in Africa is persistence of fragmentation of the African financial system, as banks are reluctant to link up with informal, semiformal and micro-finance organizations.

Inefficient financial intermediation makes the situation even more formidable. Financial intermediary is a bank that collects deposits and transforms them into bank loans. Flexible regulatory policies can enable fostering of direct and indirect linkages between the formal and informal institutions. It can provide for easier flow of credit right across the system. This integration of financial market can, help fill in the credit gap, which SMEs face. Many new options are emerging to cater for SMEs financial needs. Commercial banks, micro-credit institutions and venture capital investments are coming to the rescue of SMEs. Along with it, governments can also assist SMEs by removing some of the policy and regulatory obstacles. African Development Bank is playing an increasingly crucial role in supporting private sector. Public-Private partnerships are coming up to provide funds to SMEs. Even Algiers stock exchange has made three compartments in the stock exchange and one of them is the market dedicated to the SMEs. Moroccan government and the BVC have taken measures to support SMEs that include tax incentives and 50 per cent exemption on corporate tax.

Role of the African Development Bank

The African Development Bank (AfDB) has been supporting the private sector and markets in regional member African countries. Hussain (2000) notes that initially in the 1970s, the Bank provided mainly indirect support to the African private sector in four major areas. First, the Bank has provided lines of credit and resources to national development banks. Second, through policy-based lending, the Bank Group has encouraged to adopt favourable macro-economic policies. Third, by financing public sector infrastructure projects, the Bank has looked beyond the immediate impact of the projects to the long-term effect of providing basic services required for private sector development. Fourth, the Bank has provided institutional support for private sector development. The United Nations Development Programme (UNDP), the International Finance Corporation (IFC) and the African Development Bank Group (AFDB), with the support of a group of international private companies and a number of multilateral and bilateral donors launched in 1989 the African Training and Management Services (ATMS) Project. The African Development Bank Group reports that the ATMS Project is a unique program for assisting the private sector and particularly SMEs. It seeks to develop sustainable, locally managed companies by providing managers for a period of two to three years. As an integral part of its services, AMSCO (African Management Services Company), its operational arm, designs and executes comprehensive training programs for local managers and staff, so that they can take over the responsibilities of providing managers and sustain the performance of the enterprise at the end of contract. The African Development Bank provided support in the form of a grant to support provision of management service, management development and training activities to SMEs in Africa. Only SMEs are eligible to such grants. The African Development Bank, UNDP, IFC and other donor, co-sponsored the creation of the African Project Development Facility (APDF). APDF primarily facilitates consultative services to African entrepreneurs in establishing SMEs.

Grant to Private Enterprise Partnership (PEP) Africa Initiative

Private Enterprise Partnership for Africa (PEP Africa) was established in 2005 to stimulate private sector growth. PEP Africa is a new initiative led by IFC with the support of the Private Sector and Microfinance Department (OPSM) of the AFDB as a regional sponsor and the involvement of many other donors aiming at supporting private sector and SMEs development in sub-Saharan Africa, in an integrated manner. The three main objectives of PEP Africa are to enhance the enabling business environment, to strengthen the growth and competitiveness of SMEs, and to stimulate private sector investments. It will assist particular countries to improve their business environment while supporting enterprise development by building capacity of Business Development Service Providers and Financial Institutions. PEP Africa will constitute one of the Bank's implementation arms of direct assistance to SMEs to better respond to the needs of the private sector in Africa and in a more cost-effective way (African Development Bank Group).

The AfDB's President Donald Kaberuka, officially announced the launch of the African Guarantee Fund (AGF) on 1 June 2012. It is a market-friendly guarantee scheme intended to provide finance to SMEs in Africa. The AGF, designed and funded by the AfDB in partnership with the governments of Denmark and Spain, will provide financial guarantees to financial institutions to stimulate financing to SMEs and unlock their potential to deliver inclusive growth in the region (AfDB supports access to finance for African SMEs with the official launch of the Africa Guarantee Fund). The AGF will be a public-private partnership, and with other investors will provide more funds so as to scale up the operations. Very few of the African SMEs have a line of credit from a financial institution. This limitation of the SMEs will be addressed by the AGF. These funds have been in the form of credit-guarantee schemes and direct-credit funds through government-owned institutions. In particular, the provision of guarantees complemented by development of bank's capacity to engage in SME lending seems to be one of the most effective policy instruments for easing access to credit for SMEs (Small and medium enterprises as drivers of productive capacity and job creation in Africa, 2012). The AGF will be a permanent regional conduit for channeling guarantees and technical assistance to financial institutions in Africa with the objective of generating enhanced growth in the SME sector, hereby creating increased employment opportunities in the economy, particularly for youth (*ibid.*). The AGF will operate as a non-bank financial institution. If the legal and regulatory environment are reformed, it will help SMEs to get more support from AfDB. The AGF will provide support to African SMEs with a valid operating license regardless of sector, industry, location, and ownership. AGF activities will be accomplished in nine to fourteen countries in Africa within the first two years, but by the end of 2016 the whole continent will be covered.

SMEs and Stock Markets

In order to develop SMEs and to increase the options to finance SMEs, capital markets can play a very crucial role, especially in the initial phase, when it can significantly reduce the growth time. Oteh (2010) believes that capital markets are an important source of long term finance and a financial system that is built on the two pillars of banking and securities markets is stronger than a system that is built solely on banking credit since a well-functioning system would be comprised of various sources of finance. Therefore, capital markets should be actively promoted as an important alternative source of finance for SMEs, particularly long term finance through equity financing. Equity and debt financing can be made available as well as venture capital funds. He explains that equity financing is a strategy for obtaining capital that involves selling a partial interest in the company to investors. The equity, or ownership position, that investors receive in exchange for their funds usually takes the form of stock in the company. This provides small business owners with a broader scope in terms of financing as they gain access to multiple funding sources. In contrast to debt financing, which includes loans and other forms of credit, equity financing does not involve a direct obligation to repay the funds. Instead, equity investors become part-owners and partners in the business, and, thus, are able to exercise some degree of control over how it is run. Oteh (2010) provides one solution to the problems SMEs face when attempting to tap into the capital markets and that is the creation of exclusive stock exchanges for SMEs. There are many SMEs, which are excluded from the listed category in spite of having a good track record of growth because they do not meet the listing criteria. He insists that a SME-focused stock exchange is likely to boost the confidence of SMEs planning to tap the capital market to raise low cost capital. Some examples of SME dedicated stock exchanges include AltX, Africa's first alternative exchange for SMEs, a partnership between the Johannesburg Stock Exchange Ltd. (JSE) and the Department of Trade and Industry.

Stock markets in Africa are not very old and most were established only around 1990s. UNDP (2003) notes that there are more than 20 active stock markets in the African continent. Except for South Africa, most of these markets are characterized by low capitalization and low liquidity. Economic Commission for Africa (2012), in its report, mentions that many entrepreneurs, be it small or large companies, are not keen to list on the stock exchanges in Africa as a vehicle for raising capital. In most of these small markets, the growth in the number of firms listed has mainly emerged from the privatization of state enterprises and not the transformation of private firms to public-listed firms. Often SMEs are operated as sole proprietor, a governance structure that is not compatible with participation in the stock markets. The Report also notes that three countries in Africa have established alternative stock markets or boards with less restrictive listing requirements and rules to provide opportunities for SMEs to raise long-term capital. These alternative stock exchanges exist on the JSE as an alternative board, Alternative Stock Exchange (AltX) as noted above, the SEM as the Development and Enterprise Market (DEM) and the Egyptian Stock Exchange as the Nile Stock Exchange. The differences with the main boards are in terms of minimum-capital requirements, proportion of shares in public hands, historical published financial statements (at least a year) and the listing fees. The report also mentions that the AltX on the JSE serves as an incubator for the main board and focuses on small and medium sized growth companies eligible for listing if they appoint and retain the services of a registered designated advisor and satisfy directors' education requirements. Oteh (2010) says that AltX allows smaller companies to float shares with a more flexible regulatory system as compared to the main market. It shows how the requirements for the AltX market have been relaxed to cater to SMEs. The number of companies listed on alternative exchanges in Africa, similar to the main boards, is small relative to the population of SMEs.

Algiers stock market has introduced new measures to improve small and medium enterprises' access to the Algerian financial market as reported in 'Algiers Stock Exchange Improves SMEs' Access to Financial Markets'. The move is expected to help SMEs find new sources for funding, which will stimulate their development and country's economic growth. Following the recommendations of the committee for capital markets reform, the institution has decided to reorganize the domestic stock market by creating three compartments, including a main market for large companies, a market dedicated to SMEs and a third one for the trading of Treasury bonds. The listing requirements at the Algiers Stock Exchange are now less rigid for SMEs. The SME dedicated stock exchange will provide SMEs another avenue to generate finances only if the entry requirements are relaxed and enabling. But the situation here is not very encouraging as despite the opening of SME dedicated stock exchanges, the number of companies listed are small conveying either the stock market finances are of limited service or SMEs are unable to satisfy even the relaxed eligibility requirements for procuring finance from stock markets.

SMEs and Venture Capital Funds

Venture capital can be an alternative valuable source of non-banking financing for SMEs. This finance is available in addition to credit provided by commercial banks. It is quite widespread in developed countries for small or medium firms. Memba, *et al.* (2012) say that venture capitalists are organized providers of financing for winning, but risky business proposals by small and medium firms that have a promising but as yet unproven idea. Venture capitalists provide investment finance to SMEs in the form of equity or quasi equity instruments and, therefore, finance is available at a lower rate and without the requirement of collateral. These may not be traded on a recognized stock exchange. Memba, *et al.* (2012) insist that if the venture capitalists are convinced that a business idea is promising, they will take an ownership stake in the business and provide the needed fund, while sharing the risk. It is expected that many of the country's small businesses whose growth has been constrained by shortage of capital or increased cost of borrowing will have another source of finance. Also venture capitalists do not just provide funds but add value to SMEs, that is, they are not only involved in financing but also spur entrepreneurs, who are responsible for economic growth. Venture capitalists provide long term financing and will engage themselves in the firms to make their investment successful. Venture capitalists get the returns either by the sale of equity in the firms or as income from dividends of the investments they have made or from the capital gains as the value of stock rises. Being provider of the finance, venture capitalists investment in SME enables wealth creation and facilitates smooth flow of finance during all the phases of SME development. Venture capital has been seen as one of the best vehicle to realize growth of SME and its positive effect can be seen on the growth of sales, profit generation, increased assets and improvement in value addition and in management of finance and other resources. Venture capital not only assists SMEs in the provision of funds, but also in the internal operations of the business, especially in policy formulation and management. Thus, they reduce information asymmetries that help to improve the status and track record of SMEs along with providing managerial skills, the absence of which can significantly constrain the development of SMEs.

Integration of SMEs into Local and External Value Chains

Increased globalization has made value chains become 'global', when their component activities are geographically dispersed across borders to multiple country locations. Herr (2007) says that a value chain is a sequence of target-oriented production factors, which combine to create a marketable product or service—from conception stage through to the final consumption. This includes activities such as design, production, marketing, distribution and support services to the final consumer. The activities that comprise a value chain can be contained within a single firm or divided among different firms, as well as within a single geographical location or spread over wider areas. He says that the term value chain refers to the fact that value is added to preliminary products through the combination with other resources (for example tools, manpower, knowledge and skills, other raw materials or preliminary products). As the product passes through several stages of the value chain, the value of the product increases. Globalization of value chains has posed additional challenge to the SMEs in Africa as goods and services are fragmented beyond countries and regional boundaries. Since the local SMEs are used to servicing local and national markets, the standards and qualities required prior to integrating to the global value chains were often inadequate and sub-standard. This may be due to lack of necessary management, technology, knowledge, skill and financing and hence they were unable to compete effectively in global markets. Thus, integration into a value chain either enhances the standards expected and accepted internationally or those unable to compete are stifled out. By adopting global requirements and standards, SMEs could achieve competitiveness and growth and sustainability.

Strategies to Strengthen SMEs

SMEs can get support from business organizations like Chambers of Commerce. In South Africa, the Zululand Chamber of Commerce has facilitated linkages between Trans National Corporations (TNC) and small entrepreneur and established a system of accreditation that assures TNCs of accredited organization's capabilities. This can enable small companies to become competent enough to establish themselves in regional and global markets. It has been seen that forging networks and forming clusters contribute to business competency and continuity. SMEs should be organized in such a way that they can innovate, compete, sustain and grow. Ramachandran and Shah (1999) found that African entrepreneurs are short of joint action and networking because of which they lack the necessary knowledge and information on markets, capital and resources. Networks, clusters and other such organizations provide not only the required information, but promote innovation and transfer of technology and skills. Thus, networks and clusters can enable new entrants to enter as entrepreneurship as it lowers information costs and lowers risks in the new venture.

Networks

Networks, according to Hussain (2000), is a collection of firms working in cooperation, though not necessarily in the same place. It includes interaction across a supply chain without the necessity of having either formal links or equity participation. The main characteristic of a network is that it does not require geographical proximity to be efficient: it can link firms whose activities are distributed around the world. Lechner and Dowling (2000) found that network relationships are an important intangible resource supporting SMEs lacking sufficient finance as it assists SMEs to develop the links with suppliers, distributors and customers, or utilization of social contacts, including acquaintances, friends, family and kin. Klerk and Havenga (2004) found that networks in Africa focus on entrepreneurial networks and social capital. Innovation networks fulfill the function of improving firm performance by allowing information about the world to flow between members, whilst a second type, called solidarity networks, are designed to reduce uncertainty. The latter type of network dominates in Africa due to the fact that the uncertainty faced by African entrepreneurs is paramount.

Clusters

Clustering is a modern concept and this notion has been developed by Michael Porter of Harvard Business School in 1990s. It involves developing the backward and forward linkages across supply chain of a business in a geographic area to increase their overall competitiveness. Porter argued that competitive advantage lies outside a given company and possibly outside its industry. Hence, it is the region instead of nations that are the major competing forces in world markets. The main slogan behind this nature of competition is "think global, act local". Clustered firms have access to bankers, trusted consultants and business centres. The geographic boundaries of clusters are set by distances till where employees are willing to travel to work. United Nation's report on Small Scale Enterprise Development and Foreign Direct Investment (FDI) in Africa notes that clusters provide small scale enterprises the opportunity to take advantage of FDI and global value chains by being able to position themselves to access capital, technology and markets. By doing so, they strengthen their comparative advantages in a sustainable manner and become attractive sites for FDI. Clusters are defined by the combination of two characteristics: sectoral specialization and geographical location. Clustering help SMEs to grow and upgrade more easily. SMEs can even enter global markets if a high degree of interfirm specialisation and their geographical proximity to complimentary businesses can compensate for the disadvantage of lacking scale (Attenburg and Meyer-Stamer 1999). Clustering enables SMEs to improve efficiency through collaboration and team work. Clusters have been identified as important for African entrepreneurs, but are not common in Africa. The interdependence between SMEs and clusters may become potential source of finance. Apart from South Africa, Kenya, Nigeria and Zimbabwe, clusters formed in this way are not common in most African regions. African countries can organize individual enterprises into cluster for collective efficiency, economic gains and for attracting suppliers and buyers.

Alliances

According to Hussain (2000), an alliance is formed by firms coming together in some contractual arrangement. He mentioned several types of contractual arrangements that include subcontracting, licensing, joint venture, strategic alliance and consortium. Sub-contracting involves buying supplies from another firm and working closely on detailed specifications for a complex product. Licensing includes permission to manufacture a product under license, to distribute a product and to include product in another design. Joint-venture involves the creation of a third firm to manufacture or market a product, which had been developed by the entrepreneurial firm. Equity was usually shared by the partners. Strategic alliance is essentially a joint-venture without the creation of a third firm and no equity is involved. Consortium is usually a group of firms joining together in a buying group to purchase components or equipment, which they mutually share. Hussain goes on to say that alliances between large companies and SMEs usually take the form of vertical linkages where inter-firm relationships are forged along the lines of the production and marketing chain within a specific industry. It essentially represents the contractual relationships between a parent firm and its ancillaries. The parent firm depends on its specialized ancillaries for the timely delivery of high quality components and services, while the ancillaries owe their livelihood to regular sub-contracting from the parent firm. In order to ensure the quality of the goods and services it receives, it is sometimes necessary for the parent firm to extend financial, operational and managerial assistance to the ancillaries. He further says for their part, the ancillary firms strive to achieve quality-assurance and maintain a technological edge in order to remain within the sub-contracting chain. It is not uncommon for contractors to become fully independent, specialist entities in this process. This form of networking is most prevalent in manufacturing concerns requiring a wide range of processed, and standardized inputs. These forms of alliances allow for value addition, which most African countries need to diversify their economies. Since individual enterprises are too small to meet the exigencies and global competition challenges, alliances can address the problems such as access to market or procuring finance.

Franchising

African Development Bank Report notes that franchising is widely recognized as one of the most successful ways of doing and strengthening business. In both developed countries and emerging markets, franchising has been effective in ensuring business growth with private ownership and skills transfer. More specifically, for new business/start-ups and SMEs, franchising can be viewed as a means of nurturing and developing the entrepreneurial talent, promoting good corporate governance and transparency, and attracting the informal sector business to the formal sector, through certain contractual terms are used in franchise agreements. To reduce the risk of failure, international and popular local brands permit the franchisee to use its brand name, technical know-how and strategies.

Conclusion

SMEs have been contributing significantly in the growth of African economies and creation of substantial employment. Despite these benefits, SMEs failure rate is high. There are several factors that dampen the growth of SMEs and make them non-competitive and under-performing. The most crucial constraints that SMEs face is financial constraint. Large business have banks supporting them, micro-institutions have micro-credit at their disposal, but SMEs do not have any institution dedicated to finance them. Most SME owners generate their own resources informally from their own savings or by taking loans from their associations. Access to formal capital is very low due to inadequate and under-developed financial institutions in Africa. Also, deficiencies in SME setups discourage financial institutions to provide finance to SMEs. The biggest disadvantageous factor is lack of confidence in the success of SMEs due to its well prevalent failure rate. This problem, which is endemic to SMEs in most African countries, can be addressed by replicating the East Asian experience. This requires establishing networks and clusters, which are very active in East Asia. Besides, African SMEs can look for other options of generating finance like access to venture capital, by listing on stock exchange and also from other sources like, IFI and AfDB.

African Development Bank is providing much of the required support to SMEs by provisioning management services, management development and training to SMEs through AMSCO. It enables SMEs to be able to sustain the performance even after the support of the Bank is withdrawn. APDF provides consultative services to African enterprises to establish SMEs. PEP Africa is AFDB's implementation arm of direct assistance to SMEs. It helps SMEs to strengthen its competitiveness, enhance the enabling business environment and stimulate private sector investment. The AGF is one such PPP that provides more funds to enable escalation of the operations of SMEs. The AGF operates as a non-banking financial institution with a policy of easing access to credit for SMEs by providing funds in the form of credit–guarantee schemes and direct credit funds through government-owned institutions. Capital markets are actively providing an alternative source of financing to SMEs through equity finance. Equity financing is a long term finance and in return for their investment, the investors usually get ownership of stock of the company. Some countries have established alternative stock exchange or boards with less restrictive listing requirements for SMEs to raise long term finance. These stock exchanges allow smaller companies to float their shares. Finance is available at lower rate and without the requirements of the collaterals. Another source of finance for SMEs is venture capital. Venture capitalists do not just provide finance to promising business ideas, but also engage themselves in the firms by taking an ownership stake in it and involvement in policy formulation and management. Venture capital enables wealth creation. It has been seen that venture capital is one of the best vehicles to realize growth of SMEs. Integration of SMEs into the international value chain inspires innovation and promotes competitiveness and also SMEs are forced to adopt the international standards of their industry.

These agencies invest in SMEs on flexible terms and conditions. The investors, by participating in the management of business, help reduce the risk and enable upgrading of the product quality. They also ensure to reduce the informational asymmetries that boost the confidence of the creditors. By taking adequate measures to access new markets and engage in international networks and enter into e-commerce options, they can out-perform their markets. Other strategies that could strengthen the SME sector are by organizing into cluster, entering into alliances and franchising. This would reduce the risk of failure by comparatively easy availability of funds, information and skill transfer. At the same time, underscoring the importance of playing an active role in domestic and regional markets, they can become potential drivers of economic growth of their countries.

REFERENCES

Abor, J. and Quartey, J. (2010). Issues in SME Development in Ghana and South Africa. *International Research Journal of Finance and Economics.* Issue 39. *http://www.eurojournals.com/finance.htm.* Accessed on 14/11.2012

Activities: African Development Bank Group
http://www.afdb.org/en/topics-and-sectors/sectors/private-sector-development/activities/. Accessed on 21/3/2013.

AfDB supports access to finance for African SMEs with the official launch of the Africa Guarantee Fund. *http://www.afdb.org/en/news-and-events/article/afdb-supports-access-to-finance-for-african-smes-with-the-official-launch-of-the-african-guarantee-fund-9362/.* Accessed on 15/11/2012.

African Development Bank. (2012). Bridging the Missing Middle Gap in Africa: Role and Activities of the AfDB and Its Partners. *Expert Group Meeting on Financing Small and Medium Scale Industries in Africa,* 26-28 June 2012. Lusaka: United Nations Economic Commission for Africa.

Allen, F.; Otchere, I. and Senbet, L.W. (2010). African Financial Systems: A Review. *http://fic.wharton.upenn.edu/fic/papers/10/10-11.pdf.* Accessed 1/4/2013.

Attenburgy and Meyer-Stamer. (1999). How to promote clusters; Policy experience from Latin America. *World Development*, Vol. 27(9).

Ayyagari, M., Beck, T. and Demirgüç-Kunt, A. (2007). Small and Medium Enterprises across the Globe. *Small Business Economics*, Vol. 29. 415–434.

Bachama, Y. N. (2010). Economics of Small Scale Industries: A look at Programmes for the Growth and Development of Small Scale Industries in Nigeria. ICBI. Accessed on 14/11.2012 from http://www.kln.ac.lk/uokr/ICBI2010/4.pdf

Calice, P., Chando, V. M. and Sekioua, S. (2012). Bank Financing to Small and Medium Enterprises in East Africa: Findings of a Survey in Kenya, Tanzania, Uganda and Zambia. African Development Bank. Working Paper No. 146.

Doing Business Report: Smarter Regulations for Small and Medium-size Enterprises. 10th edition. The World Bank and the International Finance Corporation. *http://www.doingbusiness.org/~/media/GIAWB/Doing%20Business/Documents/Annual-Reports/English/DB13-full-report.pdf.* Accessed on 15/3/2013.

Financing Small- and Medium-Scale Industries in Africa. (2012). United Nation Economic Commission for Africa. ECA/EDND/17/12. Accessed on 5/2/2013.

Herr, M. L. (2007). *An Operational Guide to Local Value Chain Development*. ILO. Accessed on 5/5/2013.

Hussain, N. (2000). Linkages between SMEs and Large Industries for Increased Markets and Trade for SMEs: An African Perspective. *http://www.afdb.org/fileadmin/uploads/afdb/Documents/Publications/00157642-FR-ERP-54.PDF*. Accessed on 22/3/2013.

Klerk, G. D. and Havenga, J. J. D. (2004). SME Networks and Clusters and Their Impact on Economic Growth: An Exploratory Overview of Africa. *http://www1.kmu.unisg.ch/rencontres/RENC2004/Topics/DeKlerk_Havenga_Renc_04_Topic_C.pdf.* Accessed on 15/3/2013.

Lechner, C., and Dowling, M. (2000). The evolution of industrial districts and regional networks: The case of the biotechnology region Munich/Martinsried. *Journal of Management and governance.* Special issue. Vol. 99(3): pp 309-338.

Liedholm, C. and Mead, D. (1999). *Small Enterprises and Economic Development: The Dynamic Role of Micro and Small Enterprises*. London: Routledge.

Literature Review on Small and Medium Enterprises' Access to Credit and Support in South Africa. (2011). National Credit Regulator. Accessed on 10/3/2013.

Memba, S. F., Gakure W. R. and Karanja, K. (2012). Venture Capital (VC): Its Impact on Growth of Small and Medium Enterprises in Kenya. *International Journal of Business and Social Science*, Vol. 3(6).

Merchant, S. (2012). Africa: Investing in African SMEs – A New Approach to Private Equity. *http://allafrica.com/stories/201211061411.html*. Accessed on 25/2/2013.

Ojowo, O. (1989): Industrial Policy for Economic Development. A Review of the 1988 Industrial Policy of Nigeria as it Affects Small Scale Industrial Development. *National Workshop on Small Scale Industries.* University of Jos.

Osotimehin, K. O., Jegede, C., Akinlabi, B. H., and Olajide, O. T. (2012). An Evaluation of the Challenges and Prospects of Micro and Small Scale Enterprises Development in Nigeria. *American International Journal of Contemporary Research.* Vol. 2(4).

Oteh, A. (2010). Making Capital Markets Work for SMEs in Africa. Accessed on 30/3/2013 from *http://www.proshareng.com/reports/2620*.

Radelet, S. (2010). *Emerging Africa: How 17 Countries are Leading the Way.* Washington, DC: Center for Global Development.

Roxburg, C. (2010). *Lions on the move: The progress and potential of African economies*. McKinsey Global Institute. McKinsey and Company.

Ramachandran, V. (2010). Lions, Cheetahs and More: The Potential for Doing Business in Africa. *http://www.huffingtonpost.com/vijaya-ramachandran/lions-cheetahs-and-more-t_b_624781.html* June 25th. Accessed on 2/4/2013.

Ramachandran, V. and Shah, M. J. (1999). Minority entrepreneurs and private sector growth in Sub-Saharan Africa. Discussion paper. RFED. 086. The World Bank. Washington.

Small and Medium Enterprises (SMEs) as Drivers of Productive Capacity and Job Creation in Africa. Background Note Prepared by Consultant: Ousmane Diallo. Regional Preparatory meeting for Africa. 25 March 2012. Addis Ababa. Accessed on 22/3/2013 from *http://www.un.org/en/ecoso/newfunct/pdf/background* note on sme development 2012 pdf.

SME Africa (2012). *http://www.fleminggulf.com/conferenceview/SME-Africa-2012/315*. Accessed on 2/4/2013.

Tadesse, A. (2009). Perspective on SME Finance in Africa. *Private Sector and Development.* Issue 1. May.

United Ntions Development Programme. (2003). African Stock Markets Handbook. New York.

United Nations Economic Commission for Africa. (2005). Annual Report 2005. Addis Ababa, Ethiopia.

United Nation's report on Small Scale Enterprise Development and Foreign Direct Investment in Africa: Challenges and Opportunities. (2009). Accessed on 14/11/2012 from *http://www.un.org/africa/osaa/reports/FDI_study_2008_2.pdf*

Uzor, O. O. (2004). Small and Medium Scale Enterprises Cluster Development in South-Eastern Region of Nigeria. Institute for World Economics and International Management. pp. 5-15.

Xavier, S. R., Kelly, D., Kew, J., Herrington, M. and Vorderwulbecke, A. (2012). Global Entrepreneurship Monitor. 2012 Global Report.

World bank (2006). Making Finance Work for Africa. World Bank.

Part III

Society and Culture

9

Modernizing Process of Religious Identities in African Societies

A.S. Yaruingam

Religion has been an integral part of African societies since times immemorial. Religion permeates all parts of individual and social life so much so that it is not possible for an African to exist without religion in African traditional societies. To believe in a supernatural power/god is not a choice, but an inborn inherent part of the Africans. An African is born in a religious social milieu, grows up in it, works in it and dies in it. Hence, it is completely impossible to isolate religion from other aspects of social life. Being such the place of religion in African society, religion exerts probably the greatest influence upon the thinking and living of the people (Mbiti, 1969). While Africans have changed over time to adopt and adapt other religious and secular practices, African Traditional Religious (ATR) beliefs continue to affect the way people think and act, even though they may not profess them.

Despite the onslaught of modern rational thoughts and ideas, Africans' penchant for religion has not changed; rather people seem to have become more religious that manifests in different forms of religious activities. It is in this context that Eunice (2006) writes, "Today African may not be professing that they belong to the African Traditional Religions, as it was practiced in the 19th century, but the dynamic characteristic is common in all religions." Similar ideas are expressed when Awolalu (1997), who is a specialist in African Traditional religion, writes, "Though the nomenclature of the religion is being changed, African Traditional Religious belief is being practiced in various forms and various shades and intensities by a very large number of Africans, including individuals, who claim to be Muslims or Christians." Thus, though apparently many Africans have abandoned their old traditional religion, they have not truly given up their core of belief; rather they practice it in a new forms under the shade of Christianity and Islam. Today, the two most popular religions of the world—Christianity and Islam—have emerged as the most convenient religious thoughts through which Africans could find shelter in their search for new religious identity in the fast changing modern world and also express their religious identities.

This chapter is an attempt to explore and analyze the process of changing religious identities of Africans in the twenty first century. The chapter critically looks into the nature and ways in which Africans project their religious identities under the shade of different Christian denominations, keeping the core philosophical belief of traditional religious beliefs unchanged. The chapter would mainly focus on Christianity, which is generally known as a western religion, though this is not correct in true sense of the term. This paper would further examine and analyze the basic principles of different Christian denominational beliefs which the former find convenient to take shelter and identify themselves with. In other words, the paper is an attempt to examine the Africans struggle to indigenize western religion, Christianity, retaining the core belief of the traditional religion and parts of their cultural practices, while espousing to different Christian denominations as external identities which fit them into the post-modern social and cultural environment. In this context, it is realized that Pentecostal Church of Christian denomination is the most suited denomination that could meet the requirement of common Africans to attain their aspired intention. As a result, thousands of youths are being attracted to the national and international crusades and conventions organized by the group (Pentecostal Church) across the continent. One of the most plausible theories for this is the underlining similar nature of beliefs—in the power of the Supreme Being (God)—between the African Traditional Religion and Pentecostal sect of Christianity.

It is argued that though Africans have changed their external religious identity, there has not been real change in their core philosophical belief. Africans still hold the view that the primary purpose of religion is to draw power that would enable them to manipulate the surrounding physical environment for the well-being of their existence. Thus, in traditional societies, religion is taken as a means through which powers are drawn from the supreme Being (God) for managing life peacefully. However, the changing social, cultural and political environment of the human society has necessitated them to find new religions and methods of deriving the same power. Thus, it may be reasonable to believe that their change of external religious identity is a kind of method to synchronize their religion with the modern social and cultural environment while retaining their core traditional belief. It is also further argued that globalization, coupled with boom in information and telecommunication technology and services has buttressed this process. The term 'modernization' in this chapter is being used in the sense of African's adaptation to Christianity as their new religious identity. Therefore, modernization would simply mean 'Christianity' and its various denominations.

The onset of globalization coupled with booming industries in the information technology sector, have made the world smaller. The connectivity and interactions among various people and region have become easier and quicker. Through the means of electronic media, such as television network, radio, Internet and mobile, etc. every kind of information spreads fast and reaches every destination within a fraction of second. People in the remotest villages can see the things going on in far and distant cities or towns through television channels sitting in their bedrooms. Such opportunities brought by the modern technologies have facilitated for many Africans, who live in the far flung rural settings, access to the emotionally charged religious messages from Tehran by the Imam or Christian gospel messages from Europe by the Pentecostal preachers such as Rev. Pastor Benny Hinn through the television network. Moreover, within the continent itself, many regional Church organizations pull their resources together and organize mega events of preaching messages through television that would reach millions of people. For example, the 'Gospel Flames' is an event that is being organized by the Christians of East Africa and its message reaches millions of people spread out in the region (*www.hopetv./about/*news). Such new environment has brought a complete turn in the way the religious messages are being fed to the people and, thus, provide better opportunity for Africans to embrace this new found religion.

African Traditional Religion

What is African Traditional Religion? The Traditional African Religions are popularly known by the acronym ATR. Generally, Traditional African Religion means the religion that was being practiced by the indigenous Africans since times immemorial. These traditions are not religious principles, but a cultural identity that is passed on through stories, myths and tales. African religious traditions relied primarily on oral traditions handed down from teacher to student, from father to son, and mother to daughter (Baum, 2009).

Awolalu (1997) defines African Traditional Religion as, "the indigenous religious beliefs and practices of the Africans. It is the religion, which resulted from the sustaining faith held by the forebearers of the present Africans and, which is being practiced today in various forms and shades and intensities by a very large number of Africans." He further wrote that the word 'traditional' means "indigenous, that which is aboriginal or foundational, handed down from generation to generation, upheld and practiced by Africans today". So, this indigenous religion is a heritage from the past, treated not as a thing of the past, but as that which connects the past with the present and the present with eternity. Hence African Traditional Religion is the heritage from the past which connects with present and the future.

Alfredsson and Linha (1998) wrote that each African society has its own religious system, deeply connected to the roots and traditions of that society. Quoting from Mbiti, he wrote, "In African society, a person has to be born into the society in order to assimilate into the religious system and to detach oneself from the religion of one's group would mean to detach oneself from one's roots, foundation, context of security, kinship and the entire group." According to Richard (2001), "African religion is not a separate set of doctrine and practices as in the West adhered by certain group of people, who have interest in it, rather religion is a 'part of the whole of life'." For Africa, religion is a way of life and is part of all of life experience. Richard in his study of ATR in the light of Christianity said that "religion centered on man is the basic distinguishing mark of African traditional religion from Western religion, 'Christianity'". To Africans, the whole purpose of religion is to gain power to manage human life well. Thus, ATR centers on man and his whole lot of interest in life, (*Ibid.* 29). He quoted the technical term used by John Mbiti, 'anthropocentric', when he talked about this aspect of African religion. To an African, God is the explanation of man's origin and sustenance; God exists for the sake of man. This view of African religion is different from the Western religion, Christianity, in particular where God is the center of religion and man exists for God.

Eunice (2006), in his case study of the religious movement in Kenya, finds that traditional African religions are widely practiced all over Kenya in real sense. In fact, most Christian denominations have combined aspects of Christianity and traditional religious beliefs. Those, which overtly acknowledge this move, are referred to as African indigenous Churches.

According to her, while it is difficult to enumerate the number of adherents to the Traditional African religions, it is accurate to observe that most Kenyans, who profess other religions, are significantly influenced by African Traditional Religions.

Further, she viewed that traditional societies/nations in Africa were characterized by a theo-centric worldview founded on the acknowledgement of God as the ultimate designer, creator, sustainer with purpose and destiny of everything in the created order. She seems to suggest that God is the creator and man is the creature. In this sense, God is the center of religion. If this is true, her views seem to be a departure from Richard (2001), who believed that man is the center in Traditional African Religion. God exists for man to draw necessary power to manage the present life.

Eunice argued that the African worldview was also 'anthropocentric' in that the human person was recognized as the center of creation and he is the steward under whom the Supreme Being (God) entrusted the responsibility of managing the creation. There was cultural and religious homogeneity within each autonomous State in traditional African societies with clear socio-political governance, educational, health, ethical and recreational structures. Besides, the general principles or worldview, each of these structures had clear guiding principles and objectives with a lot of emphasis on human rights for every individual person, but in the context of community. In Traditional African Religion, she argued, human life is considered to be of the highest value and healthy relationship between humans and God, among humans and between humans and the rest of creation was considered the goal of life that needed to be adhered to. From this, it follows that relationship is an important element in African Traditional Religion. According to African spirituality, the ultimate purpose of life was relationships; relationships between the Creator and created, and among the created. As the designer, author, purpose and destiny of the created, the Creator determines relationships between the Creator and created and among the created. For the traditional Africans, the will of God was expressed in nature and was very easily understood by humans who saught to understand it in humility and truth. Unhealthy relationships were easily identified as they lead to anti life situations. As a writer wrote, "…unlike many western religions, the focus is on maintaining relationship within this world and not on obtaining salvation. African religions focus heavily on the presence of spirits, magic, and invisible forces that govern everyday life. Therefore, much of the focus is on renewing community bonds and healing broken social relationships.

This emphasis on the current world and social relationships leads to conflict when problems arise" (Timmins, 2009).

According to African's traditional beliefs, the ultimate destiny of life is God, who ensures perpetuation of life through healthy relationships from one generation to another through birth and rebirths. God maintains the cycle of life as human persons and all other creations transit from one stage in life to another; from pre-birth to birth to rebirth through death. All creation is designed to work together in unity and rhythm: when healthy relationships flourish among all creations, life is promoted for all creations and all creations rejoice together, but when there are unhealthy relationships, life is threatened and all creations suffer together. Life was, therefore, understood as unitary whole where individual elements of creation were understood as part of the whole creation, as they are all interdependent. A systematic process of formulating and passing on this education existed basically in the form of rites of passage from pre-birth to ancestor hood.

African Traditional Religion also centers round the power. Religion is a means through which the supernatural powers are being drawn and used for life purposes as Cyril (1987:6) puts it in his study of the Igbo religion, "the Igbo seeks power that emanates from the religious form." This power is not for the sake of power, but an over ridding concern for spiritual power from a mighty God to overcome all enemies and evils that threatened human life and vitality.

Traditionally, Africans believed that there is a Supreme Being (God) through whom all things emanated and he is the main source of power. Robert Baum (2009) wrote, "…I would suggest that in every case in which I am familiar, African religions have at their center, a concept of a supreme being, who is seen as eternal and the source of all power in the universe." By virtue of it, this Supreme God is the owner of all the things that exist. Some tribes believe that this God dwells in a place far from the human as Baum further wrote, "Many have suggested that the supreme being is relatively remote and inactive, what has often been called a *deus otiotus*, the source of all life power, but relatively inaccessible to ritual supplication." Africans believe that this power originated from the supreme power and circulates around the universe and world. Because of this, they used the term, 'High God', for this supreme God. These people believe that the Supreme God lives in a high distant place and is not accessible or visible to men. As Mbiti (1969) wrote, for most of their life, many African people place God in a transcendental plane (high, distant, lifted up) making him seem remote. These people believe that he, the

High God, entrusted the work of managing his creation to the lesser gods (Gehman, 2001).

Gikuyu, one of the major tribes in Kenya believe that this High God, who dwells in far and unreachable, visits his creation time to time and brings blessings. Apart from his visit, he is also being called upon by the family, when they have to go through the event of rites of initiations, such as birth, marriage, death, etc. (Bloom and Ottong, 1987). Among the Igbo of Nigeria, the High God is know by the name *Osanobua.* They believe that *Osanobua* created the world. He dwells in the highest place, is above all and his interaction with men is occasional. He is the source of all things, but he does not deal with them directly. He keeps in touch with his creation through lesser gods. He involves himself in human affairs only during important events, such as birth, death, harvesting, rain, etc. In most African religions, there are also lesser deities or lesser spirits.

Among the Yoruba of Nigeria, Benin, and Togo, they are known as *orisha* and there are 401 of them; many of whom were, at one time or another, incarnates among human beings. They have rich theographies or bodies of myth, which describe their different powers and their interactions with other gods and humans. These spirits are not described in very specific personal terms, but more in terms of their specific functions. The lesser spirits or lesser gods control many aspects of daily life. Among the Yoruba, there are *orishas* associated with women's fertility, the fertility of the land, kingship, various forces of nature, iron and war (recently expanded to include chauffeurs, factory workers, etc.) and disease. Among the Diola, lesser spirits known as *ukine*, govern many aspects of life from male and female initiation and fertility, to rain rituals, blacksmithing, and even the decisions of the Town Council as they set wages, prices, and collective labor obligations (Baum, 2009).

Like the Gikuyu, Ibos also believe that the High God entrusted the work of managing the daily affairs of his creation to the lesser gods. According to Ibo's tradition and beliefs, the lesser gods have different names according to their functions and each god performed their duties dealing with the day-to-day affairs of human beings. In some traditions, these lesser spirits make their presence known to the people through possession. This possessed person speaks and moves in the manner of spirit and communicates its desires to an assembled congregation.

The ancestor spirit is another important feature of traditional African religion. Bomki (2008) wrote, "Although dead, an ancestor is believed to enjoy a sacred super human status with special magico-religious powers that can be beneficial or even harmful to the earthly kins. Due to his nearness to the Supreme Being, an ancestor is believed to possess the ability or power to exist everywhere, even though they have *loci* of preference, like shrines or sanctuaries, particular trees, tombs, and large bodies of water.... There are some sacred places where sacrifices are offered...where living persons communicate with the ancestral world through sacrifices and incantations." Africans believe that the spirits of ancestors never die; it oversees the living and interferes in their day to day work of life. If he is not being treated well and pleased, he causes/ harm to the people. In other words, Africans attribute most of the misfortune occurring in the family to the ancestor's spirit. They believe that the family has not been able to please the ancestor's spirit and he is displeased. As a result, he is showing his displeasure to the family and, thus, causes misfortune to them. They have to obligate him through proper propitiation in order to avoid any misfortune to happen in their lives. Failing to please the ancestral spirit would cause great harm to the family and their descendants. Beliefs in Witchcraft is another elements of traditional Africans religion. Witchcraft is mainly utilized by the people, who are in trouble due to relationship with others as a means of revenge. In traditional African societies, there is widespread practice of witchcraft.

Thus, it is seen that traditionally, Africans lived in the world deeply embedded in a different world of religious ethos, entirely different from the western world. Every behavior, action and thought was guided by their belief. It was a society that insulated itself from the rest of the human societies. The coming of western religion into Africa with a new philosophy and religious thoughts and ritualistic practice was one of the historical events in African social and cultural history. This marks the point of bringing out the world of Africa from isolation and paving the way for assimilation into the rest of the universal civilization.

The Advent of Christianity

The advent of Christianity was not just the introduction of a new religion and philosophy. It was the coming of a new civilization, which was different from the existing African civilization. Thus, the meeting of Christianity and African Traditional Religion was the encounter of two great civilizations—the western civilization and African civilization. It brought a new thought, philosophy of life and views of the world outside. These changes in their belief came along with many ritualistic activities that greatly affected the way of life and relations among them and the world outside. In the thought of westerners, this process is the 'mission of civilizing Africans from their un-civilized heathen world'.

Eunice (2006) in her article on religious movement in Kenya has given detailed account on the presence of Christianity in Africa in the first century itself. She tried to connect how the history of Christianity dates back to the Pentecost event where the apostles assembled to await the Holy Spirit as promised by Jesus Christ. In his last words, Jesus mandated the apostles to be his "witnesses in Jerusalem, in all Judea and Samaria and to the ends of the earth". Among the first places of "the end of the world" where Christianity spread within the early times is Africa. Thus, the first seed of Christianity was sown in North Africa in the first century.

The very fact that when Jesus, the founder of Christianity, was born, his mother Mary took him to Egypt in order to escape from the hands of Herod, who issued a decree to eliminate all the children, is the first tradition that connected Christianity to Africa. This is followed by several traditional beliefs. For instance, the man called Simon, who met Jesus on the way to Golgotha to be crucified and was forced to carry the cross, who later became a Christian, was from Cyrenia of Libya, which was a Roman province during that time. Thus, Christianity was not a new religion to Africans. In fact, looking into the account of the first disciples of Jesus, several of people, who were present during crucifixion of Jesus and were dead, were Africans. Hence, African were already exposed to Christianity before it reached other parts of the world.

Because of this Mbiti (1969) wrote, "Christianity in Africa is so old that it can rightly be described as an indigenous, traditional and African religion" (Eunice). Baur supports this view based on numerous scriptural evidence. Sanneh (1983) wrote that ".... Both from the fact of centralized administration of the empire under Rome and from the personal contribution of individual Africans, the early Church struck firm root on African soil".

However, there was a break in the work of Christian mission from 7th century till the arrival of colonial rulers and new Christian missionaries, when Islam from the Middle East swept across the region. In this regard, Sennah (1983) wrote, "The attempt to establish the Church in North Africa suffered a major setback, and it was much weakened that it was swept away by the rising tide of Islam in the seventh century. The Muslim armies quickly spread over Egypt and North Africa to which they gave the name '*Maghrib*', an Arabic word meaning 'the West'. Christians remnants were easily mopped up or squeezed into acquiescence, while Islam obtained a bridgehead for attack into Iberian peninsula." The coming of Europeans to Africa in 15th century led by the Portuguese Catholic mission till the arrival of Protestant mission in 20th century was the period of the most intensive work of Christian missions in Africa.

The Portuguese first established contact with African peoples in the Canary Islands, Cape Verde Islands, along the Guinea coast. The Portuguese had a dual agenda. First, to establish trade and secondly, to spread the Christian religion. In their attempt to convert Africans, they followed the strategy of converting the chiefs or the rulers of the tribe and through them, they converted the followers. They believed that if the rulers converted, their people would follow the example set by the ruling class. Despite many setbacks, this strategy worked well and they could spread their mission to several African countries, such as present Gabon, Mozambique, two Congo, Kenya and Angola. The biggest success of Portuguese mission was in Kongo Kingdom. Their King Nzinga, a Nkuwu, was baptized as a Christian, and he allowed his son Nzinga Mbembe to be taken to Portugal where he received a Catholic education. When he returned to the Congo, he replaced his father as king and changed his name to King Alfonso I. This paved the way for the expansion of Christian mission in Africa in general and Congo region in particular.

The Wesley Revival Movement in England, beginning in the early eighteenth century until African colonies became independent, had great impact on the Christian missions in the world in general and Africa in particular. Many mission organizations and churches from Europe and North America began to send missionaries to all over the world, to Asia and Africa in particular as the civilizing work of the heathen un-civilized people. The primary agenda of the missionaries was to spread Christianity through the conversion of as many people as they could reach with their message. This work of missionaries could be summed up as the 'civilizing mission', which has invited severe criticism from the academics and intellectuals and, most of all, from the African writers themselves.

Process of Modernizing under Different Denominational Identities

The primary goal of Christian missionaries was to convert as many Africans to Christianity as possible. To facilitate the achievement of this goal, missionaries focused their efforts on teaching and preaching about Christianity. Bible was translated into local dialects and made available to the local people to read by themselves. This was followed by setting up educational institutions such as schools and other training centers. All over Africa, wherever missionaries went, they opened schools. Missionaries believed that the ability to read the Bible was of vital importance in the conversion process. At first, the main focus of these schools was to teach reading and religious instructions. As the colonial era progressed, mission education expanded to include full primary and secondary schooling.

In addition to their work in education, some mission societies were actively engaged in health care work by opening up hospitals and clinics in rural and, sometimes, remote areas. Such kinds of social humanitarian works attracted many Africans to Christian missions. Hence, apart from the mission of teaching the bible, their other social humanitarian and educational works greatly helped in advancing Christian missions in Africa.

However, the relationship between the missionaries and local converts were not without any problem. In course of time, relational problems began to occur between the missionaries and the local Africans. And this was the starting point where Africans began to look for their own religious identities in order to maintain their own traditions and culture, while adapting to Christian rituals. Thus, the concept of African Independence African Church came into being in African societies. When an African entered into a Christian fold several problems associated with the practices of indigenous traditions and customs began to surface in the relationship between the missionaries and the converted African Christians. In certain cases, these differences led to indirectly linking up religious interests with political and national issues.

The emergence of several Christian sects with different doctrinal practices, objectives and ways of worship and rituals provided golden opportunity for the local Christians to choose any denomination, which was compatible with their objective. Such a situation catalyzed the African to look for their new religious identity based on the teaching of Christianity. In a sense, this was the beginning point of Africans search of new religious identity –the identity that would suit their indigenous social, cultural and political environment. Africans took the new western religion without completely giving up their traditional and customary practices. This was one of the reasons why numerous local Christian organizations sprung up in different parts of African societies. Most of these newly founded Churches of Africans created new religious identities compatible with the existing African traditions and culture, political and economic environment.

Today, Christianity in Africa can be broadly classified into two main groups:

1. Missionaries Church (MC)
2. African Independence Church (AIC)

Missionary Churches are run and maintained by the mother Church having its administrative office outside Africa. All the administrative works, funding and policies are done by the sponsored mission organization, which is usually based in Europe or North America. Under the missionary Churches, the division is primarily based on the denominations or the country from where the Church originated. For instance, the Church that is identified as Baptist is mainly from North America (United States), the Catholic Churches are mostly from France and Portugal and the Methodist Churches are generally from England. The level of conflict and struggle among them are relatively at very low level. These Churches mainly focus on evangelizing Africans. Their only interest is to convert Africans to Christianity adhering to the fundamental teaching of the Bible that those, who do not believe in the gospel, will perish and they need to be saved. They believe in the command of the Jesus 'to go and preach the good news to all the creations'. In order to improve the quality of life among the converts, these Churches also take up many auxiliary activities apart from preaching the Bible, such as imparting training on various livelihoods such as poultry farm, agriculture, horticulture, carpentry and so on.

The acronym African Independence Church (AIC) was first coined by Sundkler (1961) in his book, '*Bantu prophets in South Africa.*' The term basically denotes the Church established and governed by Africans themselves. The very term itself signals that they are independent in their origin and organization. The term is also understood in the sense that the Church came into existence by the initiative of the Africans. However, it is pertinent to know that AIC is basically the offshoot of the Missionary Church. Most of them broke out from the Missionary Church due to relationship problem.

Several factors have been responsible for this. The first one is the clash between the teaching of the Bible and the African Traditions. Missionaries considered that many of the traditional practices of Africans have originated from their heathen philosophy, which is not acceptable to Christian teaching. Thus, the missionaries insisted that the converts should give up their old traditions and way of life. But many African, even though they had converted and became member of the Church continued to retain their old traditional way of life. One of the traditional practices of Africans, which was seriously objected by the missionaries, was polygamy. Polygamy had been a normal practice in African societies. There was nothing wrong in their thought; rather having more wives was a matter of prestige and status in their tradition. In fact, in African societies, the number of women a man could marry is a status symbol. And only those, who are wealthy, could afford to have more wives. Such practices of the Africans were in complete contrast to the teaching of the Bible in which a man is supposed to have only one wife. Thus, Christian teaching strongly condemned their tradition of polygamy. However, since this had been a deep rooted tradition, it was hard to give up. As a result, many African could no longer continue to remain in the Missionary Church and left the latter. These people found their own local Churches so that they could continue to worship in the same manner as Christians do and, simultaneously, practice their traditions and customs.

The second reason according to Ojo (2009) for the people having AIC was the leadership problem. Many missionaries could not trust Africans. They had the perception that Africans were unreliable since they did not keep their words and commitments. And some time, they did tell lies. They changed their words and commitment easily according to their situation and convenience. Because of this, the Church, which was under the control of the missionaries, did not give any leadership positions to the Africans, but allowed them to take responsibility for the Church administration. Such attitude on the part of the missionaries towards the local converts was greatly resented by educated Africans, who were looking for respect and dignity in the society. As a result, they decided to leave the Missionary Church and set up their own Churches so that they themselves would be the owner and leader of the Church. Indigenous African Church leaders, who started agitation since 19th century for more scope for African leadership in the Churches and the quest to make the Church more indigenous, resulted in secession from the Mission Church.

The third reason for the establishment of AIC was racial discrimination. Sundkler (1961) wrote, "There it was unlawful for any minister or member of a religious movement 'not under European control' to 'address meetings or assemblies of natives'—the fear on the part of colonial officialdom, steeped in the values of the new imperialism, of any movement 'not under European control'." This writing expresses the deep rooted bias and discriminative attitude of the missionaries toward Africans. No African church members was allowed to address the public without the permission of the Church. In other words, African Church members or leaders were under the tight control of the white missionaries. This created a great sense of grievance among the educated African Christian leaders. Thus, the reason for Africans leaving the Church run by the missionaries and establishing their own African Independence Church was on the ground of alleged discriminations against Africans by the white missionaries. On several occasions, many Africans felt that the local people were discriminated against by the missionaries due to their colour, so they felt insulted and hurt by such attitude of the missionaries. Hence, the only way they could be free from such discrimination was to have their own Church. The people, who left the Missionary Churches on this ground, ultimately, linked up with political movement—to liberate Africa from the white regime, who they felt, were discriminating them on the basis of skin colour.

The 'African Independence Church' was initially known to one particular local Church in South Africa among the *Bantus*. But, today, every African Church that got separated from the missionaries' Church, comes under the same nomenclature. Thus, there are several African Churches under AIC today, each one having different interest and objective based on the social and cultural suitability to a local situation. Hence, the nomenclature 'African Independence Church' is an umbrella term that includes all the Churches, which are under the leadership of Africans.

According to Pobee (2002), the following are some of the basic features, which identify African Independence Churches. The AIC represents, first of all 'a place to feel at home'. Western missionaries were largely negative about African culture and Africans were alienated from the gospel dressed in European garb. To that extent, the AICs represents an indigenizing movement in Christianity. They, in effect, protest the verbal and cerebral mode, which puts Western Christianity beyond the reach of people's comprehension and experience. Instead, the AICs offer a celebrative religion, making considerable use of symbols, music and dance. Thus, they represent cultural renaissance in reaction to the cultural imperialism of the mission work of the historic Churches.

Second, while Western churches emphasize Christology, the AICs make the Holy Spirit the focus of belief and practice. While they firmly believe in the person of Jesus Christ, they appear more at home with the Holy Spirit, especially since Christ has ascended into heaven. This affirmation of the Holy Spirit does not just emphasize sanctification, as in Methodism, but also points to the Spirit as power that manifests in healing, exorcism, glossolalia and mission. This emphasis on the Spirit asserts both continuity and discontinuity with many spirits of the heritage of traditional African religious epistemology and ontology. It also represents an experiential supernaturalism, which takes seriously the promise of Christ to send his Spirit. To that extent, the phenomenon is a protest against the tendency of the historic Churches to institutionalize every manifestation of the Spirit.

Third, the AICs represent a radically Biblicist movement. Taking off from the Protestant claim that the Bible is an open book for individual interpretation, the AICs have seen the Bible as a source to legitimate a wide variety of basic Christian patterns, often of special relevance to local conditions or of special appeal to local people. Thus, in Southern Africa, the biblical stories regarding the bondage of Israel have become a paradigm for their circumstances. Old Testament accounts of polygyny (e.g. Solomon) and taboos are very much of interest to them. There is importance of dreams, visions and trances as media of God's revelation. The penchant for such visitations reflects the mysticism of the AICs, an experience of the divine on earth.

Fourth, the Churches of the West and their daughter Churches in Africa have the stamp of individualism, which characterizes the society after the industrial revolution. That goes against the ethos of African societies, which proverbially view life in communitarian terms. The AICs, thus, act as a surrogate or auxiliary tribe, creating a self-selected community. This sense of community is manifested in pilgrimages to their holy cities, mutual aid in resources, and the sharing of a common vocabulary (Pobee, 2002).

African Independence Church exists under several Christian identities. Separatist Church was originally the term, which was being used for a certain Church in Nigeria. The group split away from the Church of Missionary Societies in Nigeria. However, in later days, the term Separatist Church includes many of the indigenous African Churches which split away from the Churches run and maintained by the missionaries. 'Spiritual' or 'Pentecostal' is another group, which gives strong emphasis to the power of the Holy Spirit and experiencing Pentecost anew, and offers a range of techniques for the emotional enhancement of religious experience. The best example is the Musama Disco Christo Church of Ghana, which broke away from the Methodist Church of Ghana.

The 'Ethiopian movement' emphasizes the importance of Africans controlling their own affairs in both religious and secular spheres. 'Ethiopian Church', which was the first type of African indigenous Church, was started as schisms from white-led denominations that their leaders saw as racism or paternalism.

The Ethiopian church stands on the slogan 'Africa for Africans' (Jose: 1993). The name 'Ethiopia' comes from the fact that Ethiopia the first Christian kingdom in Africa, is the symbol of pride for all the Africans because of achieving the uncontrolled status by the colonial rulers. The African Independent Church takes this name to show that Christianity is not the religion that belongs to the West, but to Africa. The name, thusm symbolizes African pride. Thus, African Ethiopian Church stands for three things:

1. To symbolize that Christianity is not an imported religion; its African religion with its origin from its soil,
2. Politically to escape/free from the rule of the white,
3. Culturally to incorporate African world view into their beliefs and practices.

Thus, Ethiopian Church of Africa tries to project itself as the indigenous Christian church that had its origin in Africa itself rather than being imported from the west. They symbolically stand for the fact that Africans want to be free from the domination and influence of the outsiders, the West in particular. Through this, Africans seek, indirectly, political independence from the foreign rule. Hence, it is to be understood that Africans tried to find their new religious identity in Christianity projecting it as their own rather than the followers of the west. Thereby, they try to evolve their identity as global community rather than getting isolated from the rest of the world.

Stephen (1992) opined that whereas Ethiopian Church was founded due to racial discrimination by the Missionary Church, the Zionist was founded primarily due to differences in doctrinal belief. Stephen wrote that "the Zionist and Apostolic movements, which started about fifteen years later than the Ethiopian movement, were different in origin and indeed shared common roots with many of the white-led Pentecostal movements in South Africa. Though they eventually became racially segregated, this was a more gradual process, brought about by the pressures of South African society rather than any ideological conviction. What they shared with the Ethiopian movements was the characteristic of not being under 'European control', so they have been classified together as a 'phenomenon', which has been studied by Government officials, politicians, missionaries, social anthropologists, sociologists and political scientists and perhaps many others."

The Zionist Churches, such as the Christian Catholic Apostolic Holy Spirit Church in Zion, founded between 1917 and 1920 by Daniel

Nkonyane, are primarily interested in the adaptation of Christian teachings and liturgy to indigenous cosmology and ways of worship; they stress expressive and emotional phenomena and cater to the strong fears of witchcraft among Africans.

The Zionists primarily emphasized on the power of the Holy Spirit—the power of healing, power of speaking in local tongue, spontaneity and emotionalism in religion. They opposed the western technique of education, medicine and other methods of curing diseases. These groups are mainly found in west Africa, where vast number of African Independence Churches belong to this group. The church basically originated from the Aladura Church in Nigeria. It is widely believed that this Church resorted to such a belief in the power of healing and other miracles, because they were deprived of the facilities for such things by the western dominated Churches. Thus, as an alternative to the western technique and their traditional means of healing through witchcraft and magic, they adopted such a new technique to meet their practical needs. In this context, some scholars on African religion view that Zionist is the bridge through which the old traditional religion of heathenism is brought back to where they come from (Sundkler, 1961).

Scholars have suggested several other names for AICs of different types, such as 'Witchcraft Eradication Movement', because of their preoccupation with exorcism with the power of the Holy Spirit; 'Messianic movements', built around a messianic leader, 'Prophetic movements' because they are built on a strong leader, a prophet. 'Syncretistic movements' reflect a judgment that these Churches mix Christian beliefs with traditional African customs and ethos. Some of these are also classified on the basis of denominational practice or doctrine, such as Anglican, Roman Catholic, Orthodox, Pentecostal, and Methodist AIC traditions. It is also to be noted that AICs have also demonstrated a strong missionary tendency, and that were actively involved in spreading Christianity throughout Africa in the 20th century and contributed to African Independent Churches (*www.patheos.com.library*).

According to Patheo.com.library, one of the sources of data on world religion, in 1981, AICs constituted 15 per cent of the total Christian population in sub-Saharan Africa. At present, assuming a growth estimated at more than two million per year, their adherents, probably, number over 83 million, thus constituting a significant section of African Christian demography.

Today, AICs represent well over 10,000 independent Christian denominations in Africa. Though they are found in every region and country in Africa, they are more prominently prevalent in West Africa and Southern Africa. Despite the denominational, ritual, and linguistic diversity of these Churches, which makes it difficult to analyze and classify, the common thread uniting all of the Christian Churches is that they were all established by African initiative rather than by foreign missionary agendas (*www.patheos.com.library*). Even though many of these Churches have traditional denominational names and relationships, they are not defined by these traditions; rather they focus more on emphasizing that they are established and led by Africans. A salient feature of AIC, which marks out its uniqueness from others, is giving strong inclination on the inclusion of African cultural norms into their modes of worship, theology, and practice. Because of this very nature, some scholars claim that African Independent Churches are syncretistic in that they combine indigenous African religion with Christian beliefs.

The most significant feature of religious movement in Africa is the proliferation of Independence African Churches in the form of Charismatic movement. In this regards, Ojo (2009) wrote, "The most significant development in African Christianity in independent Africa is the emergence of the Charismatic movements. Since the 1970s, there had been a dramatic rise in the activities of Pentecostal and Charismatic movements, most of which go by the name of ministries or fellowships or evangelistic associations. This new trend is promoted by literature, crusades, fire or Holy Ghost or Power conferences, etc. The members are mostly the young educated elite and those, who are fluent in English, or in French or Portuguese in the non-English speaking countries. This new religious phenomenon constitutes a milestone in African Christianity since the movements are trans-cultural and international in scope."

Ojo further wrote, "Charismatic missions have responded appropriately to the traditional African world-view, which emphasizes magical and spiritual powers, by emphasizing in turn the incidence of power encounters and spiritual warfare in missions. Every African missionary is conscious that what represses people and keeps them in spiritual and economic degradation is nothing but 'Satanic bondage', which also manifests as witchcraft and sorcery among unreached people. Among these people, spiritual warfare is very real and is taken most seriously. Charismatic missionaries, relying on the gifts of the Holy Spirit, have initiated power encounters by the working of miracles and divine healing."

Historically, Christianity was not an alien religion to Africans. The religion came to the region from the first century when the first apostle, who was believed to be baptized by the holy spirit, went to North Africa and spread the message. However, for centuries, there was silence on Christian movement in Africa due to Islamic invasion. The dawn of 21st century coupled with information technologies has once again rekindled the Christian movement in Africa. However, it is in a different context; African Christian leaders try to contextualize and indigenize Christianity in accordance with the requirement of the local situation. Today in many AICs, though Christian ritual practices have been emulated, the social, cultural and traditional practices of the indigenous African remain a core part of the African Independence Churches and this makes the Africans changing religious identity a paradox.

REFERENCES

Alfredsson & Linha. (1998). *Where God Lives: An introduction to a study of the independence churches in Maputo Mozambique*' http://www.worldcat.org/title/where-god-lives-an-introduction-to-a-study-of-the-independent-churches-in-maputo-mozambique/oclc/641893607

Awolalu, J. O. (1976). What is African Traditional Religion? *Studies in Comparative Religion.* Vol. 10 (2). World Wisdom, inc.www.studiesincomparativereligion.com.

Baum, Robert. (2009). The forgotten South: African Religious traditions and their Global Impact. Paper Presented at the American Theological Library Association Annual Meeting, St. Louis.

Bloom, Leonard and Ottong. (1987). *Changing Africa: An Introduction to Sociology.* London: Macmillan.

Eunice, Karanja Kamaara. (2006). *Religion and Emerging Religious Movement in Kenya* http://international.iupui.edu/kenya/resources/Religions-and-Emerging-Religious-Movements_Paper.pdf.

Gehman, Richard J. (2001). *African Traditional Religion in the light of the Bible:* Baraka Press and Publisher

Jose, Antunes da Silva. (1993). African Independent Churches Origin and Development. *URL:http://www.jstor.org/stable/40463748.*

Makhubu, P. (1988). *Who are the Independent Churches?* Johannesburg: Skotaville.

Mbiti, S. John. (1969). *African Philosophy and Religion.* Heinemann

Neill, S. (1964). *A History of Christian Missions.* Harmondsworth: Penguin.

Ojo, Matthews A. (2009). The Dynamics of Indigenous Charismatic Missionary Enterprises in West Africa. *http://reocities.com/missionalia/ojo1.htm.*

Okorocha, Cyril C. (1987). *The Meaning of Religious Conversion in Africa.* USA: Avebury Aldershot.

Oosthuizen, G.C. (1979). *Afro-Christian religions.* Leiden: Brill.

Pobee, John S. (2002). African Instituted (Independent) Churches. Dictionary of the Ecumenical Movement published jointly by the World Council of Churches.

Senneh, Lamin. (1983). *West African Christianity, The Religious it Impact.* London: C. Hurst & Com.

Stephen, H. (1992). African Independent Churches: Judgement through Terminology. *Missionlia*, Vol. 20(2) pp. 139-146.

Sundkler, B. G. M. (1961). *Bantu prophets in South Africa*. Oxford: Oxford University Press.

Sundkler, B. G. M. (1976). *Zulu Zion and some Swazi Zionists*. London: Oxford University Press.

Timmins, Kelly. (2009). Witchcraft in African Religions. http: Contributor.yahoo.com/user/.

www.patheos.com.library.

10

Rising Africa and India's Role in Strengthening Education Sector

Suresh Kumar

The post 1990 Africa has encountered effectively the challenges of the hunger, drought, famine, war, disease, etc and has moved towards the progress. The classical economic theory of comparative advantage teaches that all nations would benefit and more wealth created if every country should:

(a) specialize in an economic activity in which it has relative efficiency (or comparative advantage); and
(b) trade with other countries in activities in which its efficiency is less (Goldstein, 1999: 345).

Comparative advantage can occur as a result of a natural niche or, as scholars who have criticized the classical theory argue, through deliberate government policy (Zysman, 1983). How such advantage comes about should not detain us unduly so long as a country has it. Post 1990 Africa is on the way of changing economic and political domain through globalization and needs a serious orientation towards education sector to strengthen political, social and economic development and accountability towards people; at the same time avoiding the colonial pattern of education.

It is the time to recall the colonial period under which the education was given to fulfill colonial master's economic needs and to mould social orientation of African societies for their vicious motives. The colonial brutal reality is that the access to education remains a privilege- not a right- available to only a small minority and the schools and universities opened to only a small sector in Africa to reflect the social values of the minority they served. Along with it, the most damaging legacies of colonialist presences in Africa is the separation of education from the overall political, economic, social and cultural development of peoples. And yet, neither educational institutions nor the policies which govern them can be neutral because of their link to the economy and the dominant social values of the society of which they are a part. 'Colonial education had a special function: to provide necessary support personnel for the church, state or colonial economy. If the Africans receiving this education yearned for more knowledge or through their ingenuity read prohibited books or "misinterpreted" their sources, such as the Bible, and exposed the prevailing contradictions to the colonialists, they were considered dangerous to the existing colonial infrastructure and were often incarcerated in colonial jails because of their beliefs. During colonial times, education provided produced both the "docile" or cooperative Africans and others who were able to penetrate the colonizers' minds and expose the colonizing myth for what it was in reality: the deliberate exploitation of the uneducated masses with the active collaboration of the new educated elite' (Rodney, 1974: 249, 253). The analysis strongly highlights the perspective of schools and universities that were reinforcing rather than challenging the existing patterns of dependence and inequity which impeded relevant development in colonial Africa. Julius K Nyerere opined, "Indigenous African education was relevant and closely linked to the spiritual and material aspects of social life before colonization by European imperial powers. There was neither little separation of learning and productive labor nor any consequent division between physical and intellectual labor. This educational process reflected the realities of African society and produced people with an education which equipped them to meet the material, spiritual and social needs of the society" (Nyerere, 1968: 268).

Infact, colonial cultural expansion meant the expansion of school system that measured cultural and scientific advance by the number of students who could clearly demonstrate (by examination) that they had been pumped full of a foreign heritage. Thus, the colonial school was primarily a channel of social upward mobility for a tiny minority rather than a means of educating the entire population. As Walter Rodney has observed, it was never thought necessary to educate the masses "because only a minority of the [African] population entered the colonial economy in such a way that their fully in keeping with the overall objective of colonial education, to produce an indigenous elite to ensure that the colonial settlers and various public services of the conies could meet the personal requirements of the settlers themselves (Rodney, 1974: 269).

Post independent Africa (1950-70) worked for the growth of the education sector and has produced large numbers of graduates, at both the secondary school and university levels, but severe financial constraints and political pressures had prevented the economies from diversifying and have greatly reduced the numbers of jobs, relative to the numbers of school-educated people qualified to fill them. The result has been a massive brain drain from Africa to the developed industrialized states of Europe (whosoever acted as colonial power earlier), which has exacerbated the inherited problems of inequality, dependence, and underdevelopment. The period of 1950-1990 dealt with the education pattern tied to a colonial heritage and has contributed immeasurably to the magnification and dramatization of the social distances between the educated and the uneducated. Broadly, the theory and practice of colonial education was to train Africans to help man the local administration at the lowest ranks and to staff the private capitalist firms owned by Europeans. 'In effect, it meant selecting a few Africans to participate in the domination and exploitation of the continent as a whole. It was not an educational system that grew out of the African environment or one that was designed to promote the most rational use of material and social resources. It was not an educational system designed to give young people confidence and pride as members of African societies, but one which sought to instill a sense of deference to all that was European, American and capitalist culture. Education in Europe was dominated by the capitalist class. The same bias was automatically transferred to Africa; and to make matters worse the racism and cultural boastfulness harboured by capitalism were also included in the package of colonial education. The colonial school education was meant for subordination, exploitation, the creation of mental confusing, and the development of underdevelopment' (Rodney, 1974:241: emphasis mine).

After stating that avoiding the colonial pattern of education today and coming back to the arguments of refreshing education sector of post 1990 Africa, the need is to understand the role of education in building the agriculture, industrial, health, defence, science and technology and civil society. African democratic leaders exert to foster the spirit of self-reliance and sustainable development today that is accomplished through rejuvenated education sector as per the need of the people.

Education has been a means of transmitting one's culture from one generation to another. It is the process of bringing about a relatively permanent change in human behavior. The philosophy of traditional education was very pragmatic and was designed to form a gateway to the life of the society. Africa needs to pursue an educational policy aiming at shaping the individual into a sound, well informed, useful and patriotic citizen of his country. In order to achieve this objective, the country provides educational opportunities for all citizens at primary, Secondary and tertiary levels. Today, the education system and its products of any country are the pre-requisite for its development and prosperity. Human resources is the most important part of infrastructure where in as good the system, as much will be the availability of manpower. One thing to be taken into account is to provide secure employment opportunities to the graduates so as they don't leave the colleges disheartened as it was happened in the 1970-1990s with the graduates of African universities. The pattern of Education must produce enough students with post-secondary education to satisfy the nations need for high level manpower.

Demographically, Africa's median age at present is 20 and that is the strongest pillar of human resource and hence needs better education and employment opportunities in their respective countries. 'Former British Prime Minister Gordon Brown noted at one World Economic Forum session that currently 61 million school-aged children in Africa are not being educated. The demands on educational infrastructures suggested by these numbers are almost beyond comprehension—not least because of the dearth of qualified, or in many cases even literate, teachers' (Shapiro 2013). The planning and control of education to which the African countries governments are committed as part of the general planning of national development require a concentration of power in the hands of the government sufficient to secure orderly growth and to overcome sectional obstacles to growth. 'A concentration of power does not, of course, imply dictatorship, since the schools cannot be run without the willing co-operation of a great many people, and such co-operation can only be obtained on terms that imply a measure of decentralized responsibility. The questions that have to be answered are how much responsibility is it right and necessary to delegate to local bodies in order to secure their enthusiastic help for running schools and whether this measure of delegation is compatible with the central government's responsibilities for planning and general control' (Carter, 1966: 18).

Rightfully, the question arises 'Is Africa rising? Judging by the buzz and optimism of the young business leaders and political trailblazers from across the continent who gathered in Cape Town for the World Economic Forum on Africa recently, the answer is a qualified "yes". The African

Leadership Network—co-founded by Stanford graduates Fred Swaniker, now the CEO of the African Leadership Academy, and Achankeng Leke, director of McKinsey's Nigerian operations—is emblematic of a new generation of leaders who brim with sophisticated confidence about Africa's emergence. They are part of the coming elite whose ideas shaped the discussion in Cape Town' (Shapiro, 2013). The world economic outlook had made a comparative study of GDP at constant prices change and found the rising position of Sub-Saharan Africa (Table 10.1) that shows the rising Africa. It has projected the future growth of the region (2013-2018) and this debate of rising Africa has positive reports. The last decade has shown the six of the world's ten fastest-growing countries belong to Africa (Figure 10.1). It has grown faster than East Asia and the IMF expects Africa to grow by 6 per cent this year and nearly 6 per cent in 2012, about the same as Asia (IMF, 2013 and Figure: 10.1).

Criticizing the rising Africa, it is observed that the continent's future appears to be bright, but do growth figures reflect an improving quality of life? The problem, though, is that most of this wealth is extractive. Patrick Smith said, "there is lack of value addition on the African side. The energy companies are seeing massive domestic demand from Asia and they are capitalizing on that" (Smith 3 August 2013). The value addition has become the most important issue in the African economy and post 1990 Africa has taken it as a serious aspect of its economic development. To begin with, it is entitled that rising Africa and India's role in strengthening education sector enshrines value addition in its relationship with the continent. India shares humane concern and develop its own understanding on food security, climate change and energy security in the current international setting. It takes energy security both as an opportunity as well as a challenge because of its trans-national character that desires a coherent global response. India is dependent on oil and gas and Africa is contributing 15 per cent share in reducing India's dependency on oil. India believes that refinery technology using for crude oil should access to all. India is leading a campaign to re-write intellectual property rights (IPR) in favour of all the developing countries particularly for oil clean technology. It shows a major difference as compare to other countries practicing foreign economic policy. 'We urge the international community to give real and immediate effect to commitments on climate change, especially in the areas of technology transfer, financing and capacity building. There is also need for a closer look at the IPR regime to ensure cost-effective transfer of appropriate and advanced clean technologies to developing countries' (Delhi Declaration, 2008: 3). India respects value

Table 10.1: GDP, Constant Prices Percentage Change (Report for Selected Country Group and Subject)[1]

Country Group Name	*Subject*	*Unit scale*	*2000*	*2001*	*2002*	*2003*	*2004*	*2005*	*2006*	*2007*	*2008*	*2009*	*2010*	*2011*	*2012*	*2013*	*2014*	*2015*	*2016*	*2017*	*2018*
World	GDP, constant prices	% change	4.7	2.3	2.8	3.6	4.1	4.5	5.2	5.4	2.8	-0.5	5.2	3.9	3.1	3.3	4.1	4.3	4.4	4.5	4.4
Advanced economies	GDP, constant prices	% change	4.1	1.4	1.7	2.1	3.1	2.6	3.1	2.8	0.1	-3.4	3.1	1.6	1.2	1.2	2.2	2.5	2.6	2.6	2.4
Developing Asia	GDP, constant prices	% change	6.9	5.9	6.9	8.2	8.5	9.4	10.4	11.5	7.8	6.9	9.9	8.1	6.6	7.1	7.3	7.6	7.7	7.7	7.7
Latin America and the Caribbean	GDP, constant prices	% change	3.9	0.4	0.3	2.1	6.1	4.6	5.6	5.7	4.2	1.5	6.1	4.5	2.9	3.3	3.8	3.8	3.8	3.8	3.8
Sub-Saharan Africa	GDP, constant prices	% change	3.5	4.8	7.1	4.8	6.1	6.1	6.3	7.1	5.6	2.7	5.4	5.2	4.7	5.5	6.1	5.8	5.6	5.45	5.4

Source: IMF World Economic Outlook Database, April 2013.

http://www.imf.org/external/pubs/ft/weo/2013/01/weodata/weorept.aspx?pr.x=89&pr.y=2&sy=2000&ey=2018&scsm=1&ssd=1&sort=country&ds=.&br=1&c=001%2C110%2C505%2C205%2C603&s=NGDP_RPCH&grp=1&a=1: accessed on 5th August 2013

1. Mr. Utsav Kumar Singh, M.Phil-II scholar of Department of African Studies, University of Delhi has provided all the data used here particularly IMF World Economic Outlook Database, April 2013 that helped in the scientific analysis of the article.

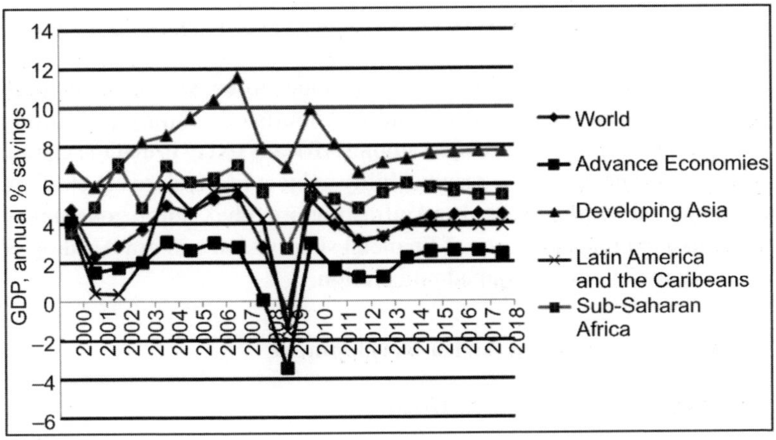

Fig. 10.1

Source: World Economic Outlook Database, April 2013.

addition in exploration, assisting in settling their different sectors including education and committed its partnership developing Africa's capacity building as per the need of individual countries. The transfer of technology needs educated and professional African entrepreneurs and India's role in strengthening education comes here and will be elaborated later.

The other criticism is raised in terms of that 'the Africa's real rise will only come about if resources can be taken control of by educated Africans and used to lessen inequality and spread wealth. As with many countries in the West, a so-called "rise" could really just mean a triumph of free market economics and an increase in inequality. This might suit an elite group of African power-players and Western CEOs, but it won't do anything for ordinary men and women across the continent' (Kwapong, 1988). This economic growth cannot go long if there is a disparity between educated work force and development. The similar opinion is felt by Ian Shapiro and he stated, "Then there are concerns about the shape of economic growth. Unless economic resurgence steers Africa's economies in more diversified directions, the dangers of cronyism and misgovernment long associated with the oil curse will remain. Winner-take-all economics begets loser-lose-all politics. Mozambique's natural gas bounty could do for it what North Sea oil did for Britain and Norway, but there are also the Libyan, Venezuelan and Russian possibilities. Ditto for Nigerian oil" (Shapiro, 2013).

Politically, Africa is moving towards democratization and elected government and as a result, around 47 countries have adopted parliamentary system. Positively, Africa has youth in majority today and need education and skill development that will act as a front runner force to run the economic development. The runner force will act as the right working force as being educated and will nourish the family and society in large. The common consensus among Africans today is that the central government must take the responsibility subject to standards in staffing, curricula and building school and infrastructure. The Central government must take the responsibility of financial supervision and grant-aiding of local organs of educational administration.

Need of Education and Africa Development

The Period of 1950-1990 in Africa

The post 1950 Africa educational system has not developed and fails to solve the socio-economic problems of the population, which is mounting urban unemployment, the problem of underemployment, shortage of critical and relevant skills, dependence on foreign countries for subsistence, and critic availability of basic comforts of life. There is genuine rationale to emphasize the fundamental task of education in the sectoral development in Africa. Jawaharlal Nehru rightly pointed out, "Standard of education and even now the opportunities for education there are meager. But now African students are able to come to India and other countries too for their studies. They will be able to shoulder more responsibilities in the advancement and progress of their country. We are passing through many strange phases of human history. The future of humanity depends on the issues now before the Great Powers. The colonial revolution started earlier in Asia has gone far, but in Africa conditions are different. Nothing can be said how long it will be before the revolution there is complete but it is certain that its pace will gain speed and Africa is bound to play an important role in world affairs" (Jawaharlal Nehru, 1953).

Education is an intrinsic part of life and development. Education is a prerequisite to development. The basic parameter of education is to get satisfaction of human need for knowledge, offers to meet other basic needs and accelerate sustainable development. The market economy respects skilled manpower for both the formal and informal sectors of the economy and facilitates the means of developing the knowledge, skills, and productive capacities of the labor force, and acts as a catalyst in encouraging modern attitudes and aspirations. Criticizing the present education system in Africa, Alexander rightly pointed out, "One of the major problems in our educational effort has been that we have been concerned with literacy in its different forms up to university. We called this education. As a result, you have now educated people, but educated for what—referred to as the popular dilemma in education? What is our philosophy for education as countries and as a continent? We have been stimulating basically a salary-oriented education, where the fact that one is educated was considered enough to be able to earn a salary. Not enough emphasis was laid on the ideals of productivity and bettering a country' (Kwapong, 1988:26). Further, the military rule and lack of democratic accountability in most of the African countries till 1990 has ignored the education system completely and eaten foreign assistance cam for the education sector. Hope Eghagha critically observed by saying, "Africa suffers from a persistent imbalance of disparity in educational development between different provinces, inadequate funding, scarcity of educational equipment and supplies, overcrowded classrooms, inadequate library and laboratory facilities, insufficient student housing, violence arising from the activities/operations of cultist student organizations, exam malpractice and general erosion of academic standards, insufficient places for students seeking admission into universities and other institutions of higher learning, and migration to other countries of teachers and other personnel in institutions of higher learning due to repression and infavourable conditions of service (the brain drain) (Eghagha, 1999), among other problems.

Besides, the oil and rich mineral resources African countries (had no democratic system during this period) started earning and had US dollars in their reserve has a comparative advantage in their education system. Education begets critical human/labor resources without which economic development is made difficult, if not possible. These countries having rich resources harness its advantage simply by proper performance of the manpower development function and not aiming beyond this limited level. The comparative advantage the country should actually be aspiring for is making education its number one industry and a foreign exchange earner just like countries like Europe, USA and India. Only advantage achieved at this higher level holds the change of diversifying the country's economy and yielding the other benefits such as depositing in the Swiss Banks and so on. Diamond observes, "Democracy is defined as a political system that meets a set of pluralist conditions or requirements, among them the existence of political parties, entrenchment of basic fundamental guarantees like free speech and free press, accountability to the electorate, and regular elections, to name just these requirements" (Diamond, 1995:

notes 6-7). The similar argument is raised in the international media explaining the real meaning of democratic system with example of Nigeria in Africa. Paul critically said, "But democracy of the kind we elaborate here, to truly depart from authoritarian military rule, must rise beyond minimalist requirements and procedures. It must be qualitative and its principles must be dynamic rather than fixed, the idea being progressive extension of democratic principles to all aspects of the national culture and political system, including relations within and among groups, governance of educational institutions, and decision making concerning allocations of educational resources, to name but these few elements. Democracy is not something solders just return to civilians after they have claimed their time at the trough. Any democracy that does not soar beyond the experiences of the First and Second Republics or depart qualitatively from the "military democracies" (Niwabuikwu, 1999) of yesteryears will not work in Nigeria.

As a result of the broken democratic structure in African countries, the educated youth had left no option except to move to developed world. The remaining youth without the proper system of adequate education had no sufficient employment opportunities. But this stagnant political chaos did not work out with the people and more and more demands has cropped up in the ninties.

The Period since 1990 in Africa

The post 1990 witnessed the major changes in the international politics and independence of South Africa was one of them. The market open economy has started linking the society into a global village. One of the major linking chains is the Information and Communications Technology (ICT) through the advancement of computer technology. Post 1990 African Societies realized that the future depends largely on the quality of its Citizen's education. The experiences of unstable political system that forced the African educated youth to migrate in search of employment opportunities. One of the current trends of international African migration is its reorientation towards new geographical destinations. These alternative topographies relate to global transitions towards a new multi-polar world order, in which European and North American destinations gradually lose their attraction: Entry into the so-called Global North has become highly restricted, controlling state practices are applied more rigidly, and expressions of xenophobia and islamophobia are more common than even before. Additionally, labour markets in the Global North shrank due to the global financial crisis of 2008, wages declind and rights to old age pensions needed to be readjusted. As a consequence, many migrants moved for more promising opportunities in other geographical areas. They turned East (to Asia and the Arab World) or West (to Latin-America), mostly with the aim of establishing business or trading partnerships, to find work or to improve their, education. In some cases, they could build on historical alliances, a shared language or religion. In others, they gave preference to countries that provided relatively easy access and seemed receptive to migrants' entrepreneurial spirit or their specific skills. In this sense, South-West or South-East African migration challenges the theorization of trans-nationalism and circular migration by questioning ideas of center and periphery that have typically entailed a crossing of hemispheres. Here the question is raised that there is a need to change the education system that should fit in the existing market environment to absorb the educated African youth on the land itself and avoid any more brain drain in Europe or America. It needs a major overhauling in the education sector. There is nothing magical about what proportion of its national spending a country sets aside for education-except that such allocation can be a good measure of an affected country's "commitment to development through education (Habte, 1993: 690). Africa seeks to renew the education system by adding the implant and authenticating social values, tackling the collapse of values and anomie so prevalent in the national society, instilling desirable values like cooperation, honesty, equity, justice, consensus, and collaborating and attacking on extant regionalism antithetical to national integration. Briefly, the knowledge that comes from education is necessary for good governance and constitutional guarantees like the free and compulsory education and equal opportunities for the employment barring the regional divisions in the society. Democracy actually needs more participation of people that will provide the basis or environment for the pursuit of higher education. Only democracy can effectively deal with certain constitutional issues such as education, specifically, here, the imbalance in favor of the central government. A constitution in different countries in Africa generally makes education a subject on the concurrent list, meaning it is a responsibility of all three levels of government, local, state, and national, especially the sharing of the last two. This must change and federal balance restored through devolution and decentralization in managing the national educational system. Moreover, democracy and education are the two sides of a coin and the relationship between the two is a two-way traffic. Education can promote democracy; democracy has also been known to benefit education. As Thomas R. Dye recounts, tracing the early history of public education in America, "the logic of democracy led inevitably to public education. The earliest democrats believed that the safest repository of the ultimate powers of society was people themselves. If the people make mistakes, the remedy was not removed power from their hands, but to help them in forming their judgment through education" (Dye, 2000: 457).

The education strengthens the means of income today and paves the way for secured education, higher income and better employment for future generation. Education influences social welfare through its indirect effects on health, fertility, and life expectancy and helps to increase the profitability of other forms of social and physical investment. Broadly, the development is the integral element of education throughout the world including Africa with the following objectives such as:

Firstly, the young human resource of African society needs education and human and financial resources permit, with the ultimate goal of developing a comprehensive scientific system of education of all levels and for all age groups

Secondly, the African governments should pursue free and compulsory education taking care of equitable distribution of educational opportunities in urban as well as rural areas to minimize the existing inequalities based on sex, economic status, and geography.

Thirdly, Africa needs to accomplish modern education policy for the betterment and optimum use of resources and avoid the students dropping out or repeating grades. The University of Delhi in India has adopted a four year bachelor program with the understanding to minimize the drop out of students on the one hand and provide the certificate (diploma after two years, graduate degree after passing three years and graduate honors degree after four years) as per their qualifications.

Fourthly, the modern education policy should be directly connected to the job market that will equip the students with the knowledge and skills needed to find employment. The University of Delhi has common foundation course in the first year in their respective disciplines (Art, Commerce, Science and Social Sciences students), discipline course-I in the second year, discipline course-II in the third year and application course in the fourth year. The scope of the students after having diploma can be good teachers in schools with relevant prequalification, can work in NGOs, in retail business, run a crèche or play schools. Similarly, after having Bachelor degree, students can work in NGOs, retail sectors, BPO industry, technical jobs in media industry and fashion houses and after completing four years, students are more specialized in their respective disciplines.

Fifthly, Africa needs to strengthen the institutional capacity to formulate and carry out education policy and to plan, analyze, manage, and evaluate education and training programmes and projects at all levels.

These broader parameters of the education policy will enable universal education in Africa. The market based education system strengthens the external and internal efficiency and enhance output quality. The external links of the policy relates to schools, universities, or training institutions provide the necessary skills for the smooth running of the economy and absorbing the school-leavers or graduates into the labor market, find the jobs and the earnings as per their qualifications using their skills in employment. The new education pattern balances the general education, diversified schools, technical institutes and vocational schools, on-the-job training, and non-formal educational programmes. The higher education under the education pattern effectively coordinated or integrated into the overall national educational and research programmes and acts as an effective interface in developing the agriculture, industry, and commerce.

Overall, there is need to improve the quality and relevance of education in the post 1990 Africa. Only a small proportion of children are reaching the minimum required competencies and Africa's education systems are not performing to the standards as per the expectation of the changing political and economic environment. Primary education should serve to help the child towards self realization and to relate to others through mutual understanding. The Socio-economic progress among the industrialized states has been propelled by advances in science and technology. The objective of science and technology policy was to e-orient the entire society towards scientific thinking in order to develop new technologies and adopt existing ones to improve societal well being and security.

Along with it, the teachers need to be well trained and have a desired motivation for their refresher as well as orientation courses. The education pattern in Africa should be geared towards self realization, better human relationships, self and national economic efficiency, citizenship and national reconstruction. 'Sub-Saharan Africa pursues an educational policy with aims at shaping the individual into a sound, well-informed, useful and patriotic citizen of his country. In order to achieve these objectives, Africa is moving forward to provide educational opportunities to all the citizens at primary, secondary and tertiary levels. Education must make one great attempt at making an individual socially efficient, adequately equipped not only with all mean for earning his bread, but also imbued with the spirit of playing an efficient role in society with the object of making it a richer better and more attractive a medium to breathe in.

African governments have the principal responsibility for adequate financing of basic education and the democratic governments are willing to strengthen this sector as per their needs. The governments need to facilitate the partnership at all levels with civil society, agencies, the private sector, NGOs, religious groups, communities, parents and teachers associations, teachers trade unions and families. The African education system needs to play an important part in strengthening economic development through adopting the following parameters such as:

- To accomplish the socio-economic needs of the children, it must review and redesign education curriculum and teaching methods.
- The reading material should be developed, produced and distributed at affordable prize.
- Integrate education into family, community and the work place.
- Introduce democratic values and practices into the conduct of teaching and learning.
- Develop field work/project work/excursion/co-curricular activities and linkage the education with the industries, NGOs, social sector and others.
- The print and television media network should encourage in organizing the public discourse on current educational issues in school, colleges and universities.
- Develop the internet network to connect the education system of home countries with the international education pattern spreading awareness worldwide.

India's Role in Strengthening African Education

Going back to history, post independent India was seriously concerned about education in Africa right from the days of first Prime Minister Jawaharlal Nehru, when he mentioned, "The whole object of our giving scholarships to African students to come to India must take some positive measures to meet the situation. In fact, we should not mind spending some money. I am told, however, that it is not money that is required, but rather the human approach. They must be made to feel at home in India" (Note to the Secretary General, 1954). Earlier, Nehru sent a note to Cabinet Secretary on New Delhi, 8 September 1952 and a copy was sent to Ministry of Education, regarding *Scholarships for African Students* mentioned that 'I agree entirely with the proposal to increase the number of Scholarships from 70 to 100. I would specially encourage Africans from Africa to come to India, as facilities for their education are terribly limited and they are looking towards India (Note to Cabinet Secretary, 1952: 380-81). Indian government keenly shared their available resource in the education sector. Nehru further urged, "Perhaps, you know that we have got nearly a hundred Government of Indian scholars from Africa in India, and we would like to increase them. Their hunger for education is tremendous. They want to get going. Thousands and thousands of schools are being started in East Africa from the pennies of the people. Whether these schools are good or bad, it is immaterial, I do not know, they may have been bad, but it shows their hunger for education. And it is a terrible thing that this desire to make good, is frustrated. It is crushed, because then all that turns into terrible bitterness, and I fear that bitterness is spreading in other parts of Africa too, all parts. And if that becomes, well, strongly entrenched, it is a bad outlook for the future for millions and millions of people in Africa. It inevitably takes a racial aspect, as it must. Of course, the principal economic problem of Africa is land. They have been deprived of their land. Then there is this racial discrimination problem, and unless this is met constructively you get the basis for future racial conflict on a big scale. That is why I am greatly worried about it" (Press conference on Urge 10 June 1953: 400). Respecting their freedom struggle of that period, Nehru further stressed, "A variety of reasons has prevented people of Africa from attaining the standard of education and even now the opportunities for education there are meager. But now African students are able to come to India and other countries too for their studies. This pace will gain speed and Africa is bound to play an important role in world affairs." (Travail of Africa, 1953: 639-40).

Continuing the education support to Africa, different governments after Nehru supported this task. Surendra Pal Singh writes, "As for the material assistance to the people belonging to these colonies, the Government's efforts have been primarily directed towards enabling them to equip themselves with necessary education and expertise to that they can carry forward the political awakening of the masses in their countries. Towards this end, India has been providing education and training facilities to a number of people from these territories. For example, 24 Angolan students received training in nursing and other technical fields in India. India has also been assisting in a modest way the FRELIMO in running its Mozambique Institute at Dar-es-Salaam. (Singh, 1970: 4-8).

Hundreds of students from Africa came to India and received degree in the various disciplines right from sciences, law, medical sciences, agriculture, veterinary and social sciences till 1990s and served in their home countries in different capacities such as the former President of Malawi Mr. Bingu Wa Mutharika received his first degree from the University of Delhi. Keeping this tradition alive, University of Delhi had honored President Mutharika with honorary doctorate on 5th November 2010. Many of the students, who attended Indian Technical and Economic Cooperation Program (ITEC) courses, have risen to top positions in their respective fields, and some have gone on to become ministers. In Botswana, many officers in the defence establishment have been trained under this programme. In Tanzania, over 24 percent senior government officials have been through the ITEC experience (ITEC, 2013).

Post 1990 India has gained its expertise in the science and technology and strengthened education in all spheres of human activities. Dr. A P J Abdul Kalam, the former President of India during his inaugural address to the African Parliament in Johannesburg on 16th September, 2004, proposed to connect all 53 AU member countries with Indian institutions with a satellite and fibre-optic network to share India's expertise in the fields of Education and Health care for accelerated socio-economic development of Africa. Africa Union (AU) accepted the Indian proposal and signed an umbrella MOU with Govternment of India (through Ministry of External Affairs—Nodal Ministry). Government of India appointed Telecommunications Consultants India Limited (TCIL) as the turnkey implementing Agency of the project network through VSATs in 169 locations in Africa.

The ICT Equipments (Computer hardware, system software, networking equipment, studio equipment and UPS) at 170 locations in Africa (53 LC,53 PEL, 53 VVIP Node, 5 RUC, 5 RSSH and 1 DC at hub) and 19 locations in India (7 UC, 12 SSH and DC at Delhi) has connected the tele-education and tele-medicine application software.

The network would primarily provide e-Services with priority on tele-education and tele-medicine. It is a non-commercial project, funded by the Govt. of India at a budgetary cost of USD116 million. Different Indian Universities has been selected for providing Tele-Education services such as Indira Gandhi National Open University (IGNOU), New Delhi, University of Madras, Chennai, University of Delhi, New Delhi, Birla Institute of Technology and Science (BITS), Pilani and AMITY University, Noida. Along with it, Indian super specialty hospitals selected for Tele-Medicine such as All India Institute of Medical Sciences (A.I.I.M.S.) Delhi, ESCORTS Heart Institute and Research Center, New Delhi, Moolchand Hospital, New Delhi, FORTIS Hospital, Noida, Apollo Hospitals, Chennai, SRI Ramchandra Medical College and Hospital, Chennai, Narayana

Hrudayalaya, Bangalore, Health Care Global Enterprises, Bangalore, CARE Hospitals, Hyderabad, Amrita Institute of Medical Sciences (AIMS), Kochi, Dr. Balabhai Nanavati Hospital, Mumbai and Sanjay Gandhi PGI, Lucknow.

The leading regional universities and super specialty hospitals of Africa selected by the AU such as Makerere University, Uganda, Kwame –Nkrumah University of Science and Technology—Ghana, University of Yaounde, Cameroon, Alexandria University, Egypt, Ibadan Hospital—Nigeria, Brazzaville Hospital—Republic of Congo, Sir Seewosagur Ramgoolam National Hospital, Mauritius and Alexandria University Hospital, Egypt. The major responsibilities of the AU member states is to arrange to nominate a national coordinator, prepare the identified sites with necessary civil and electrical infrastructure and other required facilities, custom clearance of all materials imported into the country, including the exemption of customs duties and arranging necessary clearances from various regulatory agencies (VSAT, room for X-ray machine etc). Out of total, the beneficiaries African Countries are 47 as of now. As a result, Pan-Africa e-network is connected with 17 Super Specialty Hospitals (India—12, Africa—5), 12 Universities (India—7, Africa—5), 100's of specialist doctors of India and Africa, 100's of educational experts/professors of India & Africa, national coordinators, consignees, university coordinators, medical coordinators of African countries and beneficiary doctors, patients, nurses, paramedical staff, students, equipment operation staff in African countries.

The major benefits intended for African nations towards capacity building is by way of imparting education to 10,000 African students over 5 year period (2009-14) in different courses such as 2000 in PG Programs, 3000 in UG Programs and 5000 in skill enabling Certificate, Diploma and Post Graduate Diploma Programs. The tele-medicine components provides online medical consultation for one hour everyday to each country for 5 years, offline advice for 5 patients per day to each country for 5 years, continuing medical education for practicing Doctors and working Nurses/Physicians' Assistants, to update their medical knowledge and upgrade their clinical skills.

The country-wise implementation status of tele-education refers to 43 countries such as Benin, Botswana, Burkina Faso, Burundi, Cameroon, Cape Verde, Central African Republic, Chad,, Congo, Comoros, Djibouti, D.R. of Congo, Eritrea, Ethiopia, Egypt, Gabon, Gambia, Ghana, Guinea, Ivory Coast, Lesotho, Libya, Liberia, Malawi, Mauritania, Mauritius, Madagascar, Mozambique, Nigeria, Niger, Rwanda, Sao Tome and Principe,

Senegal, Seychelles, Sierra Leone, Somalia, Sudan, Tanzania, Togo, Uganda, Zambia and Zimbabwe. The tele-education work has accomplished in Namibia, Swaziland, Mali and Kenya in 2011. The AU has showed interest in 5 broad areas of education. Along with it, the educational programmes offers various programs in different universities mentioned in Table 10.2.

Table 10.2: Educational Programmes Offered in Different Universities

Sr. No.	*Diff. Courses*	*University*
Post-Graduate programs (4/5 semesters)		
1.	MBA (HR/Marketing) (English)	IGNOU
2.	MBA–International Business	AMITY
3.	M.Sc.-IT	University of Madras
4.	Master of Tourism Management	IGNOU
5.	Master of Finance and Control	AMITY
6.	MBA (HR, Marketing—French)	AMITY
Under-Graduate Programs (3 years/6 semesters)		
1.	BBA (in English)	University of Madras
2.	BBA (in French)	AMITY
3.	B.Sc.-IT	AMITY
4.	Bachelor of Finance & Investment Analysis	AMITY
5.	Bachelor of Tourism Studies	IGNOU
Diploma Programs (1 year)		
1.	French Language	AMITY
2.	PG Diploma—IT	AMITY
3.	Business Management	AMITY
4.	Tourism Studies	IGNOU
5.	Early Childcare and Education	IGNOU
Certificate Programs (6 months, 1 year)		
1.	Database and Information System (1 year)	BITS
2.	Networking and Operating System (1 year	BITS
3.	Electronics and Instrumentation (1 year)	BITS
4.	English Language	Delhi University
5.	Accountancy	Delhi University
6.	German Language	University of Madras
7.	Arabic Language	University of Madras
8.	Tourism Studies	IGNOU
9.	Nutrition and Childcare	IGNOU
10	Environmental Studies	IGNOU
Medical Disciplines offered		
General (Internal) Medicine, Radiology, Adult Cardiology, Pediatric Cardiology, Neurology, Dermatology, Endocrinology, Infectious Diseases/HIV-AIDS, Gastroenterology, Nephrology, Pathology, Psychiatry, Pediatrics, Medical Oncology, Urology, Genetics, Gynecology and Ophthalmology.		

Source: ITEC, 2013. *www.tcil.com:* accessed on 6th August, 2013.

Overall, the feedback from the participating nations about this education networks relates to 4,000 students who have registered for various courses so far. Seychelles experience the actual reduction in health education budget, Senegal experiences of patients saving time and money, Ethiopia achieves success in all the fields and overall Africa's demand for extending tele-education and tele-medicine in Rural Areas through Public Private Partnership (PPP) model. Along with it, the government strengthens the environmental protection, Science & Technology and Information and Communication Technology (ICT) to integrate local with the international community. The use of ICT provides opportunity to skilled human resource development to get the employment in the country and abroad accordingly. It helps the business community introducing their agro & other products, diversifying export and supply the processed goods as per the demand accordingly. The introduction of scientific agriculture implements, irrigation facility and environment friendly fertilizer and seeds, strengthening this sector on the one hand and generating skill-based employment opportunities, infrastructure development on the other hand and thereby strengthens the stability of the government. The investment in horticulture and floriculture are promoted and the government is looking for the Public-Private-Partnership in these sectors. Pan-Africa network has already covered 43 countries in Africa such as: Benin, Botswana, Burkina Faso, Burundi, Cameroon, Cape Verde, Central African Republic, Chad,, Congo, Comoros, Djibouti, D.R. of Congo, Eritrea, Ethiopia, Egypt, Gabon, Gambia, Ghana, Guinea, Ivory Coast, Lesotho, Libya, Liberia, Malawi, Mauritania, Mauritius, Madagascar, Mozambique, Nigeria, Niger, Rwanda, Sao Tome and Principe, Senegal, Seychelles, Sierra Leone, Somalia, Sudan, Tanzania, Togo, Uganda, Zambia and Zimbabwe.

Along with it, the Indian Technical and Economic Cooperation (ITEC) programme in 2008 transforms capacity building and skills transfer to hundreds of thousands of students, professionals, and mid-career diplomats in 160 countries across continents, including Africa, Asia, Latin America and East and Central Europe. In-fact, ITEC programme was launched in 1964 as a bilateral programme of assistance; India has been "sharing its knowledge and skills acquired in its own development process with other developing countries going through the same process of development. India is helping 161 countries, with many in Africa, Latin America and Southeast Asia, in a big way in capacity building under ITEC. Under capacity building, the ITEC partner countries send officials to India for training in fields like IT, entrepreneurship and English language, or India sends its experts to advise on how to set up similar institutions. One major part of ITEC is the scholarships—for courses in IT, English and entrepreneurship—provided to countries as part of capacity building, covering the airfare, course fee, accommodation, project allowance and living allowance. The success of the venture can be gauged from the fact that in 2012, India offered 8,000 civilian courses and 1,500 defence courses. There are 47 empanelled institutions with 280 courses on offer. Around 900 slots were given to African countries", Kumar Tuhin, joint secretary, development partnership administration-II, in the external affairs ministry, told IANS (India-Africa Connect 2013). Similarly, "India is very advanced in areas of education and science and technology. India's developmental experience is very relevant for the African continent," says Dr Salim Ahmed Salim, a former Prime Minister of Tanzania and a former Ambassador of Tanzania to India in the 1960s. In a similar vein, Togo's Prime Minister Gilbert Fossoun Houngbo, a former UN official, sees India as "the world's most populous democracy and a leader in frontier areas of knowledge" (ITEC, 2013).

The success of the solar engineering training would ensure that it will become a regular feature of the ITEC. Over the next three years, more than 150 women would train to spread the light in their homelands, as it were. They were from different African countries, ranging from Sudan in the north to Namibia in the south and from Senegal in the west to Tanzania in the east. On an average, India spends about Rs.500 million ($10.8 million) on varied ITEC activities. Since 1964, India has provided nearly $2.5 billion worth of technical assistance to developing countries, including neighbouring countries. Over the years, India has spent around $1 billion over ITEC-related activities involving African countries (ITEC, 2013).

Against the backdrop of the burgeoning popularity of the ITEC programme in African countries, India's Prime Minister Manmohan Singh announced an additional 500 slots for African students at the maiden India-Africa Forum Summit held in New Delhi in April 2008. "We will enhance opportunities for African students to pursue higher studies in India. As an immediate measure we propose to double our long-term scholarships for undergraduates, postgraduates and higher courses and increase the number of training slots under our technical assistance programmes from 1,100 to 1,600 every year. Both India and Africa are blessed with young populations. It is only by investing in the creative energies of our youth that the potential of our partnership will be fulfilled," he said in the presence of African leaders (Forum Summit, 2011).

Besides empowering them with life-sustaining skills, the ITEC programme also gives students from different countries a taste of the multicultural and pluralistic ethos of India. "Networking and bonding is incredible among students. Many of them have tears in their eyes when the course ends and most of them retain their bonds forged during this short programme," recalls Primrose Sharma, who handled ITEC in India's foreign office a few years ago. The ITEC has also become a powerful instrument of projecting India's soft power and its cultural diplomacy as most of these students retain a life-long association with India long after their brief stay in the country. The extended fraternity, as an ITEC alumnus said, carries a bit of India in their hearts wherever they go (ITEC, 2013).

Indian Investors and Africa Education

Jindal Steel and Power Limited (JSPL) has awarded scholarships to five Liberians to study for a Master's degree in engineering at the O.P. Jindal Global University (JGU) for the next academic year, company spokesperson Rashika Kaul told IANS. The students, nominated by the Liberian ministry of education, underwent an online entrance examination as well as interview by faculty members of JGU. The company awards scholarships to students from countries across Africa where it operates. "This is not the first time as we have offered scholarships to students in other parts of Africa," Kaul said in an email communication. Announcing the offer of the scholarships, JSPL's president of Global Ventures for North and West Africa, Milind Oza, said the award of the scholarships was the company's way of contributing to human capacity lding in Liberia. "JGU is committed to offering scholarship in the amount of one million rupees—the total cost for the entire course. This is in keeping with the Liberian Ministry of Education request for a 100 percent scholarship. It's worth about US$ 80,000," Oza said. "JSPL has always believed in upliftment of the countries it operates in—a key element to this sustainable development focuses on providing world-class professional education to the youth to enable them acquire skills rendering to lifetime employment", Oza said. "The best way to provide value for what we do is through education. The scholarship is a full hundred percent one. From start to finish, we take care of them", he added. Liberia's Minister of Education Etmornia Tarpeh has commended the company for offering the scholarships (Indiaafrica connect, 2013).

Along with it, Amity University, offers online 'IT degrees and diplomas to 100,000 students on the African continent over the next five years. The 100,000 IT students will be trained at 53 learning centers in the 53 African Union countries under the Pan-African E-network project. The Pan-African e-Network project is a joint initiative of the government of India and the AU and is funded by India at an estimated cost of US $ 116 million (Amity University, 2012). The project has three components of tele-education, tele-medicine and diplomatic communications, which is coordinated by the ministries of ICT wherever it has been adopted. Uganda, has hosted the tele-education component at Faculty of Computing and Information Technology in the Makerere University. The faculty, a partner institution with Amity University, has invited applications for interested students. The courses offer a Bachelor of IT, a post-graduate diploma in IT and a diploma in IT. Amity University will provide virtual educational services through e-learning technology and video-conferencing facilities set up at Makerere University. Makerere University, in turn, will be providing support to universities in eastern Africa. Eligible students enrolled in various programs will be required to attend classes in the learning centers set up in each member country as part of the project. Learning centers would offer pre-defined lecture schedules available at a tele-education portal. The experienced faculty staff delivers the live, interactive lectures from the tele-education studio set up in India and provides the offline access to the lecture content.

Similarly, NIIT has training and educational centres in the different African countries (Table 10.3). NIIT, the leading Global Talent Development Corporation, ventured into the Africa over a decade ago by setting up its first IT education centre in Botswana in 1997. For more than a decade now, NIIT has been involved in creation of skilled ICT manpower in the continent and has trained nearly 150,000 students till date. The talent development company is touching over 20,000 learners every year, through three dozen learning centres in 8 African countries such as Nigeria, Ghana, Senegal, Libya, Sudan, Botswana, South Africa and Zimbabwe. Similarly, the DNIIT program is the most popular IT training program in many African countries. NIIT has enabled thousands of young people in these countries to join the global IT workforce, many of whom are working in large IT and non-IT organizations such as Debswana, Govt of Botswana, Zenith International Bank, Shell Corporation, Total, Dunlop, Chevron Texaco, Tower Aluminum, Unilever, Mobitel, Grant Thorton, Barclays, Standard Bank, Multilink, Shell, Afribank International, Unilever, First Bank, Union Bank, Zenith Intl Bank, UBA, Linkserve, KPMG, Ericsson etc. Along with it, NIIT regularly offers scholarship programs for students. NIIT's scholarship programs in countries such as Nigeria and Ghana have witnessed overwhelming response by over 50,000 students participating in a single event. It now plans to scale up operations and forge partnerships with more Universities and Colleges to extend its IT training offerings for the youth in Africa (NIIT 2013: emphasis mine).

NIIT has also been instrumental in providing IT and soft skills development programs for employees of large organizations. The talent development organization now plans to address the need for developing ICT skills among children by offering its learning solutions for the school segment, in many African countries. Confederation of Indian Industry (CII), India's apex industry body and NIIT, leading Global Talent Development Corporation have entered into an agreement to help create ICT infrastructure and foster International Software Talent in the African continent. As part of this capacity building and skill development endeavour, NIIT and CII will share high quality education resources from India and involve other appropriate players from the Indian industry to help Africa develop human capital for the global IT industry. NIIT will provide relevant IT curricula in line with international IT trends, and content for IT, soft skills and entrepreneurship for training in Universities and Colleges in Africa. CII on the other hand will facilitate internship with the Indian industry (CII, 2008). This agreement endeavours the capacity building partnership fostering talent in Africa for global IT industry. In future, NIIT and CII will work together and explore modalities of embedding NIIT's industry endorsed IT training programs in the curriculum of universities and colleges in Africa, under its 'NIIT Inside' model. Both organizations will also look at possibilities of establishing 'Centers of Excellence' for Talent Development in different African countries.

NIIT's Corporate Learning Solutions, offers integrated learning solutions (including strategic consulting, learning design, content development, delivery, technology, assessment and learning management) to Fortune 500 companies, Universities, Technology companies, Training corporations and Publishing houses.

NIIT Performance in Enhancing Education

It is better to take some case studies to evaluate the performance of NIIT in different African countries such as:

Ghana

NIIT has formed an academic alliance to offer Computing degree programmes. The Open University's widely acclaimed degree programme,

B.Sc. (Hons) Computing and its practice and the NIIT have formed the alliance. Now, the students in Ghana would have the chance to obtain an international degree in IT without leaving the country. NIIT took the initiative in the partnership of the Open University, UK, and offers the joint degree in B.Sc. (Hons) Computing & its Practice in Ghana. It gives an opportunity to address the growing need for trained IT professionals from many more countries. The unique combination of NIIT's global experience and delivery model with the Open University's distinctive competencies in supported open learning worldwide gives the alliance great potential to make a difference in the world of higher education.

NIIT offers a new curriculum 'Mastermind Series (MMS)' that incorporates the latest technologies. The students would have a chance to acquire Dual Qualifications by registering for this programme. It is a 360-credit points degree programme. 240 credit points will be achieved by completing DNIIT (Hons) programme at NIIT that comprises of first 10 quarters of MMS (Table 10.3). The duration of the Top-up Degree Programme would be one year and will lead to an award of the balance 120 credit points. B.Sc. (Hons) Computing and its Practice Degree would be awarded by The Open University, UK (Ghanaian Chronicle, 2013).

South Africa

NIIT has proposed a framework for developing ICT infrastructure in the country and flagged off series of training initiatives for the youth in the region (Table 10.3) and it can play a key role in providing talent for the global manpower needs. NIIT develops a growth strategy for the country's ICT industry in areas including Telecommunications, Broadcasting Digital Migration, e-skills development, Small Medium and Micro Enterprise support and e-Governance. According to Mr. Rajendra S. Pawar, "There will be an estimated shortage of nearly 56 million professionals in the working age group in the developed countries, by 2020. Leading African countries like South Africa can play a key role by leveraging ICT to develop large talent pool for global manpower needs" (NIIT, 2013). NIIT has added 15 more training centres and forge partnerships with more Universities and Colleges to extend its IT training offerings for the youth and launched new training programs in the area of Software Engineering for Graduates since April 2008. NIIT's plans to start ICT institute under Meraka in Johannesburg next year. NIIT, along with global technology giants Oracle and HP will be starting corporate schools for training employees of IT and non-IT companies in the country.

Table 10.3: NIIT in Africa

Sr. No	*Country*	*Educational Activities*
West Africa		
1.	Ghana	BSc. (Hons) Computing degree programmes, Software projects, transfer of knowledge, DNIIT (Hons) programme, IT Education & Training, teraining in various streams like software engineering, hardware and networking engineering, multimedia, short term programmes among others.
2.	Nigeria	providing learning solutions to individuals, institutions and enterprises by blending cutting-edge technology and education
3.	Senegal	learning career as well as non career courses, offering courses from our technology partners like SUN and ORACLE
4.	Mali	providing learning solutions to individuals, institutions and enterprises by blending cutting-edge technology and education
North & East Africa		
5.	Egypt	NIIT 6th of October Centre : 26th July St, Touristic Zone, 12568, 6th Of October, Egypt & phone: 20122 345 5002 for further details.
6.	Libya	offering MMS and CATS programs to the individuals,
7.	Ethiopia	providing learning solutions to individuals, institutions and enterprises by blending cutting-edge technology and education
8.	Kenya	providing learning solutions to individuals, institutions and enterprises by blending cutting-edge technology and education
9.	Sudan	corporate trainings on Swift and CATS programs, participates in many social activities such as Computer literacy & women empowerment,
10.	South Sudan	providing learning solutions to individuals, institutions and enterprises by blending cutting-edge technology and education
Central & Southern Africa		
11.	D R Congo	Hole in the Wall (HiWEL) project of NIIT- a Minimally Invasive Computer literacy initiative, has been implemented in different countries, developing ICT infrastructure, developing ICT manpower through its state-of-the-art IT training centres, partnerships with leading Universities and Colleges in South Africa, IT career stream programs in Networking and Software engineering, launched the State of Art Training campus in Botswana which will accommodate 7000 students in various IT streams by 2010.
12.	Rwanda	
13.	Botswana	
14.	Namibia	
15.	Mozambique	
16.	South Africa	
17.	Zimbabwe	
18.	Mauritius	

Sources: *http://www.niit.com/Countries/Libya/Pages/default.aspx*, *www.niitghana.com*
http://www.niit.com/Countries/Sudan/Pages/default.aspx
http://www.niit.com/Countries/Botswana/Pages/default.aspx
http://www.balancingact-africa.com/news/en/issue-no-322/computing/niit-to-offer-degree/en: accessed on 06/08/2013

Botswana

NIIT is present in Botswana since 1997 and is one of the leading IT Training companies having 03 centres offering career courses in Botswana such as Gaborone, Francistown and Maun. It offers different program (Table 10.3) and alliance with International Universities and the government has awarded the TEC (Tertiary Education Council) Accreditation to NIIT. This accreditation offers to students to do a program from NIIT and the government Bursary look after their education. NIIT alliance with the Open University, UK is offering international degree path to the students in Botswana and is a widely sought after course with over 6000 students being currently enrolled in their centers (Botswana, 2013).

Sudan

NIIT is present in Sudan since 2002 and is pioneering in corporate trainings on Swift and CATS programs (Table 10.3). There is a huge potential in terms of business in Telecom and other corporate sectors and NIIT is working to address this requirement. NIIT participates in many social activities in collaboration with the Government and private sectors on a regular basis as shown in Table 10.3 (Sudan, 2013).

Libya

NIIT is working in Tripoli since 2005 and offers MMS and CATS programs (Table 10.3) to the individuals, having huge potential in terms of corporate markets especially in the Government sector which can maximize NIIT's reach in every possible level and the student's performance has been excellent since inception.

Senegal

NIIT is active since 2007 having one center in Dakar with the 500 students undergoing career as well as non career courses (Table 10.3). The medium of instruction is French language.

Critical Evaluation and Conclusion

Basic education is an essential step for meaningful technology acquisition, creation and transfer. Technology is the product of a very specific human activity within certain socio-economic relations and cultural and value systems. The so-called transfer of technology is no more than the transfer of products of that technology with all the values and lifestyles in them.

The mere transfer of technologies does not lead to technology transfer unless one has the capacity to understand fully the knowledge and skills behind these techniques. Therefore, building national and regional research and development systems and improving one's educational capability should be the major prerequisite for African countries to acquire effective technology and to hold their own in these global scientific and technological revolutions. The cultural dimension must be constantly borne in mind and indeed integrated into research and development programmes. The effective application of such research in the basic sciences and engineering should thus go hand in hand with advances in the Social Sciences and the Humanities but with a different type of relationship between scientists and other peoples and between the R&D systems and the productive sector.

Overall, African higher education, at the beginning of the new millennium, faces unprecedented challenges. The higher education is recognized as a key force for modernization and development. Africa's academic institutions under PPP model can work with the Indian institutions in securing the education, research, and services. Africans should come forward considering the current realities of their social, economic, and political problems. The road to future success will not be an easy one. The access to higher education, the challenges of funding, the growing role of private higher education institutions in Africa, governance and autonomy, management challenges, gender (including the access of women to higher education and the problems faced by women students and academic staff), the role of research and the problems of scholarly communication, language issues, and the brain drain needs to be tackled under the South-South cooperation. India is supporting the Africa's future academic development by providing academic and institutional expansion. Post 1990 phase sees the emergence of democratic political systems and a civil society is positively building. The revival of academic freedom and the commitment is seen in the higher education community as building successful institutions to strengthen the viability of academic systems. India enables in providing a vital area for development in African higher education and that is seen positively. This era belongs to the developing world and African higher education with India's experience can assist in solving Africa's problem of lack of trained and educated human resource through suitable planning and effective people's elected leadership.

REFERENCES

Amity University, Issue no 468 21st August 2009. India's Amity University offers IT degrees to Africans. *http://www.balancingact-africa.com/news/en/issue-no-468/computing/indias-amity-univers/en*: accessed on 06/08/2013.

Botswana, (2013). *http://www.niit.com/Countries/Botswana/Pages/default.aspx:* accessed on 06/08/2013.

Carter J. Roger. (1966). The Legal Framework of educational planning and administration in East Africa. UNESCO.

CII. (2008). *www.cii.com*: accessed on 05/08/2013.

Delhi Declaration, India-Africa Forum Summit (8-9 April 2008), New Delhi.

Diamond, Linz & Lipset. (1995). *What makes for Democracy*? Lynne Rienner. Boulder & London. notes 6-7.

Dye, R. Thomas. (2000). *Politics in States and Communities*. 10th edition. New Jersey: Prentice Hall.

Eghagha, Hope. (1999). Editorial. Education: Casualty of Military Rule. *The Guardian*. June 3.

Ghanaian Chronicle. (2013). *http://www.balancingact-africa.com/news/en/issue-no-322/computing/niit-to-offer-degree/en*: accessed on 06/08/2013.

Goldstein, S. Joshua. (1999). International Relations. 3rd edition. New York: Longman.

HabteAklilu, TeshomeWagaw & F. J. Ade Ajayi. (1993). Education and Social Change. In Ali A. Mazrui (ed.). *General History of Africa, Vol.8: Africa Since 1935*. Heinemann & UNESCO.

IMF. (2013). *http://www.economist.com/node/21541015*: accessed on 02/08/2013.

India-Africa Connect. (2013). *http://www.indiaafricaconnect.in/index.php?param=news/6348/the-big-story/114*: accessed on 5th August 2013.

India-Africa Connect. (2013). Jindal Steel awards five Liberians scholarships. 23rd July. *http://www.indiaafricaconnect.in/index.php?param=news/6293/india-in-africa/117*: accessed on July 26, 2013.

ITEC. (2013). *http://2billiondreams.in/index.php?param=chapterdetails/10*: accessed on 5th August 2013.

Jawaharlal Nehru Speech at the inauguration of an African Students Conference in Delhi University, 26 December 1953. From the *Hindustan Times*, 27 December 1953. Extracts.

Kwapong A. Alexander. (1988). The Challenge of Education in Africa. Africa Leadership Forum. 821 UN Plaza, 7th Floor. New York.

Libya, 2013. *http://www.niit.com/Countries/Libya/Pages/default.aspx*: accessed on 06/08/2013

NIIT, 2013. *www.niit.com*: accessed on 06/08/2013.

Niwabuikwu, Paul. (1999). *The Guardian*. London. September 8

Note to Cabinet Secretary on New Delhi. 8 September 1952. And In Jawaharlal Nehru. (1972). *Selected Works of Jawaharlal Nehru.* Vol. 19.

Note to the Secretary General. (1954). A copy of the note was sent to the Ministry of Education. JN Collection. 23 May

Nyerere, K. Julius. (1968). *Freedom and Socialism*. Oxford University Press. Dares Salaam. p. 268.

Press conference on Urge for Independence in Asia and Africa in London, 10 June 1953. AIR tapes, NMML. Also from *India News*. 13 June 1953. Extracts. And In Jawaharlal Nehru. 1972. And In. Jawaharlal Nehru. 1972. *Selected Works of Jawaharlal Nehru.* Vol. 22.

Rodney, Walter. (1974). *How Europe Underdeveloped Africa*. Howard University Press. Washington D.C.

Shapiro, Ian. (2013). The Promise of Africa. *The Hindu*. Delhi. July 11.

Singh, Pal Surendra. (1970). India and Liberation of Southern Africa. *Africa Quarterly*, Vol. X, No. 1. Delhi.

Smith, Patrick. (2013). *http://www.africa-confidential.com/news*: 3 August. accessed on 03/08/2013.

Sudan. (2013). *http://www.niit.com/Countries/Sudan/Pages/default.aspx*: accessed on 06/08/2013

Travail of Africa. Nehru Speech at the inauguration of an African students conference in Delhi University. 26 December 1953. *Hindustan Times*. (1953). 27 December, 1953. And In Jawaharlal Nehru. 1972. *Selected Works of Jawaharlal Nehru.* Vol. 24.

Zysman, John. (1983). *Governments, Markets, and Growth.* Ithaca. New York: Cornell University Press.

11

Climate Change and Agriculture in Ethiopia

Tribhuwan Prasad

Climate refers to the average weather conditions in a certain region over a long period of time. The climate of a region is known as a regional climate and the average of climatic components of the world is called a global climate. One of the important trends of global climate is that the average temperature of the world is continuously increasing. This is known as global warming. The rising of average temperature of the globe is not the only factor indicating that the climate is changing. In fact, the signs around us such as changing rainfall and snow pattern, changing temperature and frequent drought shows that the climate has already changed. The Rio convention 1992 defined the climatic change as "a change of climate which is attributed directly or indirectly to human activity that alters the composition of the global atmosphere and which is in addition to natural climate variability observed over comparable time periods." The convention further states "Adverse effects of climate change means changes in the physical environment and biota resulting from climate change which have significant deleterious effects on the composition, resilience and productivity of natural and managed ecosystems and on the operation of socio-economic systems and on human health and welfare." Agriculture is one of the sectors that are most vulnerable to climate change impact. The impact is even stronger in Africa, where agriculture is truly important for the daily subsistence and where adaptive capacity is low. The changes in the climatic components have had adverse impact on agriculture of Ethiopia.

Impact of Climate Change on Agriculture

The climate change has some impact on agricultural components such as the potential of soil to support agriculture and distribution of land use. It is also influenced by the changes in soil water balance. The increase in soil water deficits that is dry soils become drier, therefore this increases the need for irrigation but it could improve soil workability in wetter regions and diminish erosion risk. Further, the effect of increased temperature and CO_2 levels on arable crops has been broadly neutral but new crop varieties may need to be selected. Horticulture crops are more susceptible to changing conditions as compared to the arable crops. The field vegetables are particularly affected by temperature changes whereas water deficit has direct impact on fruit and vegetable production.

Simultaneously, there is also an adverse impact of the climate change on the livestock sector and its suitability in Ethiopia. The piggery and poultry could be exposed to higher incidences of heat stress that influences the productivity and increase in transmission diseases at the faster growth of pathogens in the environment as well as more efficient and abundant vectors such as insects. Apart from that weeds that grow rapidly to overcome the control measures. The short lived weeds that spread vegetative evolve at the greatest rate. The rate of evolution increases in hotter, drier and in 'extreme years' conditions. It could lead to some kinds of herbicide tolerance and its becoming more common. It's possibly increasing the range of many native pests and species.

Climate Change and African Agriculture

Climate change is emerging as a major challenge to agriculture development in Africa. Increasingly the unpredictable nature of weather systems on the continent has placed an extra burden on food security and rural livelihoods. The widespread destruction of farms and homes in recent flooding in Burkina Faso and the prolonged drought in Ethiopia, demonstrate the extent of the threat posed by Africa's changing climate. The agriculture is expected to pay a major damage caused by climate change. The progress in the rural development has already been diminished by the combined effect of the global economic slow down and the food crisis, as a result hunger and malnutrition trends remain high. Without extensive adaptation the effects of climate change on agriculture, it is expected to exacerbate Africa's deepening food crisis, narrowing channels of food access and slowing efforts to expand food productivity.

The report of intergovernmental Panel on Climate Change (IPCC) 2007 provides an extensive assessment on the expected effects of climate change on agriculture in the Africa continent. It estimates that Africa is the most vulnerable to climate change globally due to the multiple stresses of poor infrastructure, poverty and governance. Temperature is likely to increase between 1.5-4°C in this century. The projections of agricultural yield reduction show a drop of up to 50 per cent and crop revenue is to fall as much as 90 per cent by 2100. The agriculture sector is also likely to experience prolonged droughts and floods during the El-Nino events. Agriculture losses of between 2-7 per cent of GDP is expected by 2100 in parts of the Sahara desert region and 2-4 per cent and 0.4-1.3 per cent in Western and Central Africa and Northern and Southern Africa respectively. The arid and semi-arid land could expand in coverage by 60-80Mha. Fisheries would be particularly badly affected due to the changes in sea temperatures that could decrease trends in productivity by 50-60 per cent. According to Overseas Development Institute (ODI), productivity in Africa could be further undermined by a reduction in fertile agricultural land availability and an expansion in the coverage of low potential land. The World Bank forecasts show that Sub-Saharan Africa (SSA) could surpass Asia as the most food insecure region inhabiting 40-50 per cent of undernourished people globally in 2080as compared to 24 per cent today. Levels of viable arable land for production are predicted to decline by 2080, with 9-20 per cent of arable land becoming much less suitable to agriculture.

In response to variations in temperature and precipitation, Africa is predicted to see an increase in crop pests and diseases in addition to altered soil fertility. Declining incomes and rising unemployment are expected to hit agriculture zones in combination to worsening health. A fall in nutrient access is likely to raise susceptibility to diseases such as malaria and HIV/AIDS. Conversely not all assessments of the impact of climate change in Africa are negative, there are likely to be some positive aspects due to changes in seasons and production cycles. Ethiopia and Southern Africa are expected to have extended growing seasons due to climate change, as a consequence of increased temperature and rainfall changes. In addition to that the livestock sector could be boosted by temperature increases, as per the findings of IPCC study. An increase in 5°C of temperature could mean that a rise in farmers' incomes by up to 58 per cent. The overall climate change presents a substantial challenge to regional agricultural development. From food security, nutrition to sustainable management the climate change is a significant threat to the welfare of millions of the continents rural poor. Without extensive current strategies on adaptation for agriculture in Africa, the region will remain vulnerable in its exposure to the widespread effects of climate change.

Climate Change Scenarios

Scenarios are images of the future, or alternative futures. They are neither predictions nor forecasts. Rather, each scenario is one alternative image of how the future might unfold. A set of scenarios assists in the assessment of future developments in complex systems that are either inherently unpredictable, or that have high scientific uncertainties (IPCC 2007).

The Special Report on Emissions Scenarios (SRES) (IPCC, 2007) are grouped into four scenario families (A1, A2, B1 and B2) that explore alternative development pathways, covering a wide range of demographic, economic and technological driving forces and resulting GHG emissions. The A1 storyline assumes a world of very rapid economic growth, a global population that peaks in mid-century and rapid introduction of new and more efficient technologies. Scenario B1 describes a convergent world, with the same global population as A1, but with more rapid changes in economic structures toward a service and information economy with reductions in materials intensity, and the introduction of clean and resource efficient technologies. B2 describes world with intermediate population and economic growth, emphasizing local solutions to economic, social, and environmental sustainability. Scenario A2 describes very heterogeneous world with high population growth, slow economic development and slow technological change. No likelihood has been attached to any of the SRES scenarios (IPCC 2007). In this study three SRES scenarios (A1B, B1, and A2) were used. These scenarios were constructed to explore future developments in the global environment with special reference to the production of greenhouse and aerosol precursor emissions. Each scenario assumes a distinctly different direction for future developments.

Climate Change Scenarios and Agricultural Yields

Climate models often disagree, especially with regard to changes in precipitation. The CSIRO global climate model from the IPCC Assessment Report 4 shows a decrease in annual precipitation in most highland areas of Ethiopia, while other models used in the analysis show normal to above-normal rainfall. MIROC shows a dramatic increase in precipitation over much of Ethiopia. The MIROC and CSIRO models have similar results for changes in average daily maximum temperatures during the warmest month in 2050: while some areas would experience a temperature increase of 1.5–2°C, temperatures in most of the country would only rise by

1–1.5°C. The other two models in the report projected much larger Increases in temperature. Any temperature increase will increase rates of evapotranspiration, possibly leading to a deficit in the water balance and posing a major challenge to rain fed agriculture. The Decision Support System for Agro technology Transfer (DSSAT) crop modelling software was used to compute yields for six crops in rain fed and irrigated systems under current temperature and precipitation regimes, and then again for the 2050 climate projections. The findings suggest substantial reduction in wheat yields and some loss of area, even where rainfall is expected to increase, presumably owing to heat stress. Wheat is the most lucrative crop and the third most important food crop by amount of consumption. This critical loss suggests a couple of option. The first would be more investment in heat-resistant wheat. This could perhaps be done in conjunction with international agricultural research institutes which specialize in wheat. Alternatively, research could be done in strategizing the best substitute crops to replace wheat. Furthermore, there may still be possibilities for wheat production in areas in which wheat had not previously thrived, as Ethiopia offers a wide range of diverse agro ecologies. We also used DSSAT to examine the impact of climate change on rain fed maize in Ethiopia. The CSIRO model suggested a gain in maize yields of more than 25 per cent in the eastern highlands of the edge of Great Rift Valley as well as in the north-central highlands. With a varying degrees, the model shows patches of new area gained along the eastern parts of Amhara and Tigray. But the results also reveal an equal amount of existing maize land that would be marginalized or completely unsuitable for maize, as well as a marked decrease in maize yield over the south-western and eastern parts of central Ethiopia.

Climate Change and Food Security

The research used the IMPACT global model for food and agriculture to estimate the impact of future GDP and population scenarios on crop production and staple consumption, which can be used to derive commodity prices, agricultural trade patterns, food prices, calorie consumption, and child malnutrition. Three GDP-per-capita scenarios were used – an "optimistic scenario" with high per capita income growth and low population growth, a pessimistic scenario with low per capita income growth and high population growth, and an intermediate scenario. The optimistic scenario shows GDP per capita exceeding US$ 1,000 by 2050. In the intermediate scenario it is about US$ 700 in

2050. The pessimistic scenario shows stunted growth through 2050, which nonetheless results in a near doubling of 2010 per capita income. IMPACT shows maize yield rising somewhat by 2020 and then levelling off. At the same time, it projects that cultivated area of maize would decline slightly after 2020. Together, this leads to production rising by around 25 per cent to 2020 and then falling slightly thereafter (with levels in 2050 about the same as those in 2010). With no change in maize production, the rise in consumer demand from a growing population leads to imports of maize after 2020, despite the high world price for maize. For wheat, the IMPACT results projected yields to more than double by 2050. While this appears to contradict the projections of the crop model, the IMPACT model factors in technological change. With a slight increase in area, production by 2050 increases to around 2.5 times the 2010 level. There were very little differences in yield projections across scenarios, and very little differences between climate models, suggesting that observed changes were driven by demand for wheat and by technological changes. The IMPACT model projects that the number of malnourished children will decrease between 2010 and 2050 in the optimistic scenario, reflecting lower population growth and improvement in GDP; the baseline scenario showed a more or less constant number of malnourished children; and the pessimistic scenario showed an increase. Even though the absolute number increased in that scenario, the share of malnourished children declined owing to population growth. Projections of available kilocalories per capita under multiple income and climate scenarios have clear increases under the optimistic scenario, modest increases under the baseline scenarios, and no increase under the pessimistic scenario.

Climate Change, Weather Variability and Agricultural Productivity in Ethiopia

The main crops in Ethiopia are *teff,* maize, and wheat. The population is about 79 million people. Life expectancy has been rising steadily, from less than 40 years in 1960 to about 55 years in 2008. Child mortality decreased gradually from about 270 cases per 1,000 births in 1960 to 210 cases per 1,000 births in 1980. The level remained constant through the 1990s and declined to 100 cases per 1,000 births by 2008. The combined effect of declining child mortality and increasing life expectancy has produced an overall population increase, putting additional pressure on the land to meet food requirements. More than 80 per cent of Ethiopians live below the poverty line and are therefore vulnerable to small shocks and less able to recover from them.

A range of studies of national climate trends since the 1960s show that mean annual temperatures in Ethiopia have increased by between 0.5 and 1.3°C. In addition, the frequency of cold nights (linked to frost in dry season) has decreased significantly in all seasons. Although national models and missing data obscure regional differences in variability and trends, there is evidence of a declining trend in the February to April short rains from 1981-2000, and slight increases in the June to August long rains, as well as in October and November over the same period. Given the dependence on rain-fed agriculture, these trends could have a negative impact on food security. At the same time, flood events are also reported to be becoming more common, with significant disruptions from flooding occurring in 1997 and 2006. Climate change projections are subject to uncertainties and data gaps, and can be contradictory. In Ethiopian climate models, there are high levels of confidence in projecting continuing temperature increases, though the extent of the rises depends one mission's scenarios and varies between models. A review of 18 different models and emissions forecasts predicted warming of1.2°C by the 2020s in all four seasons in all regions of Ethiopia, from 1961-2000 mean temperatures. Other study predicts that temperatures could increase by between 1.5°C and 5.1°C by 2090, (from the 1970-1999 mean) depending on the levels of emissions reductions and range given in the models.

There is less confidence in rainfall projections and less convergence between models. A slight increase in average annual rainfall is projected nationally, but with seasonal and regional differences, which may mean that some regions might experience decreasing grain fall in certain seasons. This broadly explains that more rain will fall in 'heavy events' with increased volumes over shorter periods of time. A further complication in projecting climate impacts is that Ethiopia's exposure to drought and floods is heavily influenced by the global atmospheric 'El Nino' phenomena and the impacts of climate change on these phenomena are not yet clear.

Rainfall and Temperature Variables

The interpolated monthly rainfall observations corresponding to the survey years are averaged for each year corresponding to the survey years in order to construct the average Annual rainfall measure. In addition, given seasonality of rainfall and cropping patterns in the Ethiopian agriculture, separate seasonal measures are constructed for the minor and major rainy seasons. Accordingly, the spring (*Belg*) rainfall measures include the average rainfall for the months between March and May and while the summer (*Kiremt*) rainfall is measured as the average for the months between June and September, all corresponding to the survey years in order to get the short term seasonal weather measures. The climate measure or the long term average is computed as the mean rainfall observations for the years between 1976 and 2006. Similarly, the corresponding long term means rainfall for the spring and summer seasons are calculated as the monthly average over the thirty years, for the spring and summer months, respectively. Although the use of monthly average temperature is common in climate change analyses, Deschenes and Greene (2007) argue that measuring temperature in terms of growing degree days is a better way of assessing the impact of climate change. This is based on agronomic studies that have shown that plant growth depends on the cumulative exposure to heat and precipitation during the growing season. Specifically, as plants cannot absorb heat below a specific threshold or extra heat above a ceiling, the effect of heat accumulation tends to be nonlinear. As a result, the standard agronomic approach involves converting daily temperatures into degree days, which represent heating units accounting for such non linearity's (Hodges, 1991; Grierson, 2002).

Similar studies that focus on single crops (e.g. Deschenes and Greenestone) employ baseline and upper threshold temperature values corresponding to a single crop, in order to generate growing degree days. However, as these thresholds would vary across crops, and due to the multi cropping nature of our data, we construct growing degree days specific to each crop, based on crop specific baseline and threshold temperature values. The growing degree days so constructed are then averaged over seasons and years to obtain the weather (short term) and climate (long term), annual and seasonal temperature measures.

Agriculture remains one of the most important sectors in the Ethiopian economy for the following reasons: (i) it directly supports about 83 per cent of the population in terms of employment and livelihood; (ii) it contributes over 40 per cent of the country's gross domestic product (GDP); (iii) it generates about 85 per cent of export earnings; and (iv) it supplies around 73 per cent of the raw material requirement of agro-based domestic industries (MEDAC, 1999; AFDB, 2011). It is also the major source of food for the population and hence the prime contributing sector to food security. In addition, agriculture is expected to play a key role in generating surplus capital to speed up the country's overall socio-economic development (MEDAC, 1999).

Ethiopia has a total land area of about 112.3 million hectares. Of this, about 16.4 million hectares are suitable for producing annual and perennial crops. Of the estimated arable land, about eight million hectares is used annually for rain fed crops. The country has a population of about 80 million with a growth rate of about 2.6 per cent (AFDB 2011). Small-scale farmers who are dependent on low input and low output rainfed mixed farming with traditional technologies dominate the agricultural sector. The present government of Ethiopia has given top priority to this sector and has taken steps to increase its productivity. However, various problems are holding this back. Some causes of poor crop production are declining farm size; subsistence farming partly due to population growth; land degradation due to inappropriate land use such as cultivation of steep slopes; over cultivation and overgrazing; and inappropriate polices. Other causes are tenure insecurity; weak agricultural research and extension services; lack of appropriate agricultural marketing; an inadequate transport network; low use of fertilizers, improved seeds and pesticides; and the use of traditional farm implements. However, the major causes of low level of production are drought, which often causes famine, and floods. This climate related disasters make the nation dependent on food aid. With agriculture almost completely dependent on rainfall, rain rules the lives and well-being of many rural Ethiopians. It determines whether they will have enough to eat and whether they will be able to provide basic necessities and earn a living. Indeed, the dependence on rainfall and its erratic pattern has largely contributed to the food shortages and crop crises that farmers are constantly faced with. Even in good years, the one-time harvest or crop may be too little to meet the yearly household needs; as a result, the majority of Ethiopia's rural people remain food insecure (Devereux, 2000).

Rainfall contributes to poverty both directly, through actual losses from rainfall shocks, and indirectly, through responses to the threat of crisis. The direct impacts particularly occur when a drought destroys a smallholder farmer's crops. Under such circumstances, not only will the farmers and their families go hungry, but they also will be forced to sell or consume their plough animals in order to survive. They are then significantly worse off than before because they can no longer farm effectively when the rains return (Barrett, *et al.*, 2007).

Ethiopia is one of the African countries that have recently started paying particular attention to climate change as a national as well as a global problem. Ethiopia is active in climate change negotiations representing Africa. There are also a number of activities undertaken over the past decade to address climate change. These include submission of initial national communications on Green House Gases (GHG) emissions to United Nations Framework Convention on Climate Change (UNFCCC), submission of National Adaptation Program of Action (NAPA) as well as the Nationally Appropriate Mitigation Actions (NAMA) to UNFCCC, preparation of a Reducing Emissions from Deforestation and Forest Degradation (REDD) readiness plan, and ongoing preparation of a national level adaptation program as well as a green growth strategy as part of a climate resilient green economy (CRGE) strategy. Such attempts should be supported by rigorous empirical studies on various aspects of climate change including its impacts which are very limited.

Impact of Climate Change on Agricultural Water Resources

The climate change has some negative impact on the performance of existing and planned irrigation and hydropower schemes in the Ethiopian part of the Blue Nile River. The results show that climate change will constrain the technical performance of large reservoirs with knock-on effects for agriculture and electricity production. Against this background water resource development in the basin requires interventions that bolster resilience and water security. This requires much more systematic planning of water storage and greater cooperation between the riparian states. The Blue Nile River is an important shared resource of Ethiopia, Sudan and, because it is the major contributor of water to the main Nile River, also Egypt. To date, in contrast to Sudan and Egypt, Ethiopia has utilized very little of the Nile water. This is partly because of its inaccessibility and partly because the major centres of population lie outside of the basin. However, this is likely to change in the near future. To drive economic development, the Ethiopian government plans to utilize Nile water resources for both irrigation and hydropower. Many large dams are planned, both on the main stem and on tributaries, to support hydropower and irrigation development.

If all planned development occurs, large reservoir water storage will exceed 160,000 mm^3 (i.e. approximately 14x present levels and 3x the current mean annual flow at the Ethiopia-Sudan border), irrigation will exceed 360,000 ha (i.e. 23x present levels) and installed hydropower generating capacity will be in excess of 10,000 MW (i.e. 47x present levels). There is great uncertainty about the impacts of climate change in the basin and there have been few systematic studies of the possible implications for water resource development. This research was conducted to determine the impact of one specific IPCC climate change scenario (A1B) on the performance of existing and planned irrigation and hydropower schemes in Ethiopia and the implications for flows into Sudan. This scenario was selected simply because it is a mid-range scenario resulting in climate change that lies between that anticipated by other scenarios. As such, it is a relatively conservative, but not overly cautious, scenario. Three computer models were used in combination. A dynamic regional climate model – COSMO (Consortium for Small Scale Modelling) CLM (CCLM) – was used to determine climate projections for the basin for the period 1983-2100 with initial and boundary conditions set by the The Fifth Generation Atmospheric general Circulation Model (ECHAM-5) model 3. The outputs generated from CCLM (i.e. rainfall, temperature and potential evapo-transpiration were used as input to a hydrological model Soil and Water Assessment Tod (SWAT) which was setup, calibrated and validated with observed climate and hydrological data. Land use was assumed constant throughout the scenario simulation. Results of the SWAT modelling (i.e. projections in river flow and groundwater recharge), in conjunction with projected water demand, were used as inputs to the Water Evaluation and Planning (WEAP) model which was used to evaluate the possible impacts on hydropower generation and irrigation.

There is great uncertainty on exactly what sorts of water resources schemes would be better in the basin for the better future. In order to systematically assess the impact of growing water demand on the basin's water resources, four development scenarios were identified and modelled.

- No development – this scenario simulated the basin in its natural condition without any development. It provided a baseline to enable the impact of only CC to be assessed.
- Current development – this scenario simulated water resources development in 2010. In this scenario, irrigation and hydropower schemes were the ones that are currently operating.
- Intermediate development – this simulated possible expansion of existing irrigation schemes, as well as new hydropower and irrigation schemes that are likely to start by approximately 2025.

- Full development – this simulated expansion of the near-future schemes and additional new schemes that are likely to occur in the future (i.e. before approximately 2050).

Results indicate that changes in climate will affect both water availability and demand. Under the A1B scenario, in a natural situation (i.e. no development), flows increase slightly at the Ethiopia-Sudan border in the first half of the 21st century but decrease by 20 per cent, in the second half of the century. Average annual irrigation water demand fluctuates but increases significantly, particularly in the second half of the century. The planned water resources development in the basin will cause an additional 2.6 per cent decline in flows at the border in the second half of the century. Simulated catchment average irrigation demand: a) annual values (1983-2100) b) mean monthly values over three periods 1983-2012, 2021-2050 and 2071-2100. The anticipated changes in climate will have significant impacts on both hydropower generation and water supply to irrigation schemes. The model simulations indicate that approximately 90 per cent of irrigation demand will be met and the hydropower generated will broadly match the potential until the middle of the 21st century. However, in the latter part of the century, in the Intermediate and Full Development scenarios, 40 per cent or less of the total irrigation demand will be met and only approximately 60 per cent of potential hydropower will be generated.

The increase in 'Evapotranspiration' is probably due to increased air temperatures. Moreover, it is observed that more than 60 per cent of the hydrological loss in the present system is through evapotranspiration process. This indicates that increased evapotranspiration in the future may be a significant factor leading in the direction of decreased stream flow, which may or may not be compensated for by changes in rainfall.

Climate Change Impacts on Ethiopian Agriculture, Growth, and Poverty

The impact of climate change was assessed in terms of its effect on crop and livestock farming and how these effects extend throughout Ethiopia, in terms of economic growth and poverty reduction. Looking at the two zones that dominate Ethiopia's agricultural production today—the moisture-sufficient highlands areas with cereal-based agriculture and the drought-prone highlands—their projected outcomes are somewhat different, but climate change is expected to have a huge impact on both. In the moisture-sufficient highlands where cereals dominate, which currently accounts for the largest share of agricultural production, overall productivity is projected to increase until approximately 2030 as a result of climate change, but decline sharply thereafter. This is clearly visible in the projected overall production outcomes for crops, as well as for livestock. Both crop and livestock production increase faster in the climate-change scenarios than in the corresponding no-climate-change scenarios, until land productivity begins to decline around 2030.

In the high TFP growth scenario, the increased overall productivity can compensate for the loss in land productivity until about 2040, but is unable to keep pace with the loss in land productivity after that. In the low TFP growth scenario, as a result of climate change, overall production of both crops and livestock is lower at the end of the projection period than at the beginning. In the drought-prone highlands, the situation is somewhat different. Land productivity and crop yield is expected to decline as a result of climate change more or less continuously throughout the period studied, but much of the decline occurs relatively soon. After that, deterioration slows down temporarily between 2030 and 2050. This agro-ecological zone does not have the—grace period, until 2030 that the moisture-sufficient highlands do, and crop and livestock production both decline compared with the corresponding no-climate-change scenarios. However, the sharp fall in crop production seen in other parts of the country after 2030 it means that the value of crop production increases after 2030 and actually rises above that in the no-climate-change baseline. For livestock production, unlike crops, the long-term decline in land productivity does not slow down after 2030; therefore, there is no corresponding recovery period. Instead, production is projected to decline throughout the projection period in both the climate-change and no-climate-change scenarios.

Climate Change and Poverty

Poverty continues to be a major development challenge in Ethiopia Despite a significant decline in the incidence of poverty during the past four decades, poverty is still prevalent in the country (Fig. 11.1). More than 28 million people, or 34 per cent of the population, earn less than US$ 1 per day. The picture is not different in the rest of Africa. As a result, internal policies are gauged towards fighting poverty at the Ethiopian or African level. In Ethiopia, approximately 84 per cent of the poor are located in rural areas, implying poverty is mainly a rural phenomenon, with the large majority of people depending on agriculture

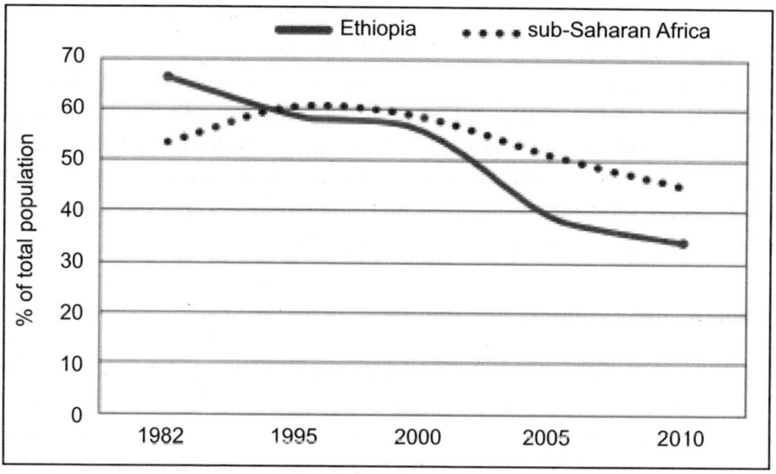

Fig. 11.1: Trend and Incidence of Poverty in Ethiopia

Source: World Bank Indicators, 2008.

for employment and income. Agricultural growth, thus, offers a potentially enormous opportunity for poverty reduction in the country, particularly when the growth is broad-based. Likewise, agricultural failure exacerbates poverty and food insecurity in such agrarian economies (DFID, 2005). Climate change and the associated environmental degradation are emerging as big challenges to Ethiopian agriculture and poverty alleviation efforts. Agriculture is the main pass-through mechanism from climate change and environmental degradation to poverty. According to DFID (2005) and Rao, *et al.* (2004), growth in agricultural production and productivity are considered essential to achieve sustainable growth and significant reduction in poverty in developing countries. This is primarily because the sector is the main source of employment and output in developing countries. There are also undeniable backward and forward linkages between agriculture and other pro-poor sectors of the economy.

Although agricultural failure can harm the rural poor, it can also have a significant impact on the urban poor. The urban poor are affected in terms of high food prices, limited job opportunities in the agro-processing industries, and expensive imported food items due to foreign exchange shortages. Climate change is also predicted to affect world cereal production and marketing (Parry, 2007; Barrios, *et al.*, 2004), the impact of which can easily be transmitted to Ethiopia through trade channels with increased import prices.

Climate change can also affect the lives of the poor by limiting access to traditional sources of energy due to the depletion of forest cover (Aster, 2010). Moreover, climate change can bring with it health threats that put pressure on quality of life and on health expenditures. During periods of extreme conditions such as serious drought and flooding, people tend to migrate and leave their original locations. Such actions can at least temporarily terminate education and other public services, which are closely related to non-income dimensions of poverty.

Climate and Economy of Ethiopia

Agriculture in Ethiopia is mainly dependents on rain. Its geographical location in semi-arid Sahelian region and topography, as well as low adaptive capacity, makes the country highly vulnerable to the adverse impacts of climate change. Poverty in Ethiopia is a chronic problem and about two-thirds of its 72 million people live on less than US$ 2 a day (World Bank, 2008). It is one of the most food-insecure countries in the world, a situation compounded by droughts and famine that cycle in and out. Over 80 per cent of the population of the country derives its livelihood from agriculture. Of the 4.3 million hectares of potentially irrigable agricultural land, less than 10 per cent is currently farmed. Smallholder farmers dominate the sector, generating about 90 per cent of agricultural output (Adenew, 2006).

Economic performance was very low during most of the second half of the twentieth century. A useful indicator is total factor productivity (TFP) growth, which measures economic growth that cannot be explained by increases in factors of production, such as labour, capital, or land. It gauges production increases that are caused by more efficient application of technology or more efficient use of existing inputs, rather than increased use of inputs. Between 1950 and 1990, Ethiopian TFP actually declined by over 01 per cent per year. In the post-1992 reform period, on the other hand, its economic growth was among the highest in Africa, with TFP growth registering over 2.5 per cent per year. Important constraints remain, however, in the forms of insecure property rights to land and a poorly developed private sector (Easterly, 2006).

Geographically, Ethiopia can be subdivided into five agro-ecological zones based on moisture and land use:

(1) drought-prone highlands with insufficient rainfall;
(2) rainfall-sufficient highland areas mainly planted with cereal-based crops;

(3) Generally dry, pastoral lowland areas (bordering on Eritrea); and
(4) Humid lowland areas further inland that primarily support crop farming.

Climate change will lead to adaptive shifts in cultivation patterns in all five regions. Whether input and output markets can change sufficiently in time, so that farmers can cope with these shifts, will be an important challenge for future adaptation policies.

Ethiopia has experienced at least five major national droughts since 1980, along with a large number of localized droughts (World Bank, 2008). These cycles of drought create poverty traps for many households, constantly consuming their efforts to build up assets and increase income. About half of all rural households in the country experienced at least one major drought from 1999 to 2004 (Dercon, 2009). With agriculture highly dependent on rainfall variability and amount, weather in general rules the lives and well-being of many rural Ethiopians. The weather determines whether they will have enough to eat, be able to provide basic necessities, and be able to earn a living. Indeed, farmers' dependence on change (Boko, *et al.,* 2007).

The country has a complex climate system, in addition to socioeconomic challenges, such as endemic poverty, limited access to capital and global markets, ecosystem degradation, complex disasters, and conflicts. Accordingly, the effect of climate change on Ethiopia's economy will likely be a function of both the macro-economy and sector-specific vulnerability. This means that the government's adaptation policies will be crucial. However, such policies are likely to be costly and, without a realistic baseline scenario, there is a risk that government programs will be evaluated against an inappropriate status quo (no cost, no climate change), rather than against the outcomes that will prevail if no government adaptation is carried out (Stage, 2010). It is important, then, to assess the impacts climate change is likely to have, if private agents are left to adapt on their own. Such a baseline impact assessment can be used to assess the effects of activist adaptation policies. Rainfall and its erratic patterns have largely contributed to the food shortages and crises with which they constantly battle. In Ethiopia, as well as many other African countries, a range of factors may undermine communities' ability to adapt to climate.

Implications of Climate Change Impact

Ethiopia is known to be one of the countries most affected by drought. Given a large part of the country is arid or semi-arid and highly prone to drought and desertification, a further decrease in precipitation could increase the frequency and intensity of droughts in the country. Also, Ethiopia has a fragile highland ecosystem that is currently under stress due to increasing population pressure. Our analysis suggests that the northern highlands of the country could experience reduced rainfalls, and hence become susceptible to even more severe drought Conditions. A dramatic reduction in precipitation or increase of actual evapotranspiration would cause soil moisture stress. The resulting negative agricultural water balance would reduction both rain-fed and irrigated agriculture productivity. A reduction in rainfall coupled with land degradation and other factors would also significantly reduce effective rainfall; that is, rainfall which could be available for crop consumption. The combined effect has the potential to cause a great agricultural drought, unless there is ample water available for irrigation. However, a reduction in rainfall may cause reduce ground water recharge, which would significantly reduce its contribution to stream flow. Lake Tana is highly sensitive to variations in rainfall, as well as in river inflows and evaporation. Setegn *et al.* (2009) showed that inflow river discharge to Lake Tana contributes over 90 per cent of the lake inflow. It is thus very likely that changes in river inflow would also change the volume of the lake and the water balance, which could ultimately adversely impact the lake ecosystem.

The Declaration of Conference of Parties (COP) 17, Durban on Climate Change

The United Nations Climate Change Conference, Durban 2011, delivered a breakthrough on the international community's response to climate change. In the second largest meeting of its kind, the negotiations advanced, in a balanced fashion, the implementation of the Convention and the Kyoto Protocol, the Bali Action Plan, and the Cancun Agreements. The outcomes included a decision by Parties to adopt a universal legal agreement on climate change as soon as possible, and no later than 2015. There are some major initiatives taken in conference; such as

Green Climate Fund

- Countries have already started to pledge to contribute to start-up costs of the fund, meaning it can be made ready in 2012, and at the same time can help developing countries get ready to access the fund, boosting their efforts to establish their own clean energy futures and adapt to existing climate change.

- A Standing Committee is to keep an overview of climate finance in the context of the UNFCCC and to assist the Conference of the Parties. It will comprise 20 members, represented equally between the developed and developing world.
- A focussed work programme on long-term finance was agreed, which will contribute to the scaling up of climate change finance going forward and will analyse options for the mobilisation of resources from a variety of sources.

Adaptation

- The Adaptation Committee, composed of 16 members, will report to the Conference of Parties on its efforts to improve the coordination of adaptation actions at a global scale.
- The adaptive capacities above all of the poorest and most vulnerable countries are to be strengthened. National Adaptation Plans will allow developing countries to assess and reduce their vulnerability to climate change.
- The most vulnerable are to receive better protection against loss and damage caused by extreme weather events related to climate change.

Technology

- The Technology Mechanism will become fully operational in 2012.
- The full terms of reference for the operational arm of the Mechanism — the Climate Technology Centre and Network — are agreed, along with a clear procedure to select the host. The UNFCCC secretariat will issue a call for proposals for hosts on 16 January 2012.

Support of Developing Country Action

- Governments agreed a registry to record developing country mitigation actions that seek financial support and to match these with support. The registry will be a flexible, dynamic, web based platform.

Other Key Decisions

- A forum and work programme on unintended consequences of climate change actions and Policies were established.
- Under the Kyoto Protocols Clean Development Mechanism, governments adopted procedures to allow carbon-capture and

storage projects. These guidelines will be reviewed every five years to ensure environmental integrity.

- Governments agreed to develop a new market-based mechanism to assist developed countries in meeting part of their targets or commitments under the Convention. Details of this will be taken forward in 2012.

Conclusion and Policy Implications

Climate change affects various dimensions of Ethiopia's economy including power generation, the country's health, education and industry sectors, and public spending on productive investments. However, estimating the impact of climate variability on agriculture is simple and easy to analyse. Given the structure of the Ethiopian economy and the distribution of poverty the assessment of the impact of climate change on growth and poverty should focus on agricultural productivity. Whatever happens to the agricultural sector it highly governs the performance of other sectors of the economy. Finally it affects the national economy and poverty incidences. In the light of this it can be stated that the possible impact of rainfall variability (one of the manifestations of climate change) on the Ethiopian agriculture is an attempts to relate climate change to poverty. The study reveals that the performance of Ethiopian agriculture is highly and significantly influenced by the trends in rainfall patterns. The study further states that the level of agricultural production is reduced by 3.6 to 6.1 per cent of current RAGDP (Real Agricultural Gross Domestic Product) as compared to the no change in climate over 1990 to 2008. The forgone output would have been used to reduce poverty and food insecurity from the country. The lost output would also have spill over effects on the performance of the overall economy. The level of reduced output is found to be in the range of 13 to 40 per cent of the current level of agricultural yield. Furthermore, unless the observed climate change induced variations are reversed the cost to the economy will continue in the near future. Extending our evaluation in the future, the present paper finds that Ethiopia will continue to sacrifice its potential agricultural production, through which the country needs to obtain food security and achieve the millennium development goals including reducing poverty as compared to the 1995 levels. The study explains that the country will lose about US$ 20 billion (i.e. 32.5 per cent of current RAGDP) of agricultural production over the coming few years due to rainfall variability. The poverty implications of climate change are severe due to the inherent characteristics of the poor. The poor normally rely on primary sectors such as agriculture, forestry, fishery, and marginal lands, which are highly susceptible to climate change. The poor also lack the expertise on climate change adaptation mechanisms which make the poor highly vulnerable to further deteriorations in their environment and the climate. At the national level, agriculture centred growth is perceived to be broad based and pro-poor as the majority of the poor rely on the sector. The smallholder agriculture and sectors with direct ties to it tend to be more labour intensive than the sophisticated high level services and industrial establishments. The studies found that sectoral distribution of growth has implications on poverty reduction. This study's attempt to explain the direct impact of climate change on poverty shows that the country had lost a 2 to 9 per cent reduction in poverty over 1991 to 2010. On the other hand, a 3 to 4 per cent potential reduction in poverty will be lost over 2011 to 2015 due to rainfall variability. At the regional level, the regions with higher vulnerability to climate change tend to have higher poverty levels.

REFERENCES

Admassu, Habtamu, Mezgebu, Getinet, Timothy, S. Thomas, Michael Waithaka. and Miriam Kyotarlimye (2012). *East African Agriculture and Climate Change: A Comprehensive Analysis-Ethiopia*. International Food Policy Research Institute. Washington, DC. USA.

Aragie, Asaminew Amerta. (2013). *Climate Change, Growth and Poverty in Ethiopia.* Working Paper No 3. The Robert S Strauss Centre for International Security and Law. Climate Change and African Political Stability Program (CCAPS). USA: The University of Texas. Austin.

Barrett. Socioeconomic Scenarios. *Global Environmental Change* 14: 53–67.

Christopher, B. and Santos, Paulo. (2013). *The Impact of Changing Rainfall Variability on Resource-Dependent Wealth Dynamics.*

Deschenes, Olivier and Greenstone, Michael. (2007). The Economic Impacts of Climate Change: Evidence from Agricultural Output and Random Fluctuations. *In Weather*. Vol. 97. No. 1. MIT. USA.

Devereux, Stephen. (2000). *Food Insecurity in Ethiopia.* Discussion Paper

Funk, Chris, Jim, Rowland, Gary, Eilerts, Emebet, Kebebe, Nigist, Biru, *et al.* (2012). *A Climate Trend Analysis of Ethiopia*. Research Project. United States Agency for International Development (USAID). Rolla Publishing Service Center, USGS. USA.

Gebreegz, Iabher Zenebe, Stage, Jesper, Mekonnen Alemu, and Atlaw Alemu. (2011). *Climate Change and the Ethiopian Economy A Computable General Equilibrium Analysis*. Discussion Paper. Environment for Development. Ethiopia.

Hassan R. (2006). *Impacts of Climate Change on Crop Farming in Ethiopia.* Diccussion Paper No. 21. Centre for Environmental Economics and Policy in Africa (CEEPA). University of Pretoria. South Africa.

McCartney Matthew. (2012). *The Implications of Climate Change for Water Resource Development in the Blue Nile River.* Discussion Paper 1251. Global Water Forum.

Parry, M.L. Rosenzweig, C. Iglesias, A. Livermore, M. and Fischer, G. (2004). *Effects of Climate Change on Global Food Production under SRES Emissions.* Department for International Development (DFID). Ethiopia/UK.

Schimmelpfennig, D. Lewandrowski, J. Tsigas, M. and Parry, I. (1996). *Agricultural Adaptation to Climate Change: Issues of Longrun Sustainability.* Agricultural Economic Report No. AER740.

Tadege Abebe (Ed.). (2007). *Climate Chamge National Programme of Action (NAPA) of Ethiopia.* National Meteorological Agency. Addis Ababa. Ethiopia.

Tadesse Debay. (2010). *The Impact of Climate Change in Africa.* ISS Paper no. 220. Institute of Security Studies. ISS Publication. Pretoria. South Africa.

Thornton, Philip and Cramer, Laura (Eds.). (2012). *Impacts of Climate Change on the Agricultural and Aquatic Systems and Natural Resources within the CGIAR's Mandate.* Working paper no. 23. University of Copenhagen: CGIAR Research Program on Climate Change, Agriculture and Food Security (CCAFS). Copenhagen, Denmark.

Vololona, Mireille Rahaingo, Miriam, Kyotarlimye, Timothy, S. Thomas, Michael, Waithaka. (2012). *East African Agriculture and Climate Change: A comprehensive analysis-Madagascar.* International Food Policy Research Institute. Washington, DC. USA.

World Bank Report. (2007). *African Development Indicators.*

World Bank (2008a). Ethiopia: *A Country Study on the Economic Impacts of Climate Change.* Development Prospects Group, Report Number 46946-ET.

World Bank. (2008b). *Agriculture for Development.* World Development Report.

www.mofed.gov.et/English/Pages/Home.aspx

www.fao.org/docrep/014/i2155e/i2155e00.pdf

www.ipcc.ch

www.unfccc.int

www.ccafs.cgiar.org.

www.undp.org

www.epa.gov.et/default.aspx

www.iied.org

12
Gender and Agriculture in Africa

Rashmi Kapoor

> Women are the only oppressed group in our society that lives in intimate association with their oppressors.
>
> —Evenly Cunningham

Discussing about African women is always a challenging task. The social transformations brought about by global economic processes show qualitative changes in African women in many spheres. Paradoxically, at the same time, there exists seemingly static status of traditional African women in whom patriarchal ideologies are adhered tightly to the bosom. There is no single defining quality describing the identity of 'the African women' representing the whole continent as there exist plurality of images informing about the African women due to extreme diversity and dynamic nature of the African society. The predominant role traditionally assigned to women in Africa is that of reserving her in the private, domestic domain, that is, into the role of mother and wife and to men that of household head with orientation towards the public sphere. This gendered division of labour has resulted in ascribing a subordinate status to women despite the fact that they play crucial socio-economic role. Most rural African women have to bear a double burden; one of actively participating in farming activities and the other of fulfilling the duties of wife and mother. What is different in Africa and at variance to most other developing societies is that women in traditional, pre colonial Africa played a central role in the polity, society and economy. Within the family, they had an important position in the decision making process. It can be said that women had some autonomy and were fairly empowered.

Industrialization and colonial policies undermined the role of women and made them dependent as in any other traditional patriarchal society. Loss of control of land was the biggest blow to their autonomy as it left women in lurch and completely dependent on men. Then with the introduction of agricultural technology, African rural women were worst hit because their access to such resources remained limited. Facilities like training programs and farm management skills again are not favorable for women to attain as either they are not educated or have little education not equipping them enough for these programs, apart from being less tech-savy. In contemporary urban Africa, some appreciable change can be observed in women's living and material conditions, but in the status and role, they are still lagging behind. Modern education and participation in industrial labor force has given women an opportunity to move out of their homes into the uncontested public spaces. These women have become active agents in transforming their physical conditions. They are proactively articulating their concerns through collective efforts. Also political impetus and various international and national initiatives and programs have resulted in significant change, but not as much as desired. So the gender gap rather than being bridged is widening and it is further affecting their life chances. This chapter will focus on the role of gender in agriculture in Africa. It will discuss how gender inequalities can affect food production immensely. The chapter will also elaborate on various initiatives and programmes to be undertaken to address the issue of gender inequality.

There are some facts regarding rural women in developing countries, which generally go unnoticed. Developing economies are primarily agricultural economies and women are pillar of strength for these economies. Gender inequalities have been one of the major causes of impediment to the growth of agricultural sector. The State of Food and Agriculture (2011) notes that just by giving women the same access as men to agricultural resources could increase production on women's farms in developing countries by 20 to 30 per cent. This could raise total agricultural production in developing countries by 2.5 to 4 per cent, which could in turn reduce the number of hungry people in the world by 12 to 17 per cent, or 100 to 150 million people. An estimated 925 million people in the world were undernourished in 2010, of which 906 million live in developing countries. IFPRI Issue Brief 62 in its Report on The Challenge of Hunger: Focus on Financial Crisis and Gender Inequality notes that countries with the highest levels of hunger also have very high levels of gender inequality. Careful deliberations on gender inequality can help in alleviating hunger and poverty in the world. To address the issue of gender inequality, it is imperative to lessen gender gap and enhance equal access to resources for men and women in an effort to reduce food insecurity, improve economic growth and bolster sustainable development.

Oyewumi (2005), while discussing about the Oyo oral traditions of Africa, says that since colonial times men and women have been invented as social categories and history is presented as being dominated by male actors. Female actors are virtually absent and where they are recognized, they are reduced to exception. This is a reflection of the extent of invisibility of women and existence of perpetual gender inequality. This is true not only for African societies, but for most developing societies of the world. Most confuse sex and gender. Biological sex is not same as gender identity. Sex refers to a person's biological maleness or femaleness. Gender is a learned attribute. Gender roles are learned through socialization and education by living in a particular society. Issacka (Realising Women's Equality Rights in Africa) opines that gender refers to the socially and culturally assigned roles and responsibilities to various human beings. Barasa (2011) says that gender refers to a group of attributes or behaviours shaped by society and culture that are defined appropriate for the biological distinction between men and women. Simone de Beauvoir says that one is not born a woman, but learns to become one. Gender determines the fixed course of social development and learning of expected social roles and cultural norms. This includes the learning of and acceptance of unequal status of woman and man. Emphasizing the unequal status between men and women, Nfah-Abbenyi (2005) says that for some feminists, gender is a system of meanings within cultures used to categorise male and female sexuality in hierarchical terms. Though learned, the gender roles vary widely within and across cultures. Tietcheu (2006) insists that these social constructs may not be objective, but more subjective and since the gendered roles in society are not given by nature and hence they can change in time and space.

Gender can, therefore, mean different things to different people since it carries the ideologies of the socio-cultural context in which it is constructed. Steady (2005) insists that without doubt, the term 'gender' carries a western bias. It tends to be myopic, inventive, and can obscure other differences. Because it is western, it reveals white western middle class biases and obscures other differences based on race, class, ethnicity, religion, sexuality and so forth. In this regard, it fails to recognize the role of women themselves in other structures of oppression. It should be noted here that gender is related to both women and men and not promotion of women only as is often understood. Also, gender is not only about the roles assigned, but also about the value placed on those roles. Gender inequality and hierarchy between genders is adversely affecting half the population of the world.

Amartya Sen (2001), in his inaugural lecture for the New Radcliffe Institute at Harvard University, while discussing South Asia societies argued that there is a need to take a plural view of gender inequality, which can have many different faces. He expressed that gender inequality exists in most parts of the world. However, inequality between women and men can take very many different forms. Indeed, gender inequality is not one homogeneous phenomenon, but a collection of disparate and interlinked problems. He demonstrated that there are seven kinds of gender inequalities. (1) Mortality inequality: In some regions in the world, inequality between women and men directly involves matters of life and death, and takes the brutal form of unusually high mortality rates of women and a consequent preponderance of men in the total population. (2) Natality inequality: Given a preference for boys over girls that many male-dominated societies have, gender inequality can manifest itself in the form of the parents wanting the newborn to be a boy rather than a girl. (3) Basic facility inequality: Even when demographic characteristics do not show much or any anti-female bias, there are other ways in which women can have less than a square deal. (4) Special opportunity inequality: Even when there is relatively little difference in basic facilities including schooling, the opportunities of higher education may be far fewer for young women than for young men. (5) Professional inequality: In terms of employment as well as promotion in work and occupation, women often face greater handicap than men. (6) Household inequality: There are, often enough, basic inequalities in gender relations within the family or the household, which can take many different forms. (7) Ownership inequality: In many societies, the ownership of property can also be very unequal. Even basic assets such as homes and land may be very asymmetrically shared. The absence of claims to property can not only reduce the voice of women, but also make it harder for women to enter and flourish in commercial, economic and even some social activities.

Each of the Social Science perspectives deal with the significance of gender and provide explanation for the existence of gender inequalities. Functionalists emphasise that gender inequality is functional and contributes to social stability. According to them, gender inequality is a product of traditional division of labor in human societies and conforming into the prescribed roles is a cause of gender inequality. Men perform instrumental tasks whereas women fill in expressive roles. These roles are presumed to be functional and important not only for the individual, but also for the benefit of the society's survival. Conflict theorists stress that the root cause of gender inequality lies in male-female power opportunities for their employment and healthy life be removed. Facilitating increased control of resources by women and enhancing women's assets can promote agricultural production and thus increase food security. For this financial support and appropriate strategies and interventions are required in different areas tailored according to the needs of women. These different areas of financing gender equality are interrelated, and all these areas should be activated to promote gender equality and empowerment of women. Policy formulations and long-term planning is not enough. There has to be a paradigm shift in the policies and financing programmes and they need to be transformative rather than selective and exclusive.

REFERENCES

Agarwal, B. (2002). Are We Not Peasants Too? Land Rights and Women's Claims in India. *Seeds*. Number 21.

Barasa, J. N. K. (2011). Gender and Higher Education in Africa: The Case of Kenya. In T. Falola and S. U. Fwatshak (eds.). *Beyond Tradition: African Women in Cultural and Political Spaces*. New Jersey: Africa World Press. pp. 301-327.

Berg, A. van den. (1997). Women farmers in pursuit of land security: and what about sustainability? In M. E. Bruijn, I. van Halsema, and H. van den Hombergh (eds.). *Gender and Land use: Diversity in Environmental Practices*. Amsterdam: Thela Publishers. pp. 87-105.

Benschop, M. (2002). *Rights and Reality: Are women's equal rights to land, housing and property implemented in East Africa?* Nairobi: United Nations Human Settlement Programme

Bridging the Gap: Financing Gender Equality. (2008). A Publication of the United Nations Development Fund For Women (UNIFEM) and The UN Non-Governmental Liaison Service (NGLS). http://www.un-ngls.org/IMG/pdf/UNIFEM.pdf. Accessed on 10/11/2012.

Bulow, D.V. and Sorensen, A. (2010). Gender and Contract Farming: Growing Tea in Kenya. In M. Trushen (Ed.). *African Women: A Political Economy*. New York: Palgrave Macmillan.

Cooper, B. M. (1997). *Marriage in Maradi: Gender and Culture in a Hausa Society in Niger, 1900-1989*. Portsmouth, NH: Heinemann.

Cotula, L. Toulmin, C. and Hesse, C. (2004). Land Tenure and Administration in Africa: Lessons of Experience and Emerging Issues. International Institute for Environment and Development. London. *http://pubs.iied.org/pdfs/9305IIED.pdf*. Accessed on 10/9/2012.

Davis, M. S. Farnworth, C. and Sundell, M. F. (2012). Transforming gender relations in agriculture in sub-Saharan Africa: Promising approaches. SIANI: Stockholm Environment Institute. Sweden.

Duran, L. A. (2012). Strengthening Financing for Gender Equality and Women's Organizations. United Nations Commission on the Status of Women. Fifty-Sixth Session. 27 February—9 March 2012. New York.

September 2003, 174 countries (90% of the members of the United Nations) have become party to the Convention. The United Nations Human Development Report (1995) refers to gender equality in terms of capabilities (education, health, and nutrition) and opportunities (economic and decision-making). The World Bank defines gender equality in terms of equality under the law, equality of opportunity (including equality of rewards for work and equality in access to human capital and other productive resources that enable opportunity), and equality of voice (the ability to influence and contribute to the development process).

Barasa (2007) said that gender equality does not simply mean equal numbers of women and men in all activities; nor does it mean treating men or women exactly the same. It should signify that men and women are able to live equally fulfilling lives. Men and women have equal opportunities and equal access to resources or equal participation in decision making process. With regards to women, gender equality entails elimination of discrimination against women and the empowerment of women to combat poverty, hunger and disease and achieving sustainable development. International Plan Parenthood Federation defines gender equality in terms of parity of status and insists that it does not imply that women and men are the same, but that they have equal value and should be accorded equal treatment. Issacka (Realising Women's Equality Rights In Africa) says that it is when women and men, boys and girls enjoy the same status and have equal conditions/opportunities for realizing their full human rights and potential to contribute to national, political, economic, social and cultural development, and to benefit from the results. Nelson and England (2002) insist that as opposed to inter-gender power hierarchy or a separatism where everyone is self-interested and autonomous, in gender equality all individuals hold a similar level of power and treat other people with respect and consideration, regardless of their sex. The above definitions of gender equality have been defined in multiple ways and stress different dimensions of gender equality. But most would agree that gender equality be regarded first and foremost as a human right that entails equal value and equality of opportunity for both men and women, it is when they have equal access to resources and equal participation in the decision making process and, thereby, are able to contribute optimally to political, economic, social and cultural development of the society. In its absence, women will remain disempowered, which will be a great barrier for reducing poverty and promoting just sustainable development.

Gender Inequality in Rural Sub-Saharan Africa

Gender inequality has been found to be a serious constraint to food production in rural sub-Saharan Africa since the crucial role played by women in agriculture sector is undermined. International Fertilizer Development Centre notes (as cited in Gender and Agriculture: Unlocking Africa's Potential) that the African farmer is primarily a woman farmer. And she is a good farmer, who can feed her family and her continent if she is given the tools and the opportunities to do so. There is a strong confidence in rural African women's potential, but at the same time, it underscores the fact that lack of facilities and opportunities is limiting them.

Most of Africa is largely rural and agrarian and a large number of agricultural activities are performed by unpaid labour, mostly women. Agricultural activities include wide range of operations and, surprisingly, women provide much of the labour in most activities. Opio (2003) takes agriculture to mean the production, processing and marketing of crops, livestock and fish from producer to consumer. Agriculture as defined is a major part of overall natural resource based activity. Other areas include forestry and wild life. Agricultural enterprises range from large capital intensive production and processing units to small scale activities forming only part of the people's livelihood strategies in the developed or industrialised countries. He further says that in contrast, the majority of agricultural products in developing countries are grown, processed and marketed by small family-operated enterprises. Women manage most farms, but do not have effective rights on the land. This is one of the critical factors contributing to the persistence of poverty and hunger in Africa.

Agarwal (2002) while discussing about securing effective land rights for women in South Asia and importance of this issue in reducing rural women's poverty and improving their economic status, says that in largely agrarian economies, arable land is the most valued form of property and productive resource. It is a wealth-creating and livelihood-sustaining asset. For a significant majority of rural households, it is the single most important source of security against poverty.... A disproportionate number of those still dependent on land are women. Women's domestic work burden, lower mobility, lesser education, and fewer investable assets limit their entry into non-agriculture, and also their range of non-farm options.... As more men shift to urban or rural non-farm livelihoods, a growing number of households become dependent on women managing farms

13

Islam and Africa

From Stereotypes to Knowledge

Pushpraj Singh

Islam is one of the world's major religions, along with Hinduism, Judaism, Buddhism and Christianity. Since its birth in Arabia more than 1,400 years ago, it grew rapidly, making a profound impact on philosophy, literature, the arts, science and medicine throughout history. Today, an estimated 1.6 billion people (Pew Research.org, June 2013) worldwide are Muslims and the Islamic traditions they follow are as varied as the nations where they live. Islam's central teaching is that there is one Omnipotent and Omniscient God, who is referred to by the Arabic name, *Allah*. In Arabic, Islam means "surrender", or "submission", to the will of God. Over a quarter of the Muslim population live in Africa and Islam is increasingly playing a central role in shaping African societies. An understanding of Islam in the world today is critical for all concerned as Islam is woven throughout the African experience. This chapter demonstrates how history, culture, and religion intersect in Muslim communities in Africa. This chapter provides an overview of the development of Muslim societies in Africa from early history (7th century) to the present with a regional focus on North Africa, the Sahara, sub-Saharan West Africa, the Horn of Africa, and East Africa. This paper will examine processes of Islamization and the emergence of regional Muslim cultures and will explore the diversity of Islam in Africa.

Understanding the Islamization Processes in Africa

One of the great cultural contact experiences in the world history involved the spread of Islam, from its initial base in the Arabian Peninsula and the Middle East to a host of areas in Africa, Asia, and Europe. Islam appealed to people in a variety of societies and cultures, bringing important changes as a result of contact while often in some respects merging with the established local belief systems. Muslims compelled new cultural contacts from about 700 CE onward as a result of conquests, far-reaching trade, and, increasingly, missionary activity. The geographical dimensions of the Muslim world were pretty well established by 1450 CE (the end of the post classical period).

The process of Islamization may be explained as occurring in three stages: Isolation, Syncretism, and Reform (Margari Hill, Stanford, 2009). Initially, Islam spread in towns through merchants, who primarily resided there and travelled between cities for trade. These merchants largely kept to themselves and the rural poor had little contact with them or their religion. During this phase, families of Muslim scholars, some of whom were also traders and merchants, also settled in these small, isolated Muslim neighbourhoods and towns. In fact, a long-lasting interpretive tradition emerged from the reality that Muslim traders travelling throughout West Africa often settled in areas where most people were non-Muslims. In the 16th century, Al-Hajj Salim Suwari, an influential Muslim scholar, who lived in parts of present-day Mali, taught tolerance towards non-Muslims. He preached that non-belief resulted from ignorance rather than wickedness, that true conversion could only occur in God's time and that *jihad* against unbelievers, was unacceptable. The Suwarian tradition, which emphasizes non-violence, flourished among groups of West African Muslim traders for centuries. During the Syncretic, or "Court" stage, Islam spread to political capitals and ruling groups. This phase often began with rulers in trade towns inviting Muslim scholars to join their courts, and/or converting to Islam at the hands of these scholars, such as at 14th century Lamu, on the coast of Kenya, or at Niani, the 14th century capital of the Mali Empire. But in this phase, Islam did not spread far beyond these scholarly families and the aristocracy of the courts. This period saw the Islamization of the empire of Ghana and rise of the great Muslim empires of Mali, Songhai, and Kanem-Borno. Mansa Musa, the ruler of the Malian Empire, went on a famous *hajj* in 1324 during which he gave away so much gold that he crashed the gold market in Cairo. This year-long journey reinvigorated the strong trade and religious ties between the Middle East, North Africa, and the Muslim courts of West Africa, as well as attracting the attention of traders in Europe.

Finally, during the third stage of reform during which large numbers of people began to convert to forms of Islam approved by the scholarly

- 100 per cent of food processing
- 50 per cent of animal husbandry
- 60 per cent of agricultural marketing
- female farmers receive less than 10 per cent of credit provided to farmers (Gender and Agriculture: Unlocking Africa's Potential)
- own only 1 to 2 per cent of all land in developing countries
- women provide 50 per cent of labour in cash crop production

Source: Manuh, 1998; Gender and Agriculture: Unlocking Africa's Potential.

Corroborating the above findings, Opio (2003) states that regarding specific farm operations, women on average contribute 55 per cent of land preparation, 65 per cent of planting, 85-90 per cent weeding, over 95 per cent of food processing, and a high proportion of rural water and wood-fuel acquisition. It is worth noting that currently, these operations are predominantly (up to 93%) accomplished using rudimentary hand tools (the hand hoe, axe, panga and machete). Where production operations are mechanized, mainly based on animal traction, men are the main beneficiaries. Most of the agricultural activities are performed by women using simple tools. But in case of mechanized farms, men benefit the most.

Remunerations for the women's work on agricultural farms range from paid to unpaid work. The State of Food and Agriculture Report 2011 notes that women work in agriculture as farmers on their own account, as unpaid workers on family farms and as paid or unpaid labourers on other farms and agricultural enterprises. They are involved in both crop and livestock production at subsistence and commercial levels They produce food and cash crops and manage mixed agricultural operations often involving crops, livestock and fish farming. All of these women are considered part of the agricultural labour force. It further reports that women in sub-Saharan Africa have relatively high overall labour-force participation rates and the highest average agricultural labour-force participation rates in the world. Cultural norms in the region have long encouraged women to be economically self-reliant and traditionally give women substantial responsibility for agricultural production in their own right. Since they do not define their activities as work, hence remain under paid or unpaid workers.

Despite considerable role that women play in agriculture in Africa, they have very limited land rights. Whatever limited land rights they have, are derived from either their husbands or some male relative. At the same time, it must be remembered that in rural Africa, most land is community owned under customary land tenure systems. The land ownership in Africa can also be secured through state system. Customary land tenure is characterised by its largely unwritten nature. In state systems of land tenure, which are usually based on written laws and regulations, ownership of land rights are registered. Though the land legislation are gender neutral or prohibit gender discrimination, legislation is largely not implemented in rural areas. In any legal matters, they resort to customary land tenure, which varies considerably from place to place. Women remain in detrimental position as they could depend only on the rights derived after marriage from those of their husbands or male relatives. Moreover, women face discrimination with respect to the allocation of individual fields, as they may be given smaller and less fertile fields. Despite cultural norms in Africa encouraging women to be economically independent, but more prevalent customary land tenure system and traditional mind-set discriminate against women, thereby discouraging their ownership of land rights or providing very limited land rights to them that has a profound impact on agricultural productivity.

Benschop (2002) found that while control of land was vested in men, houses were controlled by women (but in most cultures built by the men for their wife/wives), especially married women with sons. Most pre-colonial agricultural social groups were organised around satellite households, which were usually composed of a wife and her unmarried children. Sons, who had reached maturity, would build their own houses in a specific spatial relation to their mother's house. In polygynous marriages, each wife had a separate house within the homestead.... This separate economic unit represented the starting points of the developmental cycle of the family. Bulow and Sorensen (2010) observe that where polygamy is the dominant marriage pattern, women obtained access to the means of production—land and cattle through marriage as brideswealth. The house property system provided a certain kind of autonomy to women vis-à-vis men. Each wife was allocated land and cattle to secure her and her children's livelihood. Benschop (2002) also insists that houses were identified with women, although women inherited neither houses nor land; daughters were expected to get married and their husbands were expected to build a new house for them upon marriage. Access to land and housing, therefore, mainly existed through male relatives (husbands, brothers and sons). In general, gender relations were more complementary than hierarchical. Bulow and Sorensen (2010) say that with the introduction of cash crop, the distinction between women's

From its base in the Middle East–North Africa, Islam gained adherents in several parts of southern Europe; in sub-Saharan Africa; in central Asia, including western China; in India; and in Southeast Asia. The dates and patterns of growth varied in each case. In explaining how Islam caught on, a crucial variable involves the balance between conquest versus trade and spiritual example. Another division, when Islam spread mainly by persuasion, involves relationships between elites and masses of the receiving areas. In some cases, elites and ruling classes converted first, attracted by the religion but also by its praise for merchants and its political success; elites then disseminated the religion further. In other cases, conversion began among ordinary people, as when Sufi leaders interacted with peasant villages.

Inevitably, as Islam surged into areas of different traditional beliefs and styles, cultural amalgamations occurred. Some areas received the religion fully, including its associated artistic styles, such as the architecture of the mosques and the rich decoration of a religion that tried to forbid representations of people and animals. Other areas, however, accepted the religion, but not some of the specifics concerning art or family life. A variety of patterns of syncretism, or cultural blending, occurred. Finally, some areas saw the development of an important Muslim minority along with resistance by the majority culture. Tracing the geography of Islam means exploring these various and important results.

As Thomson (2010) points out, African rulers have been quick and generous with the building of mosques. It has been so since the days of independence. Islam dominates the north and east coast, but even throughout the rest of the continent, one can easily find a mosque (or one under construction) in just about every city neighbourhood. It's unknown what the rate of mosque-building is, but one would guess it's pretty high. One-fifth of the world's Muslim population lives in Africa, Muslims have the highest birth rate of any religious group in the world, and record numbers of people convert every year. Several African nations have ruled in the name of Islam (sometimes erroneously called Arab states) for some time. Libya, Sudan, and Mauritania, for example, have been Islamic ever since independence. Algeria came close in 1992, but the army stepped in to prevent Islamic rule. Nigeria decided to adopt *Shari'a* law in 1999 and Islamic expansionism takes the form of terrorism in Kenya, Tanzania, Somalia, Morocco, and other places. There is certainly growing support for Muslim beliefs across the continent.

There are many factors that have contributed to the Islamization of black Africa. One of the factors that can account for the spread of Islam in West Africa is adaptability and flexibility of Islam. It came to Africa through trade routes and through the Arab countries. Additionally, it developed rather differently in black Africa than its counterparts in the rest of the Islamic world. Meaning, the conversion of black Africa was peaceful. In the sub-Saharan Africa, the people were converted to the love of God without disturbing the existing indigenous religions that were already in existence. The Islamic faith merged, adapted, and retained much of the traditions of the pre-Islamic religions, "in contrast to Islam of the *ulema* and followers of other beliefs" (De George, 2000: 195). Many of the advantages of Islam were combined with practices of indigenous religions to establish legitimacy between non-Muslims. This cohabitation suited Africans since Islam offered the uprooted and disillusioned Africans a new religious framework. Furthermore, becoming a Muslim has always been easy; it only requires assuming a new name. There was no break from the old religion to the new one that would come later.

According to Westerlund (1997), the rise of Islam can be attributed to its organizational skills. Through modern organization skills, it permits Islamists to act as lobbying groups. During the colonial eras, the organizational structures of Islam were not well developed. This was attributed to the separation of church and states. This had damaging effect on the growth of Islam. As colonial rule began to phase out, and became the relic of the past, many Muslim organizations began to mushroom in Africa and other Islamic world. Several of these associations began to challenge the established organizations that they became counterpoise to the activities of conversion. They used the tactics practiced by well organized Christian missionary societies. The spread of these organizations began in the 70's and reached their crescendos in the 80's and 90's. In Nigeria, for example, governments formed organizations such as the Supreme Council of Islam, with a view of being the mouthpiece of the Muslim community. Various other organizations were also established in Nigeria such as *Jamaat nostril al-Islam* (JNS-Association for the Victory of Islam). This was considered the trail-blazer for Islamization of Nigeria (McCormack, 2005).

Even though the precise number of Muslims in the continent is unknown—due to incomplete statistics regarding religious demography, and despite the intense efforts to win converts by Christian missionary groups active in Africa—Islam is the largest religion in Africa with about 50 per cent of the population being Muslims. In contrast, about 33 per cent are Christians and less than 10 per cent are non-religious or adherents of widened the gap between the resources women and men control. Thus, the commoditization of land, inaccessibility of land and ownership of less fertile land have resulted in attaining lower incomes and high risks for women in Africa.

Beside land constraints, women face severe labour constraints. Agricultural labor refers to women's own labor and also to the labor they have access to whether it is paid or unpaid. Unpaid labour includes the labour of household members. The FAO Report 2011 records that female-headed households face more severe labour constraints than male-headed households because they typically have fewer members, but more dependants. Peters (1986) observes that in some areas, male out-migration adds to the constraint already imposed by gender-specific farming tasks. Female-headed households may receive help from male relatives, but only after the men have taken care of their own plots. The fact that female-headed households typically farm smaller plots may not compensate for the lower availability of family labour. The FAO 2011 Report found that household and community responsibilities and gender-specific labour requirements mean that women farmers cannot farm as productively as men and makes it more difficult for them to respond when crop prices rise. Depending on cultural norms, some farming activities, such as ploughing and spraying, rely on access to male labour without which women farmers face delays that may lead to losses in output. Bulow and Sorensen (2010) found that migration has resulted in loss of access to male help on farms or the money they may have previously provided. This means, to increase their yield, women have to work even harder and use more labour intensive methods to maintain soil regeneration. Another drawback due to labour constraint is that women can own only smaller number of animals in their stock and so have to depend solely on land produce, adding to it is the risk due to bad weather conditions.

It has been found by several studies that women routinely have less access to agricultural extension services than their male counterparts (Gilbert, Sakala, and Benson, 2002; World Bank and Government of Malawi, 2007; World Bank and IFPRI, 2010; Meinzen-Dick, *et al.*, 2010). Sometimes lower educational level of women may hinder their opportunity of availing training facilities as they are unable to use the educational material supplied with it. Diffusion of good farm practices and scientific and innovative knowledge regarding agriculture gets stalled due to ways and methods in which they are disseminated. Even the fixed days, time and place for the extension services can deter women from availing the facility. Fixed days or fixed places may be inconvenient and participating with men may be a constraining factor for some. Sometimes, the enabling environment is lacking.

Also, improving women's direct access to financial resources leads to higher investments in human capital in the form of children's health, nutrition and education (Why gender ::: Key facts). The FAO Report 2010-2011 cites Fletschner, 2009; World Bank, FAO and IFAD, 2008 who insist that institutional discrimination by private and public lending institutions often either ration women out of the market or grant women loans that are smaller than those granted to men for similar activities. Manuh (1998) says that many co-operatives limit membership to household heads, who are generally male. Banks demand collaterals in the form of landed property, which women don't have. Technical assistance and training is generally provided for export crops, which is invariably for men. Manuh also quotes the World Bank study in Kenya showing that if women have same production factors and inputs as men, then their output would increase by 22 per cent. If women's productivity is increased to that of men, it would solve the problem of food insecurity and hunger. Similar are the findings of the FAO Report (2011). Its estimates suggest that if women had the same access to productive resources as men, they could increase yields on their farms by 20-30 per cent, lifting 100-150 million out of hunger. Thus, it is imperative that women should have access to the same resources as men to increase the output if Millennium Development Goals of alleviating hunger and poverty and gender equality have to be achieved in Africa.

Access to new adaptable technology is critical for maintaining and improving agricultural productivity. There is wide gender gap that exists in the use of large range of agricultural technologies, including machines and tools, improved plant varieties and animal breeds, fertilizers, pest control measures and management techniques. Labour saving and productivity enhancing technologies can also help reduce women's time and poverty (Facts and Figures on Rural Women, 2011). Farmers use lesser mechanical equipment and tools in most developing countries, but female-headed households use significantly lower. Agricultural yield may be significantly reduced due to difficulty in access to factors like water, nutrients and labour, which are yield limiting or yield may be reduced due to pests and diseases, which are yield reducing factors. There are many ways available for improving agricultural production like the use of fertilizers, new breeding technology, using HYV seeds and mechanization. But these methods as such may not be suitable for the African situations. They cannot be replicated and, therefore, adaptation few years before he made his historic *hijra* or migration to Medina from Mecca, the Prophet advised his cousin *Ja'far* to take a group of Muslims to seek refuge at the court of the Christian King of Aksum (present-day Ethiopia and Eritrea). As Islam spread gradually throughout the Arabian Peninsula, most of these refugees returned to Arabia. But close trade contacts between the Horn of Africa and the newly-Muslim Arabian Peninsula fostered the growth of what is today the oldest Muslim community on the continent. Even before the first Muslims set foot on African soil, however, a large number of Africans and people of African descent living in and around Mecca converted to Islam. The most famous of these early African Muslims was *Bilal Ibn Rabah al-Habashi* (Bilal the son of Rabah, the Ethiopian). According to Islamic tradition, Bilal converted to Islam while enslaved, and his master tortured him in a vain attempt to get him to recant.

Hearing of his plight, the Prophet's friend Abu Bakr paid for Bilal's freedom, after which he became the chief *muezzin* (the person who gives the call to prayer, called the *adhaan*) of the young Muslim community. Some Muslims in sub-Saharan Africa have claimed descent from Bilal and many more have looked to him as a symbolic and spiritual forefather for centuries.

These first Muslim migrants provided Islam with its first major triumph, and Africa became the first safe haven for Muslims and the first place Islam would be practiced outside of the Arabian Peninsula. The conquest of Egypt by the Muslims during the tenure of Umar Ibn al-Khattab served as an opportunity for the Muslims to penetrate into Africa. That was in the month of *Safar* 20 A.H. (641 CE), when on the order of the Caliph, Amribn al-'As conquered Egypt. The *Khalifah* again dispatched a mission of 300 men under the leadership of Alqamahibn Mujassar al-Kaneum, to the land of Eritrea (Ethiopia) to preach Islam in the heart of Africa. The routes followed by the Muslims to spread their religion in Africa were:

- Through the Red Sea to North Africa, e.g. Egypt, Tunisia, Algeria and Morocco.
- Across River Nile, namely from the lower part of Egypt to the Sudan, through the Nubious land and across the Sahara Desert and lake Chad, Bornu, Hausa, Yoruba and Nupe lands of Nigeria.
- Through the Indian Ocean from Yemen to Somalia, Omen and Albahrain, to the Island of Zanzibar in Tanganyika (Tanzania). From there Islam penetrated into the western part of South East Africa to Uganda, Malawi, Madagascar and Comoro land.

- Morocco through Northeast Africa to the fall of River Senegal to Mali, Guinea and all parts of West Africa.

Sub-Saharan Africa

Islam reached Africa south of the Sahara in two ways. Important interactions occurred during the postclassical period, though only a minority of Africans converted (except in North Africa, which religiously merged with the Middle East). But the religious contacts were nonetheless important. They set the basis for much more extensive conversions from the late eighteenth century onward, when missionary efforts and religious wars conducted by fervent Muslims began to spread the religion to ordinary people. By the late twentieth century about 40 per cent of all sub-Saharan Africans were Muslims. Initial contacts in West Africa focused on the Sudanese kingdoms, headed at first by Ghana. These contacts had some distinctive features. Trade with Muslim North Africa developed quickly, across the Sahara Desert by camel and horseback. The trade was vital to Ghana for tax revenues and supply of horses. The king of Ghana also hired Arab Muslims to keep records, because they had writing and bureaucratic experience. But contacts also facilitated raids by Muslims from the north, often encouraged by local Islamic groups.

The kingdom of Mali, which flourished after Ghana collapsed in about 1200, regularized interactions with Muslims. Rulers like Sundiata more systematically utilized Muslim bureaucrats and converted to Islam as a gesture of goodwill toward the North African trading partners. A king of Mali, Mansa Musa, made a famous pilgrimage to Mecca in 1324, dazzling Arabs with his lavish supply of gold. Mansa Musa also organized a centre of Muslim scholarship in the city of Timbuktu, and Muslim architecture spread widely. This remained, however, a compromise contact. There was little effort to convert ordinary people, though Sufi missionaries fanned out in the common pattern, with gradual results; their efforts were limited by the lack of towns south of the Sudanic kingdoms and by disease. In the Sudanic region itself, kings continued to portray themselves as divine, in the West African tradition, despite the contradictions with Islamic faith. And even among the Muslim elite, customs such as giving a relatively prominent place to women persisted, which profoundly shocked Arab visitors, who were otherwise impressed with the culture and political organization they saw around them. Islamic punishments, such as cutting off the hands of thieves, were also rejected as too brutal.

women as active economic agents that are central to a vibrant economy. It also notes that it must also entail the design and implementation of economic policies that give women and men access to decent work, food security, social insurance and protection. Financing required for needs of women does not entail having access to funds only but it requires women to be proactive in the whole development process.

To address the constraints women face in rural Africa, policies, programmes, strategies and interventions at local, national and regional level must be so designed to meet the needs of both men and women. Achieving gender equality requires transformative strategies rather than ad hoc arrangements. Gender equality cannot be promoted without genuine allocation of resources for each purpose. There can be several strategies for which financial resources have to be allocated to achieve gender equality.

Strategies for financing gender equality:

1. To identify and develop latent faculties of women
2. To encourage equitable access to resources and to attain financial control
3. To enhance access to health and nutrition
4. To provide protection and safety

- *To identify and develop latent faculties of women*: It relates to development of women by way of providing education and training for them to become more productive and more competitive. It will enable them to be economically and socially independent. Developing the skills of women and girls through training and education will promote employability of women and thereby will empower them. Financial policies, programs, strategies and interventions that are required are as follows:

  – Promote women's education and training
  – provide legal aid services for women
  – Remove obstacles to women's participation in rural and local organisations
  – Promote employability of women through vocational training programs
  – Promote entrepreneurship in women
  – Increase awareness of women of their rights

- *To encourage equitable access to resources and to attain financial control*: It relates to providing women equal access to resources like land, cattle, financial resources so that they are independent and are able to use their capability for their and their family's growth and development. The following strategies and interventions are required:

- provide improved infrastructure to reduce women's work load
- promote more secure and gender equitable legislation for land tenure rights
- Increase women's representation in political organizations
- Expand women's access to credit and economic opportunities
- Promote equitable remuneration for equal work done
- Access to labour-saving and productivity enhancing techniques
- Access to agricultural inputs and technological resources
- Provide access to public goods and services
- Improve income-generating activities for women
- Encourage participation of women in micro-financing, general insurance schemes and self-help groups

- *To enhance access to health and nutrition*: Well-being of women depend on the provision of maternal and child health programs. It has been found that maternal and child health in sub-Saharan Africa is very poor. For women to be productive and employable, it is important that her nutrition is optimum and general health services are accessible. Several programmes and policies are required for promoting health of women and children.
  - Promote maternal and child health programs
  - Promote mental and physical health by disseminating information through mass media like radio, TV and mobile phones
  - Strengthen nutrition programmes and educate women and children regarding it
  - Encourage distribution of nutrient supplementation to girls and women
  - Promote sexual and reproductive health rights
- *To provide protection and safety:* Insecurity due to violence and conflict is endemic in Africa. Insecurity and fear of violence and conflict reduces the ability to use optimally the full capacities of women and may lead to permanent damage. To provide security to women financial commitments are required to strengthen policies for deterrence of violence and conflict.

In recent times Islam has seen a rise in previously non Muslim countries particularly Rwanda. During the Rwandan genocide mobs avoided searching in local Rwandan Muslim neighbourhoods, which were used to hide Tutsi and other persecuted people. In places like Cyangugu, it was also widely believed that local Muslims and Mosques were protected by the power of Islamic magic and the efficacious *Jinn*. Post genocide many Rwandese mass converted to Islam because of protection Islamic communities offered them.

The penetration of Islam in Africa also met with difficulties. The Islamic calendar follows the moon year, whereas African agricultural calendar followed the sun. The Islamic society is patrilineal, whereas many African societies are matrilineal. A very serious problem is that the men often accepted Islam completely, but the women continued the pagan religion because it is believed that in Islam there is only marginal involvement of females. Above all, ancestor worship had to be dropped.

Muslim Population in Africa

There are conflicting statistics on religious practitioners in Africa (including North Africa). Britannica Online Encyclopaedia, in its article "Religion: Year in Review 2010: Worldwide Adherents of All Religions", states the religious statistics of Africa in 2010, as: 488,880,000 Christians (47.32%); 421,938,820 Muslims (40.84%); 109,592,000 African traditional religions (ethno religionists) (10.6%); and 12,632.200 for all other remaining beliefs (1.22%), from the 1033,043,000 total population of Africa (100%) in 2010. Nevertheless, according to a 9 May 2009 Congressional Research Service report, there were 371,459,142 Muslims, 304,313,880 Christians, 137,842,507 who practiced indigenous religions, and 9,818,542 people who practiced other religions in Africa. Although there is no specific data on the total Muslim population in Africa, experts believe that there are approximately 300 million African Muslims in the world, which comprises roughly one-third of the African continent's population. However, regardless of the relatively large Muslim population and Islam's historical presence in Africa, African Islam has remained largely neglected in the study of Muslim politics. Academics argue that this neglect was, to a large extent, the result of an academic division of labour based on the assumption that Africa was only superficially Islamized. These scholars argue that many parts of Africa were incorporated into the world of Islam centuries ago and that African Muslims have adhered to and practiced the main pillars of Islam (including opportunities for their employment and healthy life be removed. Facilitating increased control of resources by women and enhancing women's assets can promote agricultural production and thus increase food security. For this financial support and appropriate strategies and interventions are required in different areas tailored according to the needs of women. These different areas of financing gender equality are interrelated, and all these areas should be activated to promote gender equality and empowerment of women. Policy formulations and long-term planning is not enough. There has to be a paradigm shift in the policies and financing programmes and they need to be transformative rather than selective and exclusive.

REFERENCES

Agarwal, B. (2002). Are We Not Peasants Too? Land Rights and Women's Claims in India. *Seeds.* Number 21.

Barasa, J. N. K. (2011). Gender and Higher Education in Africa: The Case of Kenya. In T. Falola and S. U. Fwatshak (eds.). *Beyond Tradition: African Women in Cultural and Political Spaces.* New Jersey: Africa World Press. pp. 301-327.

Berg, A. van den. (1997). Women farmers in pursuit of land security: and what about sustainability? In M. E. Bruijn, I. van Halsema, and H. van den Hombergh (eds.). *Gender and Land use: Diversity in Environmental Practices*. Amsterdam: Thela Publishers. pp. 87-105.

Benschop, M. (2002). *Rights and Reality: Are women's equal rights to land, housing and property implemented in East Africa?* Nairobi: United Nations Human Settlement Programme

Bridging the Gap: Financing Gender Equality. (2008). A Publication of the United Nations Development Fund For Women (UNIFEM) and The UN Non-Governmental Liaison Service (NGLS). http://www.un-ngls.org/IMG/pdf/UNIFEM.pdf. Accessed on 10/11/2012.

Bulow, D.V. and Sorensen, A. (2010). Gender and Contract Farming: Growing Tea in Kenya. In M. Trushen (Ed.). *African Women: A Political Economy.* New York: Palgrave Macmillan.

Cooper, B. M. (1997). *Marriage in Maradi: Gender and Culture in a Hausa Society in Niger, 1900-1989.* Portsmouth, NH: Heinemann.

Cotula, L. Toulmin, C. and Hesse, C. (2004). Land Tenure and Administration in Africa: Lessons of Experience and Emerging Issues. International Institute for Environment and Development. London. *http://pubs.iied.org/pdfs/9305IIED.pdf.* Accessed on 10/9/2012.

Davis, M. S. Farnworth, C. and Sundell, M. F. (2012). Transforming gender relations in agriculture in sub-Saharan Africa: Promising approaches. SIANI: Stockholm Environment Institute. Sweden.

Duran, L. A. (2012). Strengthening Financing for Gender Equality and Women's Organizations. United Nations Commission on the Status of Women. Fifty-Sixth Session. 27 February—9 March 2012. New York.

Facts and Figures on Rural Women. UN Women.mht. Accessed on 8/3/2013.

Financing Gender Equality is Financing Development. Financing for Gender Equality. UNIFEM Discussion Paper, February 2008. *http://www.unifem.org/attachments/products/FinancingGenderEqualityIsFinancingDevelopment_en_1.pdf.* Accessed on 18/1/2013.

Gilbert, R. A. Sakala, W. D. and Benson, T. D. (2002). Gender Analysis of a Nationwide Cropping System Trial Survey in Malawi. *African Studies Quarterly.* Vol. 6(1).

Grebmer, K. V. Nestorova, B. Quisumbing, A. Fertziger, R. Fritschel, H. Pandya-Lorch, R. and Yohannes, Y. (2009). 2009 Global hunger index the challenge of hunger: focus on financial crisis and gender inequality. *IFPRI Issue Brief 62.* November 2009.

Guyer, J. I. (1991). Female farming in anthropology and African history. In M. di Leonardo. Berkeley (ed.) *Gender at the crossroads of knowledge: Feminist anthropology in the postmodern Era.* California, USA: University of California Press.

Hilhorst, T. Changing rights to common pool resources and land in West Africa. http://www.kitpublishers.nl/net/KIT_Publicaties_output/ShowFile2.aspx?e=1322. Accessed on 15/1/2013.

Issaka, F. Realising Women's Equality Rights in Africa: The Delicate Balance Between Culture and Universality of Rights. *http://www.captured-edu.org/afbeeldingen/Franciska-etal.pdf.* Accessed on 10/9/2012.

Manuh, T. (1998). Women in Africa's development: Overcoming obstacles, pushing for progress. *Africa Recovery Briefing Paper Number 11.* April 1998.

Mbayo, A.S. Gender Equality, the Nexus Between the Conflict. Development and Sustainable Peace in Africa: The Case of Sierra Leone. Accessed on 23/8/2012 from the site *http://global-studies.doshisha.ac.jp/english/i18n/images/theme1/Alex_Full_paper.pdf*

Meinzen-Dick, R.; Quisumbing, A.; Behrman, J.; Biermayr-Jenzano, P.; Wilde, V.; Noordeloos, M.; Ragasa, C.; and Beintema, N. (2010). Engendering Agricultural Research. *IFPRI Discussion Paper 00973.* May 2010.

Mikkola, A. and Miles, C. A. (2007). Development and Gender Equality: Consequences, Causes, Challenges and Cures. Discussion Paper No. 159. HECER—Helsinki Center of Economic Research. *http://ethesis.helsinki.fi/julkaisut/eri/hecer/disc/159/developm.pdf.* Accessed on 23/8/2012.

Nfah-Abbenyi, J. M. (2005). Gender, Feminist theory, and Post-Colonial (Women's) Writing. In O. Oyewumi (Ed.) African Gender Studies: A Reader. New York: Palgrave Macmillan.

Nelson, J. and England, P. (2002). Feminist Philosophies of Love and Work. *Hypatia,* Vol.17(2). pp. 1-18.

Ogunlela, Y. I. and Mukhtar, A. A. (2009). Gender Issues in Agriculture and Rural Development in Nigeria: The Role of Women. *Humanity and Social Sciences Journal,* Vol. 4(1): 19-30.

Opio, F. (2003). Gender Mainstreaming in Agriculture with Special Reference to Uganda: Challenges and Prospects. *African Crop Science Conference Proceedings.* Vol. 6. 699-703.

Ovonji-Odida, I. *et al.* (2000). *Impact of Spousal Co-ownership of the Primary Household Property.* Incomplete first draft report. Kampala. April 2000.

Oyewumi, O. (2005). Making History, Creating Gender: Some Methodological and Interpretive Questions in the Writing of Oyo Oral Traditions. In O. Oyewumi (Ed.). *African Gender Studies: A Reader.* England and New York: Palgrave Macmillan.

Peterman, A. Behrman, J. and Quisumbing, A. (2010). A Review of Empirical Evidence on Gender Differences in Nonland Agricultural Inputs, Technology, and Services in Developing Countries. *IFPRI Discussion Paper 00975.* May 2010.

Quisumbing, A. R. and Pandolfelli, L. (2009). Promising Approaches to Address the Needs of Poor Female Farmers Resources, Constraints, and Interventions. IFPRI Discussion Paper 00882. *http://www.ifpri.org/sites/default/files/IFPRIDP00882.pdf.*

Report of the Expert Group Meeting. Financing for gender equality and the empowerment of women. EGM/FFGE/2007/REPORT. Accessed on 8/11/2012 from the site *http://www.un.org/womenwatch/daw/egm/financing_gender_equality/EGM per cent20Report per cent20Final.pdf.*

Rawlings, N. K. A. (2009). Mobilising African Women for Economic Development. http://jjrawlings.wordpress.com/2009/09/24/mobilising-african-women-for-economic-development-nana-konadu-agyeman-rawlings/.Accessed on 24/1/2013.

Sen, A. (2001). Inauguration Lecture for the New Radcliffe Institute at Harvard University. on. *Frontline Magazine*. Vol. 18(22). Oct. 27-Nov. 09, 2001.

Steady, F. C. (2005). An Investigative Framework for Gender Research in Africa in the New Millennium. In O. Oyewumi (ed.). *African Gender Studies: A Reader.* England and New York: Palgrave Macmillan.

Tietcheu, B. (2006). Being Women and Men in Africa Today: Approaching Gender Roles in Changing African Societies. *http://www.koed.hu/sw249/bertrand.pdf*

What is gender equality. International Plan Parenthood Federation. *http://ippf.org/our-work/what-we-do/gender/what-gender-equality*. Accessed on 7/3/2013.

Why gender ::: Key facts *http://www.fao.org/gender/gender-home/gender-why/key-facts/en/* Accessed on 15/1/2013.

Women in Agriculture: Closing the gender gap for Development. The State of Food and Agriculture. (2011). *http://www.fao.org/docrep/013/i2050e/i2050e02.pdf. Accessed on 11/1/2013*; *http://www.fao.org/docrep/013/i2050e/i2050e03.pdf.* Accessed on 15/1/2013

World Bank (WB) and Government of Malawi. (2007). Malawi Poverty and Vulnerability Assessment (PVA): Investing in Our Future. Synthesis Report: Main Findings and Recommendations. *Poverty Reduction and Economic Management 1: Report No. 36546-MW.*

Washington DC.: World Bank.

World Bank and IFPRI. (2010). Gender and governance in rural services: Insights from India, Ghana and Ethiopia. Gender and Governance Author Team. Washington, D.C.: The International Bank for Reconstruction and Development/The World Bank.

World Development Report. (2012): Gender and Development.

13
Islam and Africa
From Stereotypes to Knowledge

Pushpraj Singh

Islam is one of the world's major religions, along with Hinduism, Judaism, Buddhism and Christianity. Since its birth in Arabia more than 1,400 years ago, it grew rapidly, making a profound impact on philosophy, literature, the arts, science and medicine throughout history. Today, an estimated 1.6 billion people (Pew Research.org, June 2013) worldwide are Muslims and the Islamic traditions they follow are as varied as the nations where they live. Islam's central teaching is that there is one Omnipotent and Omniscient God, who is referred to by the Arabic name, *Allah*. In Arabic, Islam means "surrender", or "submission", to the will of God. Over a quarter of the Muslim population live in Africa and Islam is increasingly playing a central role in shaping African societies. An understanding of Islam in the world today is critical for all concerned as Islam is woven throughout the African experience. This chapter demonstrates how history, culture, and religion intersect in Muslim communities in Africa. This chapter provides an overview of the development of Muslim societies in Africa from early history (7th century) to the present with a regional focus on North Africa, the Sahara, sub-Saharan West Africa, the Horn of Africa, and East Africa. This paper will examine processes of Islamization and the emergence of regional Muslim cultures and will explore the diversity of Islam in Africa.

Understanding the Islamization Processes in Africa

One of the great cultural contact experiences in the world history involved the spread of Islam, from its initial base in the Arabian Peninsula and the Middle East to a host of areas in Africa, Asia, and Europe. Islam appealed to people in a variety of societies and cultures, bringing important changes as a result of contact while often in some respects merging with the established local belief systems. Muslims compelled new cultural contacts from about 700 CE onward as a result of conquests, far-reaching trade, and, increasingly, missionary activity. The geographical dimensions of the Muslim world were pretty well established by 1450 CE (the end of the post classical period).

The process of Islamization may be explained as occurring in three stages: Isolation, Syncretism, and Reform (Margari Hill, Stanford, 2009). Initially, Islam spread in towns through merchants, who primarily resided there and travelled between cities for trade. These merchants largely kept to themselves and the rural poor had little contact with them or their religion. During this phase, families of Muslim scholars, some of whom were also traders and merchants, also settled in these small, isolated Muslim neighbourhoods and towns. In fact, a long-lasting interpretive tradition emerged from the reality that Muslim traders travelling throughout West Africa often settled in areas where most people were non-Muslims. In the 16th century, Al-Hajj Salim Suwari, an influential Muslim scholar, who lived in parts of present-day Mali, taught tolerance towards non-Muslims. He preached that non-belief resulted from ignorance rather than wickedness, that true conversion could only occur in God's time and that *jihad* against unbelievers, was unacceptable. The Suwarian tradition, which emphasizes non-violence, flourished among groups of West African Muslim traders for centuries. During the Syncretic, or "Court" stage, Islam spread to political capitals and ruling groups. This phase often began with rulers in trade towns inviting Muslim scholars to join their courts, and/or converting to Islam at the hands of these scholars, such as at 14th century Lamu, on the coast of Kenya, or at Niani, the 14th century capital of the Mali Empire. But in this phase, Islam did not spread far beyond these scholarly families and the aristocracy of the courts. This period saw the Islamization of the empire of Ghana and rise of the great Muslim empires of Mali, Songhai, and Kanem-Borno. Mansa Musa, the ruler of the Malian Empire, went on a famous *hajj* in 1324 during which he gave away so much gold that he crashed the gold market in Cairo. This year-long journey reinvigorated the strong trade and religious ties between the Middle East, North Africa, and the Muslim courts of West Africa, as well as attracting the attention of traders in Europe.

Finally, during the third stage of reform during which large numbers of people began to convert to forms of Islam approved by the scholarly families. In West Africa, this process of reform was also facilitated through the organization of *Sufi* brotherhoods, called *Tariqahs*, such as the *Qadiriyyah* and *Tijaniyyah.* These reform movements sometimes took the form of *jihads* and spread across West Africa during the 18th and 19th centuries, affecting Muslim and non-Muslim Africans alike. Reformers challenged what they saw as the corrupt practices of urban merchants and ruling classes, such as heavy taxation and syncretic religious practices.

Islam's spread was gradual though amazingly rapid given the extensive geography and diverse regions involved. Two primary patterns were involved. In some cases, Islam spread to other cultures in a context of military conquest, even though the religion was tolerant of other beliefs. Muslims rarely forced people to convert to their religion, often preferring to levy a special tax on minority communities instead. The famous *jihad*, or holy war described by the prophet Muhammad, was mainly used for defence of the faith, not forced conversion, though there were exceptions. But the success of Muslim armies could create a context in which other people found it prudent to convert, or in which they were attracted to the religion simply because of its manifest power and triumph. In other instances, Islam spread through more spontaneous conversions as people learned of it through trade and missionary activity.

The religion was clearly attractive, with an explicit set of beliefs about what to do and what not to do in order to win access to heaven and avoid a lamentable eternity in hell. It appealed to lower-class groups because of its commitment to charity and spiritual equality; it also legitimated merchant activity more than did most belief systems at the time, and so could attract traders. The cultural and political achievements of Islam drew people eager to advance their societies in a variety of ways, including religious ones. Believing that he was divinely inspired, the prophet Muhammad, born in about 570 CE, generated the basic tenets of the newest world religion. The context for Islam involved the surge of Arab peoples, originally a nomadic group on the fringes of Mediterranean civilization that became increasingly active in trade and formulated a well established culture, including a writing system. The collapse of the Roman Empire had left a welter of small states in the eastern Mediterranean, along with a confusing mixture of religions, including Judaism and Christianity. Muhammad sought to reorganize Arab culture but also to offer a religion that would build on and perfect Jewish and Christian thinking. Islam was a rigorous monotheistic system, offering a clear statement of duties that would help assure salvation.

The *Qur'an,* the holy book that Muhammad composed under the inspiration of Allah, provided detailed regulations for many aspects of life, including family life. Muslim principles urged rulers to defend the religion above all, though their political goals were often unfulfilled; Islam came to depend on a mixture of state support and the activities of scholars and legal philosophers, who interpreted doctrine and law on a local basis and administered a system of religious courts. Islam had begun to spread rapidly among the Arabs by the time of Muhammad's death in 632 CE. This growth helped galvanize Arabs to a surge of conquest, and armies quickly spread through the Middle East, including Persia, though the Byzantine Empire long held out amid reduced Asian territory.

North Africa was another early conquest. A loose central government, the Caliphate, was established for this West Asian–North African heartland by Muhammad's successors; it lasted until the thirteenth century. Arabs for a time sought to reserve Islam for their people alone, while tolerating local religions; but many people in the conquered regions sought access, some of them adopting Arab language and culture in the process. Conquests by Muslim Arabs gradually turned into a more general spread of Islam in its Middle Eastern–North African heartland and beyond.

The Middle East had long been a centre of trade with Asia, Africa, and Europe alike. Arab and Muslim gains spurred further efforts toward achieving additional wealth, which were aided by Islam's approval of merchant activity leavened by charity. Muslim traders spread well beyond the Caliphate, and they left new cultural contacts in their wake. Finally, changes in Islam itself galvanized even more active and extensive spiritual leadership. After about 900 CE a movement called Sufism took hold. The movement emerged gradually and was fully defined only in about 1200 CE. Sufi leaders worried about the luxury and secular interests of the later Caliphs, and also the diverse intellectual life that had developed as Islam interacted with Greek scientific heritage and various literary movements. They wanted a stricter focus on religion and more intense Piety. Interestingly, Sufi leaders, who initially flourished among outlying peoples like the Turks, borrowed some ideas from the Christian monastic movement and from Buddhism. Some Sufi leaders emphasized works of charity, but others offered a highly emotional religion complete with intense rituals. Characteristically, Sufi leaders sought to spread the beliefs of Islam to new regions. Their enthusiasm and the example of their holy devotion helped to persuade many people, as they showed how to bridge the gap between Allah and ordinary mortals.

From its base in the Middle East–North Africa, Islam gained adherents in several parts of southern Europe; in sub-Saharan Africa; in central Asia, including western China; in India; and in Southeast Asia. The dates and patterns of growth varied in each case. In explaining how Islam caught on, a crucial variable involves the balance between conquest versus trade and spiritual example. Another division, when Islam spread mainly by persuasion, involves relationships between elites and masses of the receiving areas. In some cases, elites and ruling classes converted first, attracted by the religion but also by its praise for merchants and its political success; elites then disseminated the religion further. In other cases, conversion began among ordinary people, as when Sufi leaders interacted with peasant villages.

Inevitably, as Islam surged into areas of different traditional beliefs and styles, cultural amalgamations occurred. Some areas received the religion fully, including its associated artistic styles, such as the architecture of the mosques and the rich decoration of a religion that tried to forbid representations of people and animals. Other areas, however, accepted the religion, but not some of the specifics concerning art or family life. A variety of patterns of syncretism, or cultural blending, occurred. Finally, some areas saw the development of an important Muslim minority along with resistance by the majority culture. Tracing the geography of Islam means exploring these various and important results.

As Thomson (2010) points out, African rulers have been quick and generous with the building of mosques. It has been so since the days of independence. Islam dominates the north and east coast, but even throughout the rest of the continent, one can easily find a mosque (or one under construction) in just about every city neighbourhood. It's unknown what the rate of mosque-building is, but one would guess it's pretty high. One-fifth of the world's Muslim population lives in Africa, Muslims have the highest birth rate of any religious group in the world, and record numbers of people convert every year. Several African nations have ruled in the name of Islam (sometimes erroneously called Arab states) for some time. Libya, Sudan, and Mauritania, for example, have been Islamic ever since independence. Algeria came close in 1992, but the army stepped in to prevent Islamic rule. Nigeria decided to adopt *Shari'a* law in 1999 and Islamic expansionism takes the form of terrorism in Kenya, Tanzania, Somalia, Morocco, and other places. There is certainly growing support for Muslim beliefs across the continent.

There are many factors that have contributed to the Islamization of black Africa. One of the factors that can account for the spread of Islam in West Africa is adaptability and flexibility of Islam. It came to Africa through trade routes and through the Arab countries. Additionally, it developed rather differently in black Africa than its counterparts in the rest of the Islamic world. Meaning, the conversion of black Africa was peaceful. In the sub-Saharan Africa, the people were converted to the love of God without disturbing the existing indigenous religions that were already in existence. The Islamic faith merged, adapted, and retained much of the traditions of the pre-Islamic religions, "in contrast to Islam of the *ulema* and followers of other beliefs" (De George, 2000: 195). Many of the advantages of Islam were combined with practices of indigenous religions to establish legitimacy between non-Muslims. This cohabitation suited Africans since Islam offered the uprooted and disillusioned Africans a new religious framework. Furthermore, becoming a Muslim has always been easy; it only requires assuming a new name. There was no break from the old religion to the new one that would come later.

According to Westerlund (1997), the rise of Islam can be attributed to its organizational skills. Through modern organization skills, it permits Islamists to act as lobbying groups. During the colonial eras, the organizational structures of Islam were not well developed. This was attributed to the separation of church and states. This had damaging effect on the growth of Islam. As colonial rule began to phase out, and became the relic of the past, many Muslim organizations began to mushroom in Africa and other Islamic world. Several of these associations began to challenge the established organizations that they became counterpoise to the activities of conversion. They used the tactics practiced by well organized Christian missionary societies. The spread of these organizations began in the 70's and reached their crescendos in the 80's and 90's. In Nigeria, for example, governments formed organizations such as the Supreme Council of Islam, with a view of being the mouthpiece of the Muslim community. Various other organizations were also established in Nigeria such as *Jamaat nostril al-Islam* (JNS-Association for the Victory of Islam). This was considered the trail-blazer for Islamization of Nigeria (McCormack, 2005).

Even though the precise number of Muslims in the continent is unknown—due to incomplete statistics regarding religious demography, and despite the intense efforts to win converts by Christian missionary groups active in Africa—Islam is the largest religion in Africa with about 50 per cent of the population being Muslims. In contrast, about 33 per cent are Christians and less than 10 per cent are non-religious or adherents of

African religions (Pew Research Foundation, 2013). This ever-growing conversion to Islam in Africa has been made possible especially due to the intensive activity of Islamic NGOs, such as the Muslim World League, based in Saudi Arabia, World Islamic Call, based in Libya, and other organizations, within the continent during the last three decades or so. The increase in the number of Islamic NGOs in the 1970s and onwards can be largely attributed to financial sponsorship from oil-rich Muslim states in the Middle East, the Persian Gulf, and North Africa. They have been willing to finance their work, among other things, also as a means of counteracting the activities of Western-backed Christian NGOs. Saudi Arabia, Kuwait, Qatar, and the United Arab Emirates, are the main financiers of these organizations. A significant factor is the fact that this activity of the Islamic NGOs' has been directed only at Muslims or those who are willing to embrace Islam. Islamic development work among non-Muslims is performed as a form of *Da'wah* in order to gain more converts to Islam.

Due to the financial problems facing many African countries, the state welfare programs of these various countries are weak. Consequently, non-governmental organizations such as *Izala* in Nigeria had to fill the vacuum created, that they have become increasingly important by copying socio-economic activities of Christian missionary churches in attracting new members to Islam (Westerlund, 1997). In Port Harcourt, Nigeria for example, "Muslims contribute money, food and other items, which are distributed without discrimination on the basis of religion." These outreach programs are very effective in converting the poor, who depend on these handouts. The growth of Islam in Nigeria and Senegal can also be attributed to the resurgence among youths, because of a network of information available through television, radio, books and the Internet, which the youths have access to as compared to older Muslims. These available new tools serve as a catalyst to recruit the youth, not only in sub-Saharan, but the world as a whole.

A common method used to convert non-Muslims is the establishment of Islamic primary schools and colleges and educational exchanges. These collective efforts are aimed at stabilizing the Islamic faith within black Africa. In many communities, free Arabic schools are established. In Senegal, for example the *Mouvement de l'Enseignement* Arab has initiated such schools. Educational efforts are not confined to primary and secondary schools, teaching of adults and females are being included. A Friday Islamic column in Nigeria newspapers has mass readership within the country. In Senegal, Chiekh Toure's radio programs in Arabic are of importance in propagating Islam. Where many people cannot read, radio becomes an instrument to transmit Islam to non-believers (Westerlund, 1997: 326-327). Also, there is consistency in Islam. Since the Koran was revealed to Mohammed through the angel Gabriel more than a thousand years ago, it has not been subjected to various interpretations like the Bible.

One might conclude, then, that these NGOs have focused their work, first of all, on development and relief issues in sub-Saharan Africa in the name of *Jihad* and the cause of converting more people to Islam (Terdman and Paz, 2007). In this case, it should be noted that the term *Jihad* encompasses a wider range of meanings than just militant holy war. Its relevance to the subject of relief and development stems from its general meaning of "striving" or "struggling". According to this worldview, the *Zakat*—a duty every Muslim must pay—can be rightfully spent on some kinds of Jihad including: military preparedness or defence; propagation of Islam; payment of salaries to religious teachers and to others, who impart other knowledge on which the people's progress and prosperity depends; and, for bringing about improvements in matters of faith and state. In other words, *Zakat* can be used for *Jihad* in the military sense as well as for *Jihad* in the sense of propagating Islam and development.

In Africa, therefore, Islamic community development projects go hand in hand with *Da'wah* and Islamization projects (Terdman & Paz, 2007). The main reason for the Islamic NGO's growing involvement in development matters in Africa is their better ability to reach the rural poor population, than government agencies do. These same rural poor are also the main target for *Da'wah* and Islamization projects. The primary missionary feature of the Da'wah in Africa has been the training of Muslim teachers, leaders, imams, and legal experts, alongside building of mosques and of schools attached to them. Thus, since the 1970s, future imams and youth leaders have become increasingly involved with the Islamic NGOs after an initial training in Africa. Then, they have been sent by these NGOs for further education abroad in Islamic institutions, universities, and advanced seminaries. Hence, it is not surprising to find that the version of Islam that has been emphasized by these NGOs is *Salafist* or *Wahabist* or other radical versions as propagated in Sudan, Saudi Arabia, and the Gulf States.

History of Islam in Africa

Africa's first Muslims arrived on the continent in the year 615 CE as refugees fleeing the persecution of the non-Muslim Arabs of Mecca. A few years before he made his historic *hijra* or migration to Medina from Mecca, the Prophet advised his cousin *Ja'far* to take a group of Muslims to seek refuge at the court of the Christian King of Aksum (present-day Ethiopia and Eritrea). As Islam spread gradually throughout the Arabian Peninsula, most of these refugees returned to Arabia. But close trade contacts between the Horn of Africa and the newly-Muslim Arabian Peninsula fostered the growth of what is today the oldest Muslim community on the continent. Even before the first Muslims set foot on African soil, however, a large number of Africans and people of African descent living in and around Mecca converted to Islam. The most famous of these early African Muslims was *Bilal Ibn Rabah al-Habashi* (Bilal the son of Rabah, the Ethiopian). According to Islamic tradition, Bilal converted to Islam while enslaved, and his master tortured him in a vain attempt to get him to recant.

Hearing of his plight, the Prophet's friend Abu Bakr paid for Bilal's freedom, after which he became the chief *muezzin* (the person who gives the call to prayer, called the *adhaan*) of the young Muslim community. Some Muslims in sub-Saharan Africa have claimed descent from Bilal and many more have looked to him as a symbolic and spiritual forefather for centuries.

These first Muslim migrants provided Islam with its first major triumph, and Africa became the first safe haven for Muslims and the first place Islam would be practiced outside of the Arabian Peninsula. The conquest of Egypt by the Muslims during the tenure of Umar Ibn al-Khattab served as an opportunity for the Muslims to penetrate into Africa. That was in the month of *Safar* 20 A.H. (641 CE), when on the order of the Caliph, Amribn al-'As conquered Egypt. The *Khalifah* again dispatched a mission of 300 men under the leadership of Alqamahibn Mujassar al-Kaneum, to the land of Eritrea (Ethiopia) to preach Islam in the heart of Africa. The routes followed by the Muslims to spread their religion in Africa were:

- Through the Red Sea to North Africa, e.g. Egypt, Tunisia, Algeria and Morocco.
- Across River Nile, namely from the lower part of Egypt to the Sudan, through the Nubious land and across the Sahara Desert and lake Chad, Bornu, Hausa, Yoruba and Nupe lands of Nigeria.
- Through the Indian Ocean from Yemen to Somalia, Omen and Albahrain, to the Island of Zanzibar in Tanganyika (Tanzania). From there Islam penetrated into the western part of South East Africa to Uganda, Malawi, Madagascar and Comoro land.

- Morocco through Northeast Africa to the fall of River Senegal to Mali, Guinea and all parts of West Africa.

Sub-Saharan Africa

Islam reached Africa south of the Sahara in two ways. Important interactions occurred during the postclassical period, though only a minority of Africans converted (except in North Africa, which religiously merged with the Middle East). But the religious contacts were nonetheless important. They set the basis for much more extensive conversions from the late eighteenth century onward, when missionary efforts and religious wars conducted by fervent Muslims began to spread the religion to ordinary people. By the late twentieth century about 40 per cent of all sub-Saharan Africans were Muslims. Initial contacts in West Africa focused on the Sudanese kingdoms, headed at first by Ghana. These contacts had some distinctive features. Trade with Muslim North Africa developed quickly, across the Sahara Desert by camel and horseback. The trade was vital to Ghana for tax revenues and supply of horses. The king of Ghana also hired Arab Muslims to keep records, because they had writing and bureaucratic experience. But contacts also facilitated raids by Muslims from the north, often encouraged by local Islamic groups.

The kingdom of Mali, which flourished after Ghana collapsed in about 1200, regularized interactions with Muslims. Rulers like Sundiata more systematically utilized Muslim bureaucrats and converted to Islam as a gesture of goodwill toward the North African trading partners. A king of Mali, Mansa Musa, made a famous pilgrimage to Mecca in 1324, dazzling Arabs with his lavish supply of gold. Mansa Musa also organized a centre of Muslim scholarship in the city of Timbuktu, and Muslim architecture spread widely. This remained, however, a compromise contact. There was little effort to convert ordinary people, though Sufi missionaries fanned out in the common pattern, with gradual results; their efforts were limited by the lack of towns south of the Sudanic kingdoms and by disease. In the Sudanic region itself, kings continued to portray themselves as divine, in the West African tradition, despite the contradictions with Islamic faith. And even among the Muslim elite, customs such as giving a relatively prominent place to women persisted, which profoundly shocked Arab visitors, who were otherwise impressed with the culture and political organization they saw around them. Islamic punishments, such as cutting off the hands of thieves, were also rejected as too brutal.

A second strand of Islam stretched down the East African coast, propelled by Arab traders in the Indian Ocean. From Egypt, traders and missionaries worked directly southward, in the nation now known as Sudan (different from the Sudanic kingdoms); beginning with the elite, widespread conversions occurred. Farther south, Swahili merchants—the word in Arabic means "coasters or people who work along the coasts— established a lively commerce between Indian Ocean ports and interior villages. In the process, they also brought Arabic language and Muslim religion and political ideas. Many traders intermarried with the African elite, as Islam began to provide cultural unity for upper classes all along the coast. Conversions were voluntary, but Islam represented high social status and the kind of generalized religion useful to far-flung trade—a religion that local African cultures did not provide. Mosques and other literary and artistic expressions of Islam followed the shift in beliefs, and a mixed Arabic-African language, Swahili, emerged as well, ultimately providing a system of writing as well as facilitating oral communication. The intrusion of Portuguese power in this region in the sixteenth and seventeenth centuries limited further growth, but when Portugal was expelled shortly before 1700, conversions resumed along the trade routes inland.

Islam spread into Africa south of the Sahara in general as a result of the caravan trade, often by Berbers, in West Africa, up along the Nile and by the Ocean trade in East Africa. In many regions the words for "trader" and "Moslem" are synonymous. Traded goods included salt, copper, handicraft, ivory, iron, gold and slaves. The slave trade from the end of the 15th century with the cooperation of some African chiefs was an important element in the growth of Islam. Islam provided a refuge for slaves separated from their tribes and provided solidarity and tribal cohesion where people were dispersed by conquest and where traditional culture and religion had disintegrated. Islamic penetration led to a more secularized society in Africa in that the authority of old customs was undermined even in those spheres of life which were not penetrated by Islam.

Since the 19th century, another important factor in the spread of Islam, apart from the marabouts in West Africa, has been the brotherhoods: the Sanusi in Libya and the Sahara; the Qadiri and Shadili in East Africa, which converted large groups. These brotherhoods cut across kinship groups, classes, professions and lineages and integrated these units. They created a cohesive body of men. They were first of all religiously motivated, but could be oriented toward political purposes. This was in particular the case when Moslems felt their society threatened by European invasion. Brotherhoods then played a significant role in the liberation of their countries, as in the case of the Sanusi in Libya where its chief, Sayyid Mohammed Idris as-Saausi, became the first ruler on the 24 December 1951, when Libya became independents. To this day, the Islamic Brotherhood is a force to be reckoned with in Egyptian politics.

Rulers who adopted Islam for prestigious reasons brought in their subjects to the fold. In some instances, a charismatic religious leader with "blessing" appeared on the scene and established a new and greater political unity with the focus on a distinctive form of Islamic doctrine. The most famous was Usuman dan Fodio in West Africa at the beginning of the 19th century who declared a *jihad* against local rulers who claimed to be Muslims but whose Islam he denied. Out of this war there developed the Fulani Empire and the basis of the northern Nigeria of today. The most recent heads of state to convert to Islam are reportedly Emperor Bokassa of the Central African Empire and President Bongo of Gabon.

It is interesting that colonial rule facilitated the spread of Islam in Africa far beyond its former confines: the colonial rule provided better roads and other communication media and they not only recognized Islamic law, but, in the case of the British it also confirmed the power of Muslim chiefs and made use of Muslims in their administration. Another more important reason is that Islam in contrast with Christianity was not connected with the colonial overlords. It was during the colonial period that Islam made its largest inroads into the interior of East Africa. The colonial powers increased mobility between the coast and the interior in order to maximize the profitability of their colonies, and this led to greater interaction between the Muslim populations of the coast and the non-Muslim people in the interior. Perhaps more importantly, faced with the destruction of their traditional kingdoms and way of life, many East Africans saw Islam as a viable alternative to the Christianity brought by European missionaries, particularly because the Islam of their Swahili neighbours seemed culturally and religiously more familiar and acceptable than the missionary religion which forbade polygamy and had little to say about the world of spirits. *Sufi tariqahs*, particularly the *Qadiriyyah* and *Alawiyyah*, played a significant role in this process. The situation was somewhat similar in West Africa, where colonization actually facilitated the spread of Islam in Senegal and Nigeria, but Western education in the form of missionary schools led to many conversions to Christianity, particularly in English colonies. Sufi *tariqahs* also played an important role in this process of Islamization in West Africa, just as they did in resisting colonial powers.

In recent times Islam has seen a rise in previously non Muslim countries particularly Rwanda. During the Rwandan genocide mobs avoided searching in local Rwandan Muslim neighbourhoods, which were used to hide Tutsi and other persecuted people. In places like Cyangugu, it was also widely believed that local Muslims and Mosques were protected by the power of Islamic magic and the efficacious *Jinn*. Post genocide many Rwandese mass converted to Islam because of protection Islamic communities offered them.

The penetration of Islam in Africa also met with difficulties. The Islamic calendar follows the moon year, whereas African agricultural calendar followed the sun. The Islamic society is patrilineal, whereas many African societies are matrilineal. A very serious problem is that the men often accepted Islam completely, but the women continued the pagan religion because it is believed that in Islam there is only marginal involvement of females. Above all, ancestor worship had to be dropped.

Muslim Population in Africa

There are conflicting statistics on religious practitioners in Africa (including North Africa). Britannica Online Encyclopaedia, in its article "Religion: Year in Review 2010: Worldwide Adherents of All Religions", states the religious statistics of Africa in 2010, as: 488,880,000 Christians (47.32%); 421,938,820 Muslims (40.84%); 109,592,000 African traditional religions (ethno religionists) (10.6%); and 12,632.200 for all other remaining beliefs (1.22%), from the 1033,043,000 total population of Africa (100%) in 2010. Nevertheless, according to a 9 May 2009 Congressional Research Service report, there were 371,459,142 Muslims, 304,313,880 Christians, 137,842,507 who practiced indigenous religions, and 9,818,542 people who practiced other religions in Africa. Although there is no specific data on the total Muslim population in Africa, experts believe that there are approximately 300 million African Muslims in the world, which comprises roughly one-third of the African continent's population. However, regardless of the relatively large Muslim population and Islam's historical presence in Africa, African Islam has remained largely neglected in the study of Muslim politics. Academics argue that this neglect was, to a large extent, the result of an academic division of labour based on the assumption that Africa was only superficially Islamized. These scholars argue that many parts of Africa were incorporated into the world of Islam centuries ago and that African Muslims have adhered to and practiced the main pillars of Islam (including the arduous pilgrimage to Mecca required of every Muslims) for more than a millennium (Hassan, 2008).

While sub-Saharan Africa has almost twice as many Christians as Muslims, on the African continent as a whole the two faiths are roughly balanced, with 400 million to 500 million followers each. Since northern Africa is heavily Muslim and southern Africa is heavily Christian, the great meeting place is in the middle, a 4,000-mile swath from Somalia in the east to Senegal in the west. To some outside observers, this is a volatile religious fault line—the site, for example, of *al-Qaeda's* first major terrorist strike, the bombing of the U.S. embassies in Kenya and Tanzania in 1998, and more recently of ethnic and sectarian bloodshed in Nigeria, where hundreds of Muslims and Christians have been killed. To others, religion is not so much a source of conflict as a source of hope in sub-Saharan Africa, where religious leaders and movements are a major force in civil society and a key provider of relief and development for the needy, particularly given the widespread reality of failed states and collapsing government services.

Diversity found within Islam in Africa

Because Islam spread to West Africa from North Africa, Muslims there followed the *Maliki* School of law dominant in North Africa. On the other hand, in East Africa, where Islam came from the Arabian Peninsula, Muslims followed the *Shafl'i* school of law that prevailed in Arabia (Levtzion and Pouwels, 2004). Both regions, however, were exposed to the influence of the *Ibadiyya* sect. *Ibadi* merchants opened up trade across the Sahara, and were among the first Muslims who reached western Sudan-as early as the eighth and ninth centuries. But whatever converts they had made were reconverted to *Maliki* Islam by the eleventh century. The *Ibadiyya* had been established in Eastern Arabia during the first centuries of Islam and became dominant in Zanzibar after the Omani conquest of this island in the eighteenth century. The *Ibadis* of Zanzibar maintained their distinct Arab identity, and did not engage in missionary work among Africans.

Although the majority of Muslims in Africa are *Sunni*, the complexity of Islam in Africa is revealed in the various schools of thought, traditions, and voices that constantly contend for dominance in many African countries. African Islam is not static and is constantly being reshaped by prevalent social, economic, and political conditions. The *Shari'a* law broadly influences the legal code in most Islamic countries, but the extent of its impact varies widely. In Africa, most states limit the use of *Shari'a* to "personal-status law" for issues such as marriage, divorce, inheritance and child custody. With the exceptions of Nigeria and Somalia, secularism does not seem to face any serious threat in Africa, even-though the new Islamic revival is having a great impact upon segments of Muslim populations. Cohabitation or coexistence between Muslims and non-Muslims remains, for the most part, peaceful.

Nigeria is home to sub-Saharan Africa's largest Muslim population. In 1999, Nigeria's northern states adopted the *Shari'a* penal code, but punishments have been rare. In fact, dozens of women convicted of adultery and sentenced to stoning to death have later been freed. Egypt, one of the largest Muslim states in Africa, claims to have *Shari'a* as the main source of its legislation, but has penal and civil codes based largely on French law (Raday, 2003).

Sufism, which focuses on the mystical elements of Islam, has many orders as well as followers in West Africa and Sudan, and, like other orders, strives to know God through meditation and emotion. Sufis may be *Sunni* or *Shi'ite,* and their ceremonies may involve chanting, music, dancing, and meditation.

West Africa and Sudan have various Sufi orders regarded sceptically by the more doctrinally strict branches of Islam in the Middle East. Most orders in West Africa emphasize the role of a spiritual guide, *marabout* or possessing supernatural power, regarded as an Africanization of Islam. In Senegal and Gambia, Mouridism's Sufis claim to have several million adherents and have drawn criticism for their veneration of Mouridism's founder Amadou Bamba and his teaching that pilgrimage to the Senegalese city of *Touba* can replace the *Hajj* pilgrimage to Mecca. The *Tijani* is the most popular Sufi order in West Africa, with a large following in Mauritania, Mali, Niger, Senegal and Gambia.

Although African Islam remains primarily *Sunni*, *Shia* Islam has been able to make significant inroads in countries like Nigeria. In addition, fundamentalists inspired by Saudi Wahabism, a group that was virtually nonexistent when African states first gained independence, are now an integral part of the religious landscape (Hassan, 2008).

Interrelations between Islam and Other Religions in Africa

The history of Christian-Muslim relations can hardly be called a past of smooth relationships. Though at the grassroots level individual Muslims and Christians have often lived and worked together quite harmoniously, the official discourses between the two religious communities were mostly characterised by exclusivist, polemic and offensive language. Jean-Marie Gaudeul's *Encounters and Clashes (2000)* gives a chronological overview of the key participants and texts on both the Christian and Muslim side while Norman Daniel's *Islam and the West: The making of an image (1960)* provides insightful background information to understand many of the European colonial and missionary (mis)perceptions of Islam, that still linger on in many of Africa's churches.

The process of decolonisation and its aftermath of disillusions coincide, as mentioned above, with two other developments. The first was a shift in outlook of the mainline churches from the midst of the 20th century onwards to tone down the polemical approach to Islam and adopt a more respectful and dialogical attitude (Behera, 2011). Though this change was welcomed by Muslims, it was also regarded with scepticism and the suspicion, that dialogue was just another form of mission and still had conversion as its aim. The second was the emergences of groups in Christianity and Islam that, disillusioned that Independence did not bring the hoped-for change, turned to fundamentalist religiosity as an alternative for society, religiosity which was characterised by an exclusivist and often antagonistic stance towards both more liberal representations of their own traditions and towards people of other religious persuasions. This surfacing of animosity amongst certain groups of Christians and Muslims in Africa fits into the wider, global developments where with the decline and the fall of communism, Islam seems to have been branded as the new 'enemy' threatening world peace. The bombings of the U.S.A. embassies in Dar-as-Salam and Nairobi, of the Khobar Towers in Saudi Arabia, the attacks on the World Trade Centre in New York, on the hotels in Bali and the undergrounds in Madrid and London as well as the invasions in Afghanistan and Iraq can all be seen as symptoms of these increasingly strained relationships between what is perceived to be 'Christians' and 'Muslims'. The effects of these worldwide developments can also be detected in Africa.

Various reasons have been given for the hostilities; the local combatants attributing them to atrocities committed by the other side. The fighting is often dismissed as simply political and economic, with the Christians characterised generally as right wing and rich and the Moslems as left wing and poor (the opposite is the case in the Sudan). Whatever the reason is, it does not seem deliberately planned by either side. Another explanation offered is the renascence of Islam, in part caused by the wealth and influence of the devout Saudis. In view of the universality of Islam, religious revival leads to confrontation.

Less pronounced but nevertheless unhelpful is ignorance of Islam by Christian religious leaders and their use of inflammatory and offensive language in official speeches, signalled for example by Laurenti Magesa in Tanzania and Anne Kubai in Kenya. Instead of propagating peaceful relations, church leaders call upon the faithful to stop the spread of Islam in Africa or claim that Muhammad was a Christian before he founded Islam, thus fuelling the tensions (Fredericks, 2010).

Christian-Muslim relations in sub-Saharan Africa are both diverse and complex. In some areas harmonious relationships reign, whereas in other countries the tension are high. Even within countries and amongst groups the perception of the necessity of interreligious relationships varies considerably, as in both Christianity and Islam those groups that take an exclusivist and intolerant position seem to expand. The increased polarisation through the influence of fundamentalist and other radical groups in sub-Sahara Africa form part of a wider, global polarisation of relations between what are perceived as ‘Christians’ and ‘Muslims’. At the same time, the increased polarisation has also stimulated more moderately minded Christians and Muslims to work together to diffuse the tensions and strive towards peaceful coexistence and mutual respect (Behera, 2011). They have accepted the religious diversity on the continent as part of the African reality and endeavour through interreligious collaboration to work towards the betterment of societies as a whole. The trends in Christian-Muslim relations that were identified—increase in polarisation and polemics and the *shari'a* debate on the one hand and joint social action on the other—reflect the ambiguity that is part of the 21st century reality of interfaith relationships in sub-Saharan Africa.

Main Currents within Contemporary African Islam

Some argue that African Islam has both local and global dimensions (Olupona, 2006). On the local level, experts assert that Muslims (including African Muslims) operate with considerable autonomy and do not have an international organization that regulates their religious practices. This fact accounts for the differences and varieties in Islamic practices throughout the African continent. On the global level, however, African Muslims belong to the *Umma*, the worldwide Islamic community, and follow global issues and current events that affect the Muslim world with keen interest. With globalization and new initiatives in information technology, African Muslims have developed and maintained close connections with the wider Muslim world.

Analysts argue that African Muslims, like other Muslims in Asia, the Middle East and the rest of the world, seem to be locked into an intense struggle regarding the future direction of Islam. At core of the struggle are questions about the way in which Muslims should practice their faith. The scholars assert that the majority seems to prefer to remain on the moderate, tolerant course that Islam has historically followed. However, a relatively small, but growing group would like to establish a stricter form of the religion, one that informs and controls all aspects of society (Marcovitz, 2007: 91).

The rise of Islamic militancy in parts of the Sahel and Horn of Africa poses growing threats to regional stability. The appeal of these militants stems from their ability to tap into and persuadc marginalized communities, particularly youth that their grievances can be rectified by the establishment of a more pure Islamist culture. Despite breakthroughs, Islamic militants in Africa typically do not possess great military power and may not seek to govern at the state level. Rather, they tend to be home-grown phenomena, focused on local concerns. Islamic militant organizations in Africa generally only command the support of small minorities within Muslim communities. However, ill-considered interventions, especially those involving Western forces, can reinforce the militants' narrative, thereby strengthening their credibility and recruitment.

The seizure of more than half of Mali's land area by Islamic militants, the growing violence of Boko Haram in northern Nigeria, and years of religious-inspired violence in Somalia have heightened attention on Islamic militancy in Africa. In the process, violent clashes between insurgent groups and governments in the Sahel and the Horn of Africa have increased, the armed capacity of militant organizations has expanded, terrorist attacks against civilians including suicide bombings have escalated, militants' strict moral codes—enforced through stoning and amputation—have been imposed, sacred historical sites have been destroyed, and hundreds of thousands of civilians have been displaced. Militants' ability to seize and control vast territory for extended periods of time has prolonged and obstructed the process of state-building in Somalia, while in Mali it has severed the northern from the southern half of the country and exacerbated a political impasse in Bamako. Protracted instability in parts of the Sahara-Sahel, furthermore, has the potential to ripple throughout the region. The prospect of the emergence of Islamic militancy and the escalation of tensions elsewhere on the continent is likewise a cause for concern.

While the risks of escalation are significant, the gains of these Islamic militant groups are not attributable to their military strength. Rather, their expanded influence is just as much a symptom of fragile and complex political contexts. More generally, Islamic militancy in Africa today represents the intersection of broader trends in contemporary Islam and local circumstances (Ostebo, 2012). Responding to the challenge is all the more difficult in that very little is known about these often secretive Islamic groups, some of which have only recently emerged.

The emergence of contemporary Islamic movements, both violent and nonviolent, has often been seen as a response to prevailing poverty, unemployment, and socioeconomic deprivation. While economic and social factors clearly are relevant, they remain insufficient for explaining such a complex phenomenon. While such organizations draw many of their members from among the poor, militant messages are typically rejected by the vast majority of the downtrodden. At the same time, Islamic militants attract some supporters from the middle class and the affluent, including professional organizations and study groups organized at universities.

While the rank and file of Islamic militant movements may be socially mixed, a noticeable commonality is the strong presence of youth (Ostebo, 2008). This would at the outset fit the thesis of socioeconomic deprivation, as youth constitute the demographic group suffering most from unemployment and bleak economic prospects. African youth, moreover, are not only marginalized economically, but often alienated from their cultural contexts and burdened by questions of identity and belonging. Contacts with *Salafi* or Islamist groups and exposure to charismatic leaders, such as Boko Haram's Mohammed Yusuf, frame this alienation in religious terms, in which Islam is presented as the all encompassing, powerful, and only solution. Both local circumstances and global events are presented as evidence of a world threatening Islam and contradicting the will of God. In addition to being the only option for salvation, membership in *Salafi* or Islamist movements—whether militant and nonmilitant—also represents a source of empowerment. These groups may not bring an end to poverty or provide jobs, but they give disgruntled youth an alternative universal model for belonging and for social action in which disillusion is exchanged for dignity and marginalization with meaning. Moreover, the emphasis on purity and morality, coupled with the notion of an exclusive access to the truth, generates attitudes of superiority. This, in turn, produces rigid boundaries toward those on the opposite side. "Others" are seen both as threats to religious purity and as targets for expansionist activities. When such thinking is cultivated in tight-knit groups with strong leaders, the road to militancy and violence can easily be a short one (Ostebo, 2010).

In military terms, Islamic militancy in Africa does not constitute a major threat. Al Shabaab possibly commands a few thousand soldiers; Boko Haram may have a few hundred members, while the various militant groups in Mali probably count for less than a thousand each. However, the level of casualties, suffering, violations of human rights, and potential for escalation of violence make it imperative to address Islamic militancy in all its seriousness. The pertinent challenge in these advanced contexts is to identify measures that can both restore order in the short term as well as demonstrate sensitivity to local complexities. The overarching objective must be to prevent further radicalization of Muslim populations and to duly address concerns that may have produced militancy in the first place. At the same time, genuine state-building efforts are required to secure local participation, facilitate real democratic institutions to hold local regimes accountable to the people, and deal with internal ethnic, social, and religious grievances.

Conclusion

The history of Islam in Africa is a long and fascinating story of kings and slaves, scholars and Sufi mystics, empires and villages, caravans and ships, religion and culture. The African continent has left an indelible mark on Islamic civilization by shaping and giving birth to some of its greatest and most influential men and women, a number of the most important empires and kingdoms, and some of the most enduring and beautiful traditions of Islamic Art from calligraphy to architecture to *Qur'anic* recitation. Islam has also left a deep and lasting influence on the African continent. Besides governing the daily lives of nearly half the continent's residents, elements of many traditional non-Muslim cultures such as dress, mythology, art, and language bear a strong Islamic influence. For example, the traditional clothes that are commonly worn by Africans from Senegal to South Africa are actually derived from the dress of the African Muslims of the Sahel. In addition to the legacy of indigenous African civilizations and the enduring influence of modern Western civilization, Islamic civilization forms an integral part of Africa's triple heritage.

Islam in Africa today becomes an African Islam; that is Islam in African way. Thanks to brotherhoods, African Muslims worship Allah in an African way. It is more or less obvious that each sub-region in African has its particular approach and way of living the faith. Hence their vision to certain common but sensitive issues such as the place of women in Islam varies from one region to another. In one way or the other, Islam has been adapted to African context in many aspects. And this adaption is the fruit of the fact that majority of African Muslims, though they belong to the *Umma*, also long to be a member of a smaller society or organization known as *Tariq a* (Brotherhood). Muslim Brotherhoods are very prominent and successful in Africa, especially in the North, West and East. Islam has remained particularly attractive to the black man in his search for an individual identity, and stimulated by the surge of Black Nationalism in Africa. He admires the elevated ethical code of Islam, Which stresses the equality and unity of all Muslims. It makes him the brother of the incomparable champion boxer Mohammed Ali and it connects him with the fabulous wealth and power of the Arab countries. Polygamy, circumcision and an aversion to pork, fit in with his traditional way of life. Islam gives the African a feeling of power and national pride; it makes him part of the big society of the future; independent, rich and self-reliant and gives the Muslim a feeling of moral superiority over the decadent west.

While commenting on the issues and prospects for the future of Islam, Prof. John L. Esposito, Editor, *The Oxford History of Islam (1999)* raises the following fundamental questions: Whose Islam? And What Islam? Regarding the former, he observes that historically, rulers were the protectors of Islam and the *ulama* were the guardians and interpreters of Islam. The second half of the 20th century has seen rulers as diverse as monarchs, military leaders, ex-military leaders, religious leaders and students. As for the latter question, Islam like all religious traditions has been subject to multiple interpretations throughout history. The key issue here is the relationship of tradition to modernity. In other words, the issue is not change but rather how much change. There are, according to Prof. Esposito, four discernible orientations towards change: Secular, conservative, traditionalist, neo-revivalist or fundamentalist and neo-modernist. By now the stand taken by each of the above is well known. All in all, though the *Quran* and the *Sunna* of Prophet Muhammad remain normative for most Muslims, questions of interpretation, authenticity and application have become contentious items. Apart from issues intrinsic to Muslims, the other issues that have come up for debate are: the status of non-Muslims in Islamic States; and status of Muslims in non-Muslim States. It makes sense to sum up the discussion with the following remarks of Fazlur Rahman, a distinguished Muslim scholar, "Muslims need some first class minds that can interpret the old in terms of the new as regards substance and turn the new into the service of the old as regards ideals" (Rahman, 1984).

REFERENCES

Abbink, J. (1998). An Historical-Anthropological Approach to Islam in Ethiopia: Issues of Identity and Politics. *Journal of African Cultural Studies,* Vol. 11(2), pp.109-124.

Abbink, J. (2011). Religion in Public Spaces: Emerging Muslim-Christian Polemics in Ethiopia. *African Affairs*, 110/439, pp. 253-274.

Abun-Nasr J. M. (1987). *A History of the Maghrib in the Islamic Period.* Cambridge: Cambridge University Press.

Akintunde, E. Akinade. (2007). The Legacy of Arab-Islam in Africa: A Quest for Inter-Religious Dialogue. *Muslim World*, January 1 p. 1.

Bang, A. K. (2003). *Sufis and Scholars of the Sea: Family Networks in East Africa, 1860-1925.* Routledge Curzon: London.

Behera, Marina. (2011). *Interfaith relations over One hundred Years*. UK: Regnum International.

Brenner, L. (2000). Sufism in Africa. In J.K. Olupona (ed.). *African spirituality* (pp. 324-349). New York: Crossroad Publishing Company.

Brenner, L. (2007). The Transformation of Muslim Schooling in Mali: the Madrasa as an Institution of Social and Religious Mediation. In Robert W. Hefner and Muhammad Quasim Zaman (eds.). *Schooling Islam: The Culture and Politics of Modern Muslim Education*. Princeton: Princeton University Press. pp. 199-223.

Chesworth, J. A. (2006). Fundamentalism and Outreach Strategies in East Africa. In B. Soares (Ed.). *Muslim-Christian Encounters in Africa.* Brill: Leiden. pp. 159-186.

Cruise, O'Brien D. (1988). Introduction. In D. Cruise O'Brien (Ed.). *Charisma and Brotherhood in African Islam.* Oxford: Clarendon Press. pp. 1-32.

Curtin, P. D. (1971). Jihad in West Africa: Early phases and inter-relations in Mauritania and Senegal. *Journal of African History*, Vol. 12(1), pp. 11-24.

Constantin, F. (1988). Charisma and the Crisis of Power in East Africa. In D. Cruise O'Brien (ed.). *Charisma and Brotherhood in African Islam.* Oxford: Clarendon Press. pp. 67-90.

Fredericks, M. T. (2010). *Current themes in Christian Muslim relations.* Edinburg.

Griswold, E. (2010). *The Tenth Parallel: Dispatches from the Fault Line between Christianity and Islam.* Germany: Picador.

Marcovitz, H. (2007). *Islam in Africa: Africa, Progress and Problems*. Mason Crest.

Handloff, R. (1982). Prayers, Amulets, and Charms: Health and Social Control. *African Studies Review,* Vol.25(2/3), pp. 185-194.

Hanretta, S. (2005). Review Article: Muslim Histories, African Societies: The Venture of Islamic Studies in Africa. *Journal of African History,* Vol. 46, pp. 479-491.

Hassan, Hussein D. (2008). CRS Report for Congress, USA.

Hiskett, M. (1994). *The Course of Islam in Africa.* Edinburg: Edinburgh University Press.

Hiskett, M. (1984). *The Development of Islam in West Africa.* London: Longman.

Hussein, Ahmed. (1993). Trends and Issues in the History of Islam in Ethiopia. In M. Nur Alkali (Ed.). *Islam in Africa: Proceedings Conference.* Ibadan: Spectrum Books. pp. 205-220.

Ikenga-Metuh, E. (1987). The Shattered Microcosm: A Critical Survey of Explanations of Conversion in Africa. In K. Holst Petersen (Ed.). *Religion, Development and African Identity.* Uppsala: Scandinavian Institute of African Studies. pp. 11-27.

Islam, Farar, Straus and Giroux Haafkens, J. (1995). The Direction of Christian-Muslim Relations in Sub-Saharan Africa. In Y. Haddad & W. Haddad (Ed.). *Christian-Muslim Encounters.* Florida: University Press of Florida. pp. 300-313.

Levtzion, N. (Ed.). (1979). *Conversion to Islam.* New York: Holmes & Meyer Publishers.

Levtzion, N. (Ed.). (2004). *The History of Islam in Africa.* Ohio: Ohio University Press.

Lewis, I. M. (1998). *Saints and Somalis, Popular Islam in a Clan-Based Society.* Asmara: Red Sea Press.

Loimeier, R. (2003). Patterns and Peculiarities of Islamic Reform in Africa. *Journal of Religion in Africa,* Vol. 33(3), pp. 237-262.

Marchal, R. (2004). Islamic Political Dynamics in the Somali Civil War. In A. de Waal (ed.). *Islamism and Its Enemies in the Horn of Africa.* London: Hurst & Company. pp. 114-145.

Marchal, R. (2009). A Tentative Assessment of the Somali *Harakat Al-Shabaab. Journal of Eastern African Studies,* Vol. 3(3), pp. 381-404.

Martin, B. G. (1976). *Muslim Brotherhoods in 19th Century Africa.* Cambridge: Cambridge University Press.

Niezen, R. (1990). The Community of Helpers of the Sunna: Islamic Reform among the Songhay of Gao (Mali). *Africa,* Vol. 60(3), pp. 399-424.

Olupana, Jacob K. (2006*). Thinking globally about African Religion*. Oxford: Oxford Handbook of Global Religions.

Ousmane, Kane. (2007). Moderate Revivalists: Islamic Inroads in Sub-Saharan Africa. *Harvard International Review,* pp. 64-68.

Ostebo, T. (2008).The Question of Becoming: Islamic Reform Movements in Contemporary Ethiopia. *Journal of Religion in Africa,* Vol. 38(4), pp. 416-446.

Ostebo, T. (2010). *Islamism in the Horn of Africa: Assessing Ideology, Actors, and Objectives,* Report no. 2, International Law and Policy Institute.

Ostebo, T. (2012). Islamic militancy in Africa. *Africa Brief* (Nov. 2012).

Pouwels, R. (1987). *Horn and Crescent: Cultural Change and Traditional Islam on the East African Coast, 800-1900*. Cambridge: Cambridge University Press.

Raday, Frances. (2003). Culture, Religion & Gender. *I.Con special issue,* Oxford University Press and New York school of Law, Vol. 1(4), pp. 663-715.

Rahman, Fazlur. (1984). *Islam and Modernity*. California: University of California.

Rosander, E .E. (1997). Introduction: The Islamization of 'Tradition' and 'Modernity' in *Somalia's Islamists.* Africa Report no 100. Nairobi/Brussels: International Crisis Group.

Seeseman, R. & Soares, B. (2009). Being Good Muslims as Frenchmen: On Islam and Colonial Modernity in West Africa. *Journal of Religion in Africa.* Vol. 39(1), pp. 91-120.

Seeseman, R. (2006). African Islam or Islam in Africa: Evidence from Kenya. In R. Loimeier& R. Seesemann (Eds.). *The Global World of the Swahili: Interfaces of Islam, Identity and Space in 19th and 20th Century East Africa.* Berlin: Lit Verlag. pp. 229-250.

Terdmen & Paz. (2007). African occasional papers. No-2. Israel.

Thomson, A. (2010). *An Introduction to African Politics*. New York: Routledge.

Turner, S. (2009). These Young Men Show No Respect for Local Customs – Globalisation and Islamic Revival in Zanzibar. *Journal of Religion in Africa.* Vol. 39, pp. 237-261.

Waterbury, J. (1970). *The Commander of the Faithful – The Moroccan Political Elite – A Study in Segmented Politics.* New York: Columbia University Press.

Westerlund, David and Rosander, Eva Evers. (1997). *African Islam and Islam in Africa: Encounters between Sufis and Islamists*. Athens, Ohio: Ohio University Press.

Contributors

Addis Yimer is a Ph.D. candidate at Department of Economics, Addis Ababa University and Lecturer at Dire Dawa University, Ethiopia.

Alemayehu Geda is Professor of Economics at Addis Ababa University. He is also a Research Associate of the University of London (SOAS, CDPR, London), African Economic Research Consortium (Nairobi), Central Bank of Kenya and Economic Policy Research Center (EPRC, Kampala). He has published many articles on African Economies and four books published by Palgrave-Macmillan, AERC, Nairobi and Addis Ababa University Presses.

A.S. Yaruingam is Head of the Department and Coordinator of the UGC sponsored Centre for African Studies, University of Delhi. He did his Ph.D. from Jawaharlal Nehru University and joined the Department of African Studies in 1998 as a lecturer in African Sociology. He taught at Addis Ababa University, Ethiopia, from October 2003 to April 2006. He has published several articles on African culture and religion in journals. He presented papers at international conferences and seminars in India as well as abroad. He is a convener of Study Group on India-Africa Relations and Sudan Study unit of the Department.

Ian Taylor is Professor in International Relations and African Politics at St Andrews and also Chair Professor in the School of International Studies, Renmin University of China. He is also Professor Extraordinary in Political Science at the University of Stellenbosch, South Africa, an Honorary Professor at the Institute of African Studies, China, and a Visiting Scholar at Mbarara University of Science and Technology, Uganda. Focusing largely on sub-Saharan Africa he has authored 7 academic books, edited another 8 and has published over

100 scholarly articles and chapters in books and numerous working papers, reports etc.

Ivan Niranjan is a lecturer in the Department of Occupational and Health and Safety, Durban University of Technology. He is active in offering support to the South African Department of Labour on occupational health and safety issues. Currently he is an auditor for Occupational Health and Safety Assessment in the country in keeping with the International Labour Organisations norms and standards.

K. Mathews, a former Professor and Head of the Department of African Studies in Delhi University (1991–2002), is currently Professor of International Relations and African Studies at the Addis Ababa University, Ethiopia since 2003.

Kyu-Deug Hwang is an Assistant Professor, Head of the Division of African Studies at Hankuk University of Foreign Studies, Korea. He received his doctoral degree (D.Phil. in International Relations) at the Department of Political Sciences, University of Pretoria, South Africa. His research focuses on security and development in Africa, Korea-Africa relations, Asia-Africa connections in South-South cooperation.

Pushpraj Singh pursued his M.A. in History from the Department of History, University of Delhi and received his Ph.D. from the Department of African Studies, University of Delhi. He has taught as an Assistant Professor in the Department of History, University of Tripura from 2008-2012.

Rashmi Kapoor is an Assistant Professor in Swahili in the Department of African Studies, University of Delhi. She pursued her M.A. and M.Phil. in Sociology from the Department of Sociology, Delhi School of Economics, University of Delhi. She later received her Ph.D. from the Department of African Studies, University of Delhi. Her field of specialization is African Sociology in general and Swahili language in particular. She has extensively written on the Indian diaspora in Africa and also on several African issues. She is a member of Sudan Study unit in the Department of African Studies, University of Delhi.

Shubhra Parmar is a research scholar in the Department of African Studies, Delhi University. She is pursuing her Ph.D. on Ethnic Conflict Induced Displacement and Women in Africa: A Study of Rwanda. Her main research & writing interests are on contemporary African women issues, African feminism, women empowerment and their sustainable strategies in Africa. She is mainly interested in interdisciplinary perspectives on women empowerment.

Sudhir Kapoor is currently Associate Professor of Statistics at Hindu College, University of Delhi where he has taught for over three decades. He pursued his M.Sc. and M.Phil. in Statistics from the Department of Statistics, University of Delhi. He was awarded Commonwealth scholarship to pursue Ph.D. from Sheffield University, U.K. His specialization is on Statistical Inference and Characterization Theory. He went on UNDP assignment as Visiting Professor to Africa. He has several papers on Statistics and Applied Statistics published in India and abroad to his credit.

Sultan Khan is an Associate Professor in Sociology in the School of Social Sciences, University of KwaZulu-Natal. He is a nationally rated scientist and his research focus is on social policy, development and urban sociology and social issues. Prof Khan is currently working on the BRICS academic cluster to inform multilateral policies to foster south-south relationships.

Suresh Kumar is a former Head (2009-12), Department of African Studies, University of Delhi and serves as Associate Professor, Department of African Studies, University of Delhi, India. He is the Chief Editor of Africaindia.org and has traveled widely in East Asia, Europe, South America and Africa for research and teaching assignments. Recently, he participated in the last meeting of Fourth Committee October 2012 at UNO, New York. The author is active as member in the Africa Committee of Confederation of Indian Industry, an executive member of Indo-Africa Chamber of Commerce in India and member in the Advisory Group of India-Africa of Indian Council of World Affairs. About 125 articles of his have been published in different journals and newspapers. Email: skafrica2003@yahoo.com

Tribhuwan Prasad is teaching African Geography in the Department of African Studies for past two decades. He has presented papers in several national and international conferences. His several articles have been published in books and journals. He is convener of Study Group on South Africa and Study Group on Human Rights and Refugees.

Index